Computer Awareness

Highly useful for Banking, SSC, Railway, Police & all State Level Recruitment Exams

Computer Awareness

Highly useful for Banking, SSC, Railway, Police & all State Level Recruitment Exams

Author
Neetu Gaikwad

ARIHANT PUBLICATIONS (INDIA) LIMITED

arihant

ARIHANT PUBLICATIONS (INDIA) LIMITED

卐 **Administrative & Production Offices**

Regd. Office

'Ramchhaya' 4577/15, Agarwal Road, Darya Ganj, New Delhi -110002
Tele: 011- 47630600, 43518550

卐 **Head Office**

Kalindi, TP Nagar, Meerut (UP) - 250002
Tel: 0121-7156203, 7156204

卐 **Sales & Support Offices**

Agra, Ahmedabad, Bengaluru, Bareilly, Chennai, Delhi, Guwahati, Hyderabad, Jaipur, Jhansi, Kolkata, Lucknow, Nagpur & Pune.

卐 **ISBN** 978-93-25794-17-7

PO No : TXT-XX-XXXXXXX-X-XX

Published by Arihant Publications (India) Ltd.

For further information about the books published by Arihant, log on to www.arihantbooks.com or e-mail at info@arihantbooks.com

Follow us on   

CONTENTS

CHAPTER

01

INTRODUCTION TO COMPUTER

The word 'computer' has been derived from the Latin word 'computare', which means 'to calculate'. A computer is an electronic device that manipulates information or data according to the set of instructions called **programs**. It has the ability to store, retrieve and process data.

Functions of Computer

1. **Input** Information or data that is entered into a computer is called input. It sends data and instructions to the Central Processing Unit (CPU).
2. **Processing** It is the sequence of actions taken on data to convert it into information which is meaningful to the user. It can be calculations, comparisons or decisions taken by the computer.
3. **Output** It makes processed data available to the user. It is mainly used to display the desired result to the user as per input instructions.
4. **Storage** It stores data and programs permanently. It is used to store information during the time of program execution and possible to get any type of information from it.

Features of Computer

1. **Speed** The computer can process data very fast at the rate of millions of instructions per second.
2. **Accuracy** Computers provide a high degree of accuracy. They respond to the user as per the input instructions.
3. **Storage Capacity** Computers are capable to store huge amount of data, which depends on the capacity of hard disk.
4. **Versatility** Computers can do different types of work simultaneously. They can perform multiple tasks at a same time.
5. **Diligence** Unlike human beings, a computer is free from monotony, tiredness, lack of concentration, etc., and can work for hours without creating any errors.

6. **Secrecy** Leakage of information is reduced by creating login system with password protection.
7. **Reliability** Computers are more reliable than human beings. Computers always produce exact results. The possibility of errors occur only if the input is wrong, i.e. the computers never make mistakes of their own accord.
8. **Plug and Play** Computers have the ability to automatically configure a new hardware and software components.

History of Computer

Computer is not the creation of one day, rather it took a long period for the development of modern computer.

History of computer is described in this table

Inventions	Inventors	Characteristics	Applications
Abacus **1602**	China	▪ First mechanical calculating device. ▪ A horizontal rod represents the one, tens, hundred, etc.	▪ Used for addition and subtraction operations. ▪ Calculation of square roots can also be performed.
Napier's Bones **1617**	John Napier (Scotland)	▪ Three dimensional structure. ▪ Holding numbers from 0 to 9 only. ▪ Represent graphical structure of calculating result. ▪ Technology used for calculation called **Rabdologia**.	▪ Perform multiplication of numbers.
Pascaline **1642**	Blaise Pascal (France)	▪ First mechanical adding machine. ▪ This machine worked on the principle of odometer and watch. ▪ Mainly designed with regard to the pressure of liquid.	▪ Perform addition and subtraction of two numbers.
Jacquard's Loom **1801**	Joseph Marie Jacquard (France)	▪ It was first mechanical loom. ▪ Used punched card for the sequence of operation.	▪ Simplified the process of textiles.
Analytical Engine **1837**	Charles Babbage (London)	▪ First general-purpose computer. ▪ Stored program in the form of 'pegs' also called **barrels.**	▪ It was a decimal machine used sign and magnitude for representation of a number.
Tabulating Machine **1890**	Herman Hollerith (America)	▪ It used punched cards for reading numbers. ▪ It was the first electromechanical machine.	▪ It was used in the 1890 census.
MARK-1 **1944**	Howard Aiken (America)	▪ Consists of interlocking panels of small glass, counters, switches and control circuits. ▪ Data can be entered manually.	▪ Mainly used in the war effort during World War-II. ▪ Magnetic drums are used for storage.
ENIAC **1946**	JP Eckert and JW Mauchly (America)	▪ It is a combination of twenty accumulators. ▪ First electronic digital computer.	▪ Used for weather prediction, atomic energy calculation and other scientific uses. ▪ Used in IBM and other.

Inventions	Inventors	Characteristics	Applications
EDVAC **1947**	John Von Neumann (America)	▪ Electronic digital computer	▪ Logical design of a computer with a stored program.
EDSAC **1949**	Maurice Wilkes (America)	▪ It was the first computer which provided **storage capacity.** ▪ First computer program was run on machine.	▪ Capable of storing instructions and data in memory. ▪ Used mercury delay lines for memory, vacuum tubes for logic.
UNIVAC **1951**	J. Presper Eckert and John Mauchly (America)	▪ First general-purpose electronic computer with large amount of input and output.	▪ Used magnetic tapes as input and output. ▪ Use for account work.
IBM-650 Computer **1953**	IBM Company	▪ Provided input/output units converting alphabetical and special characters to two-digit decimal code.	▪ Payroll processing ▪ Oil refinery design ▪ Market research analysis

Generations of Computer

A generation refers to the state of improvement in the development of system. Each generation of computer is characterised by a major technological development that fundamentally changed the way, computers operate.

Generations	Switching Devices	Storage Devices/Speed	Operating Systems/ Programming Languages	Characteristics	Applications
First (1940-56)	Vacuum tubes	Magnetic drums (milli seconds)	Batch operating system /Machine language (Binary numbers 0's and 1's)	▪ Fastest computing device. ▪ Generate large amount of heat. ▪ Non-portable.	▪ Used for scientific purpose. e.g. ENIAC, UNIVAC, MARK-1, etc.
Second (1956-63)	Transistors (Made up of semiconductors)	Magnetic core technology (micro seconds)	Time sharing OS, Multitasking OS/ Assembly language, high level language	▪ More reliable and less prone to hardware failure. ▪ Portable and generate less amount of heat.	▪ Used for commercial production. e.g. PDP-8, IBM-1401, etc.
Third (1964-71)	Integrated Circuits (ICs) (Made up of silicon)	Magnetic core as primary storage medium (nano seconds)	Real-time system/ High level language (FORTRAN, COBOL, ALGOL)	▪ Consumed less power. ▪ Highly sophisticated technology required.	▪ Database management system e.g. NCR-395, B6500, etc.
Fourth (1971-Present)	Large Scale Integrated (LSI) circuit, microprocessor	Semi conductor memory, Winchester disc (pico seconds)	Time sharing /PASCAL, ADA, COBOL-74, FORTRAN IV	▪ More reliable and portable. ▪ This generation leads to better communication and resource sharing.	▪ Electronic fund transfer, Distributed system, e.g. Intel 4004 chip, Macintosh.
Fifth (Present and Beyond)	Super Large Scale Integrated (SLSI) chips	Optical disc	Knowledge Information Processing System	▪ Parallel processing. ▪ Intel core microprocessor is implemented. ▪ Enables mega chips.	▪ Artificial intelligence e.g. Robotics.

Classification of Computer

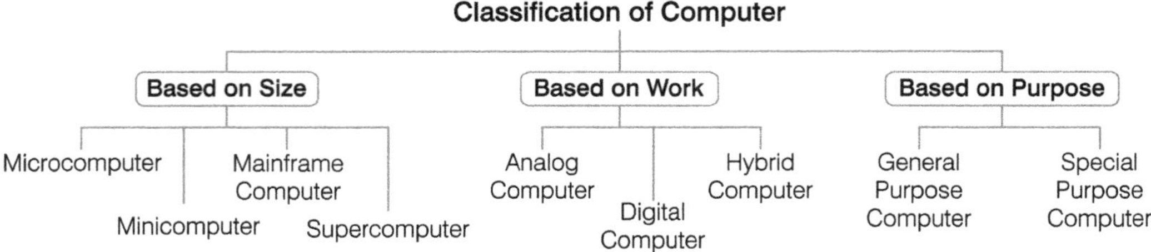

Based on Size

Microcomputer

This type of computer is the least powerful than other computers, which are based on size, yet the most widely used and is also called **portable computer**.

Some types of microcomputer are as follows

(a) **Desktop Computer or Personal Computer** (PC) This is small and relatively economical computer. This is based on the microprocessor technology (Integrated Circuit-IC).

(b) **Laptop** This computer is also known as **ultra book** or **notebook**. This is portable and lightweighted. It includes rechargeable battery, so you can work with this anywhere.

(c) **Handheld or Palmtop Computer** This is the smallest and is designed to fit into the palm. So, this is also known as **palmtop**.
It is practical for certain functions such as phone books and calendars. It uses the pen for input instead of keyboard. *For example*, PDA (Personal Digital Assistant), tablets, etc.

(d) **Workstation Computer** This computer is dedicated to a user or group of users engaged in business or professional work. It includes one or more high resolution displays and a faster processor than a Personal Computer (PC).

Nano Computer

Nano computer is a general term used to describe a computer smaller than a microcomputer, usually about the size of a credit card.

For example, Raspberry Pi, which could be used in schools to teach science to children.

Embedded Computer

It is a small size, powerful and easy to operate electronic module, based on microcontroller/ microprocessor and acts as a bridge between electronics hardware and computer software. e.g. cellphone, camera, automotive system, digital watch, etc.

Quantum Computer

Quantum computer was first introduced by Richard Feynman. It uses quantum mechanical phenomena. It is the fastest computer imitating brain working.

Minicomputer

These are smaller in size, faster and cost lower than mainframe computers. Initially, the minicomputer was designed to carry out some specific tasks, like engineering and Computer Aided Design (CAD) calculations.

But now, they are being used as central computer which is known as **server**. The speed of minicomputer is between 10 to 30 MIPS (Million Instructions Per Second). First minicomputer was PDP-8. Some examples of minicomputer are IBM-17, DEC PDP-11, HP-9000, etc.

Mainframe Computer

These types of computer having large internal memory storage and comprehensive range of software. It is considered as the heart of a network of computers or terminals that allow a large number of people to work at the same time. Some examples of mainframe computer are IBM-370, IBM-S/390, UNIVAC-1110, etc.

Supercomputer

These are the fastest and most expensive computers. They have high processing speed compared to other computers. Supercomputers are most powerful, large in size and memory, compared to all other computers.

The speed of supercomputers are measured in FLOPS (Floating Point Operations Per Second). Supercomputers are used for highly calculation intensive tasks, such as weather forecasting, nuclear research, military agencies and scientific research laboratories.

Some examples of supercomputer are described below

(i) **CRAY-1** was the world's first supercomputer introduced by Seymour R CRAY (Father of Supercomputing) in 1976.

(ii) **PARAM** was the first supercomputer developed by Vijay Bhatkar in India in 1991.

(iii) **PARAM Siddhi** is the latest machine in the series of PARAM made by C-DAC and released on 16 November, 2020.

(iv) **Pratyush**, the first multi-petaflops supercomputer was unveiled at Pune based Indian Institute of Tropical Meteorology (IITM) in India.

(v) **Fugaku** is a claimed exascale supercomputer at the RIKEN Center for Computational Science in Kobe, Japan. It is scheduled to start operating in 2021. It has defended its title as the world's fastest supercomputer.

Based on Work

On the basis of work, computer is categorised as follows

Analog Computer

These computers carry out arithmetic and logical operations by manipulating and processing of data. *For example,* Speedometers, seismograph, etc.

Analog computer can perform several mathematical operations simultaneously. It uses continuous variables for mathematical operations and utilises mechanical or electrical energy.

Digital Computer

These computers work on binary digits. A digital computer, not only performs mathematical calculations, but also combines the bytes to produce desired graphics, sounds.
For example, Desktop (PC).

Hybrid Computer

These computers are the combination of analog and digital computers. Machines used in hospitals like ECG and DIALYSIS are the commonly used hybrid computers.

Based on Purpose

On the basis of purpose, computer is categorised as follows

General Purpose Computer

General purpose computers are those computers, which are used to solve variety of problems by changing the program or instructions.

For example, To make small database, calculations, accounting, etc.

Special Purpose Computer

Special purpose computers are those computers' which are used to solve a single and dedicated type of problem.

For example, Automatic aircraft landing, multimedia computer, etc.

Tit-Bits

- **Charles Babbage** is known as the father of computer. **Alan Turing** is known as the father of the modern computer.
- **Siddhartha** was the first computer developed in India. First computer in India was installed in Indian Statistical Institute (ISI), Kolkata.
- Transistors were invented by Bell Laboratory.
- In 1958, Jack St. Clair Kilby and Robert Noyce invented the first IC (Integrated Circuit).
- ENIAC (Electronic Numerical Integrator and Computer) was the first electronic computer developed in Moore School of Engineering, USA.

QUESTION BANK

1. The word 'computer' has been derived from which of the following language?
(1) Greek (2) English
(3) Hindi (4) Latin

2. Input, output and processing devices grouped together represent a(n)
(1) mobile device
(2) information processing cycle
(3) circuit board
(4) computer system

3. Which of the following is the correct order of the four major functions of a computer?
(1) Process, Output, Input, Storage
(2) Input, Output, Process, Storage
(3) Process, Storage, Input, Output
(4) Input, Process, Output, Storage

4. Collecting the data and converting it into information is called
(1) processing (2) compiling
(3) importing (4) exporting

5. Computer cannot perform
(1) input (2) output
(3) thinking (4) processing

6. A computer cannot perform which of the following functions?
(1) Addition (2) Subtraction
(3) Bake a cake (4) Division

7. Part number, description and number of parts ordered are examples of
(1) control (2) output
(3) processing (4) feedback

8. Benefit(s) of computer is/are
(1) very fast and can store huge amount of data
(2) provide accurate output either input is correct or not
(3) think about the processing
(4) All of the above

9. A collection of unprocessed items is **[SBI PO 2015]**
(1) information (2) data
(3) memory (4) reports
(5) None of these

10. Which among the following cycle consists of input, processing, output and storage as its constituents? **[IBPS Clerk Mains 2017]**
(1) Processing (2) Output
(3) Input (4) Storage
(5) Data

11. .... is data that has been organised and presented in a meaningful fashion. **[IBPS Clerk Mains 2017]**
(1) A process (2) Software
(3) Storage (4) Information
(5) Data

12. Data or information used to run the computer is called
(1) hardware (2) CPU
(3) peripheral (4) None of these

13. The steps and tasks needed to process data, such as responses to questions or clicking an icon, are called **[IBPS Clerk Mains 2017]**
(1) instructions
(2) the operating system
(3) application software
(4) the system unit
(5) the hardware unit

14. The earliest calculating device is
(1) calculator (2) abacus
(3) difference engine (4) analytical engine

15. Abacus can perform
(1) addition (2) subtraction
(3) multiplication (4) Both (1) and (2)

16. The Napier's technology used for calculation is called
(1) Naptologia (2) Vibologia
(3) Semiconductor (4) Rabdologia

17. Pascaline is also known as
(1) abacus (2) adding machine
(3) division machine (4) difference machine

18. Punched cards were first introduced by
(1) Powers (2) Pascal
(3) Jacquard (4) Herman Hollerith

19. Punched card is also called **[RRB NTPC 2016]**

A. Hollerith card B. Video Card
C. Sound Card D. Accelerator Card

Codes

(1) B (2) C
(3) A (4) D

20. Which of the following is known as father of computer? **[SSC CGL 2015, UPSSSC 2016]**

(1) Dennis Ritchie (2) Napier
(3) Charles Babbage (4) Alan Turing

21. Who is known as the father of the modern computer?

(1) Charles Babbage (2) Alan Turing
(3) Blaise Pascal (4) Jordan Murn

22. Analytical engine developed by

(1) Blaise Pascal (2) Charles Babbage
(3) Dennis Ritchie (4) Alan Turing

23. The analytical engine developed during first generation of computers used .... as a memory unit.

(1) RAM (2) floppies
(3) cards (4) counter wheels

24. Tabulating machine was the first electromechanical machine developed by

(1) Herman Hollerith (2) Howard Aiken
(3) Blaise Pascal (4) John Napier

25. Who among the following created the Electronic Discrete Variable Automatic Computer (EDVAC) with a memory to hold both, a stored program as well as data? **[SSC CGL 2018]**

(1) Thomas H Flowers (2) Arthur Samuel
(3) Bletchley Park (4) John Von Neumann

26. The first computer which provides storage is

(1) EDSAC (2) EDVAC
(3) MARK-I (4) ACE

27. Name the first general purpose electronic computer.

(1) ADVAC (2) ADSAC
(3) UNIVAC (4) EDVAC

28. Computer size was very large in

(1) first generation
(2) second generation
(3) third generation
(4) fourth generation

29. First generation computers were based on

(1) transistors (2) conductors
(3) ICs (4) vacuum tubes

30. Computer built before the first generation computer was

(1) mechanical
(2) electromechanical
(3) electrical
(4) electronics

31. First generation computers used .... language(s).

(1) machine (2) assembly
(3) Both (1) and (2) (4) high level

32. The second generation of computers was witnessed in the years from **[UPSSSC 2018]**

(1) 1940-1956 (2) 1963-1972
(3) 1957-1962 (4) 1973-Present

33. Second generation computers can be characterised largely by their use of **[SSC CGL 2018]**

(1) integrated circuits (2) vaccum tubes
(3) microprocessors (4) transistors

34. Speed of first generation computer was in

(1) nano seconds
(2) milli seconds
(3) nano-milli seconds
(4) micro seconds

35. Time sharing became possible in .... generation of computers.

(1) first (2) second
(3) third (4) fourth

36. Third generation of computers was witnessed in the years from...... **[UPSSSC 2018]**

(1) 1940-1956 (2) 1963-1972
(3) 1957-1962 (4) 1973-Present

37. Integrated Circuits or ICs were started to be used from which generation of computers? **[IBPS PO 2016]**

(1) First generation (2) Second generation
(3) Third generation (4) Fourth generation
(5) Fifth generation

38. Chip is a common nickname for a(n) **[IBPS Clerk 2014, 15]**

(1) transistor (2) resistor
(3) integrated circuit (4) semiconductor
(5) None of these

39. Integrated Circuit (IC) or chips used in computers are made with **[IBPS Clerk 2014]**

(1) copper (2) aluminium
(3) gold (4) silicon
(5) silver

40. Who developed integrated chip?

(1) Robert Nayak (2) C Babbage
(3) JS Kilby (4) CV Raman

41. A complete electronic circuit with transistors and other electronic components on a small silicon chip is called a(n)

(1) workstation (2) CPU
(3) magnetic disc (4) integrated circuit

42. PCs are considered fourth generation and contain **[SBI PO 2014]**

(1) information (2) data
(3) vacuum tubes (4) microprocessors
(5) transistors

43. Fifth generation computers do not have **[SSC MTS 2012]**

(1) speech recognition
(2) artificial intelligence
(3) very large scale integration
(4) vacuum tubes

44. Match the following.

	List I		List II
A	First generation	1.	Transistor
B	Second generation	2.	VLSI microprocessor
C	Third generation	3.	Vacuum tube
D	Fourth generation	4.	Integrated circuit

[UGC NET June 2019]

Codes

	A	B	C	D		A	B	C	D
(1)	3	4	1	2	(2)	3	1	4	2
(3)	3	1	2	4	(4)	1	3	4	2

45. Small and cheap computers built into several home appliances are of which type? **[SSC (10+2) 2011]**

(1) Mainframes (2) Mini computers
(3) Micro computers (4) None of these

46. Desktop and personal computers are also known as

(1) supercomputers (2) servers
(3) mainframes (4) microcomputers

47. Computers that are portable and convenient to use for users who travel, are known as

(1) supercomputers
(2) minicomputers
(3) mainframe computers
(4) laptops

48. Which of the following uses a handheld operating system?

(1) A supercomputer
(2) A personal computer
(3) A laptop
(4) A PDA

49. Palmtop computer is also known as

(1) personal computer
(2) notebook computer
(3) tablet PC
(4) handheld computer

50. Which of the following is a small microprocessor based computer designed to be used by one person at a time? **[SBI Clerk 2014]**

(1) Netbook (2) Supercomputer
(3) All-in-one (4) Notebook
(5) Personal computer

51. Which of the following options correctly expresses the meaning of the term 'PCs'? **[IBPS PO 2012]**

(1) Independent computers for all working staff.
(2) Personal computers widely available to individual workers with which they can access information from layer systems and increase their personal productivity.
(3) Packed computers system formed by joining together of various computer terminals.
(4) Computer manufactured by the Pentium Company.
(5) None of the above

52. Desktop computers, laptop computers, tablets and smartphones are different types of **[SSC CGL 2018]**
(1) supercomputers
(2) mainframe computers
(3) microcomputers
(4) minicomputers

53. In the context of digital computer, which of the following pairs of digits is referred to as binary code? **[SSC CGL 2018]**
(1) 3 and 4 (2) 0 and 1
(3) 2 and 3 (4) 1 and 2

54. A central computer that holds collection of data and programs for many PCs, workstations and other computers is a
(1) supercomputer
(2) minicomputer
(3) laptop
(4) server

55. First mini computer was **[UPSSSC 2016]**
(1) PDP-8 (2) ENIAC
(3) UNISAC (4) EDVAC

56. Which of the following is generally costlier? **[IBPS Clerk 2015]**
(1) Server (2) Notebook computer
(3) Personal computer (4) Laptop computer
(5) Mainframe

57. The user generally applies .... to access mainframe or supercomputer.
(1) terminal (2) node
(3) desktop (4) handheld

58. First computer of India is
(1) PARAM (2) Siddhartha
(3) IBM-370 (4) CRAY-1

59. Where was the first computer in India installed? **[UPSSSC 2016]**
(1) Tata Institute of Fundamental Research (TIFR), Mumbai
(2) Indian Statistical Institute (ISI), Kolkata
(3) Compunational Research Laboratory (CRL), Pune
(4) Indian Railway, New Delhi

60. First supercomputer developed in India is
(1) PARAM (2) CRAY-1
(3) PARAM ISHAN (4) EPRAM

61. Pratyush is ...... fastest supercomputer in the world.
(1) first (2) second
(3) third (4) fourth

62. Example of super computer is **[UPSSSC 2016]**
(1) CRAY-2 (2) CRAY XMP-24
(3) Tianhe-2 (4) All of these

63. Which of the following is a supercomputer developed by India? **[SSC CGL 2018]**
(1) Param Yuva 2 (2) Onshape
(3) Venngage (4) Pixir

64. In 1991, India's first indigenous supercomputer named ...... was developed by Vijay Bhatkar. **[SSC CGL 2018]**
(1) Prayas 3000 (2) Prayog 2000
(3) Param 8000 (4) Pragati 5000

65. Who among the following is called the father of supercomputing? **[SSC CGL 2018]**
(1) Ken Thompson (2) Alan Perlis
(3) Seymour Cray (4) Vint Gerf

66. India's fastest and first multi-petaflops supercomputer named Pratyush was unveiled at **[SSC CGL 2017]**
(1) Indian Space Research Organisation
(2) Indian Institute of Science, Bangalore
(3) Indian Institute of Tropical Meteorology, Pune
(4) Indian Institute of Technology, New Delhi

67. Choose the odd one out.
(1) Microcomputer (2) Minicomputer
(3) Supercomputer (4) Digital computer

68. A hybrid computer is the one having the combined properties of
(1) super and microcomputers
(2) mini and microcomputers
(3) analog and digital computers
(4) super and mini computers

69. Computer system which do not require any storage device? **[RRB NTPC 2016]**
A. Analog
B. Digital
C. Hybrid
D. Third generation computer
Codes
(1) B (2) A (3) D (4) C

70. The ...... computer is the most common type of computer. It is used to process information with quantities usually using the binary number system. **[UPSSSC 2018]**
(1) Hybrid (2) Digital
(3) Analog (4) Complex

71. Calculator works on which type of computer's work method? **[UPSSSC 2015]**
(1) Hybrid computer
(2) Analog computer
(3) Digital computer
(4) None of the above

72. Which of the following computer is mainly related to convert analog output into digital form? **[UPSSSC 2016]**
(1) Digital computer
(2) Analog computer
(3) Hybrid computer
(4) Mainframe computer

73. Which of the following is not the example of special purpose computer?
(1) Automatic aircraft landing
(2) Word processor
(3) Multimedia computer
(4) All of the above

74. Which type of computer is used in automatic aircraft landing?
(1) General purpose computer
(2) Supercomputer
(3) Special purpose computer
(4) Microcomputer

75. Which of the following is the smallest and fastest computer imitating brain working? **[IBPS PO 2016]**
(1) Supercomputer
(2) Quantum computer
(3) Param-10000
(4) IBM chips
(5) None of the above

ANSWERS

1. *(4)*	2. *(4)*	3. *(4)*	4. *(1)*	5. *(3)*	6. *(3)*	7. *(3)*	8. *(1)*	9. *(2)*	10. *(5)*
11. *(4)*	12. *(4)*	13. *(1)*	14. *(2)*	15. *(4)*	16. *(4)*	17. *(2)*	18. *(3)*	19. *(3)*	20. *(3)*
21. *(2)*	22. *(2)*	23. *(4)*	24. *(1)*	25. *(4)*	26. *(1)*	27. *(3)*	28. *(1)*	29. *(4)*	30. *(2)*
31. *(1)*	32. *(3)*	33. *(4)*	34. *(2)*	35. *(2)*	36. *(2)*	37. *(3)*	38. *(3)*	39. *(4)*	40. *(3)*
41. *(4)*	42. *(4)*	43. *(4)*	44. *(2)*	45. *(3)*	46. *(4)*	47. *(4)*	48. *(4)*	49. *(4)*	50. *(5)*
51. *(2)*	52. *(3)*	53. *(2)*	54. *(4)*	55. *(1)*	56. *(5)*	57. *(2)*	58. *(2)*	59. *(2)*	60. *(1)*
61. *(4)*	62. *(4)*	63. *(1)*	64. *(3)*	65. *(3)*	66. *(3)*	67. *(4)*	68. *(3)*	69. *(2)*	70. *(2)*
71. *(3)*	72. *(3)*	73. *(2)*	74. *(3)*	75. *(2)*					

CHAPTER

02

COMPUTER ARCHITECTURE

Computer architecture deals with the functional behaviour of a computer system as viewed by a programmer. It can also be described as the logical structure of the system unit that housed electronic components. The first computer architecture was introduced in 1970, by John Von Neumann.

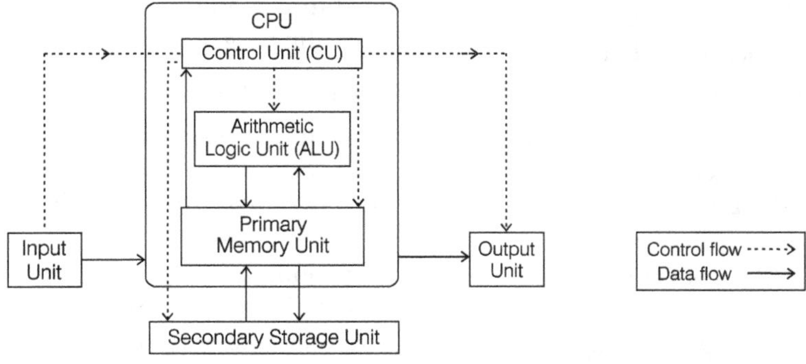

Computer Architecture

Components of Computer

1. Input Unit
2. Output Unit
3. Central Processing Unit
4. Memory Unit

Note System unit is a metal or plastic case that holds all the physical parts of the computer. The components that process data are located in it.

Input Unit

The computer accepts coded information through input unit by the user. This unit is used to give required information to the computer. *For example,* keyboard, mouse, etc.

An input unit performs the following functions

- It accepts the instructions and data from the user.
- It converts these instructions and data to computer acceptable format.
- It supplies the converted instructions and data to the computer system for further processing.

Output Unit

This unit sends the processed results to the user. It is mainly used to display the desired result to the user as per input instructions.
For example, monitor, printer, plotter, etc.

The following functions are performed by an output unit

- It accepts the results produced by the computer which are in coded form and hence cannot be easily understood by user.
- It converts these coded results to readable form which convenient to users.
- It produces the converted results to the user.

Central Processing Unit (CPU)

Central Processing Unit is often called the **brain of computer**. The CPU is fabricated as a single Integrated Circuit (IC) and is also known as **microprocessor**.

It consists a set of registers, arithmetic logic unit and control unit, which together interpret and execute instructions in assembly language.

The primary functions of the CPU are as follows

- The CPU transfers instructions and input data from main memory to registers.
- The CPU executes the instructions in the stored sequence.
- When necessary, CPU transfers output data from registers to main memory.

A CPU controls all the internal and external devices and performs arithmetic and logic operations.

The CPU consists of following main sub-systems

Arithmetic Logic Unit (ALU)

ALU contains the electronic circuitry that executes all arithmetic and logical operations on the available data. ALU uses **registers** to hold the data that is being processed.

Most ALUs can perform the following operations

(i) Logical operations (AND, NOT, OR, XOR).
(ii) Arithmetic operations (addition, subtraction, multiplication and division).
(iii) Bit-shifting operations (shifting or rotating a word by a specified number of bit to the left or right with or without sign extension).
(iv) Comparison operations (=, <, < =, >, > =)

Registers

These are used to quickly accept, store and transfer data and instructions that are being used immediately by the CPU. These registers are the top of the memory hierarchy and are the fastest way for the system to manipulate data. The number and size of registers vary from processor-to-processor.

Control Unit (CU)

CU coordinates with the input and output devices of a computer. It directs the computer to carry out stored program instructions by communicating with the ALU and the registers. It organises the processing of data and instructions.
The basic function of control unit is to fetch the instruction stored in the main memory, identify the operations and the devices involved in it and accordingly generate control signals.

Memory Unit

This unit is responsible to store programs or data on a temporary or permanent basis. It has primary memory (main memory) and secondary memory (auxiliary memory).

The input data which is to be processed is brought into main memory before processing.
Another kind of memory is referred to as secondary memory of a computer system. This unit is used to permanently store data, programs and output. This unit does not deal directly with the CPU.

Microprocessor

It is the controlling element in a computer system and is sometimes referred to as the chip. Microprocessor is the main hardware that drives the computer.

It is a large **Printed Circuit Board** (PCB), which is used in all electronic systems such as computer, calculator, digital system, etc. The speed of CPU depends upon the type of microprocessor used.

Intel 4004 was the first microprocessor made by Intel in 1971 by scientist Ted Hoff and engineer Frederico Faggin.
Some of the popular microprocessors are Intel, Intel Core i7, Intel Core i9, Dual Core, Pentium IV, etc.

Motherboard

The main circuit board contained in any computer is called a motherboard. It is also known as the main board or logic board or system board or planar board.

All the other electronic devices and circuits of computer system are attached to this board like, ROM, RAM, expansion slots, PCI slots and USB ports. It also includes controllers for devices like the hard drive, DVD drive, keyboard and mouse.

Components on Motherboard

(i) CMOS battery	(ii) BIOS chip
(iii) Fan	(iv) Expansion slot
(v) SMPS	(vi) PCI slot
(vii) Processor chip	(viii) Buses

Interconnection of Units

CPU sends data, instructions and information to the components inside the computer as well as to the peripheral devices attached to it.

A **bus** is a set of wires used for interconnection, where each wire can carry one bit of data.

In other words, bus is a set of electronic signal pathways that allows information and signals to travel between components inside or outside of a computer.

A computer bus can be divided into two types

1. **Internal Bus** The internal bus connects components inside the motherboard like CPU and system memory. It is also called the **system bus**.

Internal bus includes following buses

(i) The command to access the memory or the I/O devices is carried by the **control bus**.

(ii) The address of I/O devices or memory is carried by the **address bus**.

(iii) The data to be transferred is carried by the **data bus**.

2. **External Bus** It connects the different external devices; peripherals, expansion slots, I/O ports and drive connections to the rest of computer. It is also referred to as the **expansion bus**.

Instruction Cycle

It represents the sequence of events that takes place as an instruction is read from memory and executed.

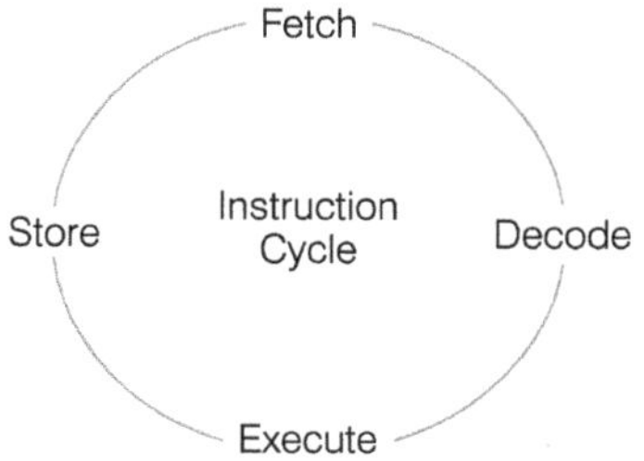

A simple instruction cycle consists of the following steps

1. **Fetching** the instruction from the memory.
2. **Decoding** the instruction for operation.
3. **Executing** the instruction.
4. **Storing** in memory.

In above steps, steps 1 and 2 instructions are same and known as fetch cycle and steps 3 and 4 instructions are different and known as execute cycle.

Tit-Bits

- **UPS** (Uninterruptible Power Supply) is an electrical apparatus that provides emergency power to a load when the input power source or mains power fails.
- **Power strip** is an electrical device that is used to expand the capacity of a wall outlet in terms of the number of devices it can accommodate.
- **Instruction code** is a group of bits that instruct the computer to perform a specific operation.

QUESTION BANK

1. .... forms the backbone for building successful computer system.
(1) Computer architecture
(2) Computer model
(3) Computer instructions
(4) None of the above

2. The first computer architecture was introduced in
(1) 1970 (2) 1968 (3) 1971 (4) 1973

3. Which circuit board is used in all electronic systems such as computer, calculators, digital system?
(1) Architecture (2) Printer
(3) Value (4) Register

4. The system unit
(1) coordinates input and output devices
(2) is the container that houses electronic components
(3) is a combination of hardware and software
(4) controls and manipulates data

5. Which of the following is metal or plastic case that holds all the physical parts of the computer? **[IBPS Clerk Mains 2017]**
(1) System unit (2) CPU
(3) Mainframe (4) Platform
(5) Microprocessor

6. The components that process data are located in which of the following? **[IBPS Clerk Mains 2017]**
(1) Input devices (2) Output devices
(3) System unit (4) Storage component
(5) Expansion board

7. Which of the following is not responsible for the performance of the computer? **[IBPS Clerk Mains 2017]**
(1) Number of keys in the keyboard
(2) Format of the video/graphics word
(3) Memory in the video/graphics word
(4) The clock speed of the processor
(5) Number of cores available in the processor

8. A(n) .... device is any device that provides information, which is sent to the CPU.
(1) input (2) output
(3) CPU (4) memory

9. Which of the following includes as a type of input?
(1) Data (2) Programs
(3) Commands (4) User response
(5) All of these

10. Information that comes from external source and fed into computer software is called **[IBPS RRB PO Mains 2017]**
(1) output (2) input
(3) throughout (4) reports
(5) process

11. Input unit converts data in computer in .... form.
(1) suitable (2) acceptable
(3) understandable (4) rejectable

12. This unit sends the processed results to the user.
(1) Input (2) Output
(3) Memory (4) CPU

13. Output unit includes
(1) plotter (2) printer
(3) monitor (4) All of these

14. This component is required to process data into information and consists of integrated circuits.
(1) Hard disk (2) RAM
(3) CPU (4) ROM

15. The Central Processing Unit (CPU) in a computer consists of
(1) input, output and processing
(2) control unit, primary storage and secondary storage
(3) control unit, arithmetic logic unit, memory unit
(4) All of the above

16. Which instruction is used for loading data into CPU accumulator register from memory?
(1) Load (2) Storage
(3) Machine (4) Access

17. Where does computer add and compare data?
(1) Hard disc (2) Floppy disc
(3) CPU (4) Memory chip

18. In computer, which of the following unit is responsible for processing and also known as brain of computer? **[SSC CGL 2019]**
(1) CPU (2) Keyboard
(3) Hard disk (4) RAM

19. The main job of a CPU is to
(1) carry out program instructions
(2) store data/information for further use
(3) process data and information
(4) Both (1) and (3)

20. The main purpose of time-sharing techniques used in computers is to make the best use of the
(1) CPU (2) peripherals
(3) secondary storage (4) floppy discs

21. The CPU is made up of two smaller components
(1) ALU and CU (2) ALU and RAM
(3) RAM and ROM (4) RAM and CU

22. The CPU comprises of control, memory and ..... units.
(1) microprocessor (2) arithmetic/logic
(3) output (4) ROM

23. What is the responsibility of the logical unit in the CPU of a computer? **[IBPS Clerk 2015]**
(1) To produce result
(2) To compare numbers
(3) To control flow of information
(4) To do maths work
(5) None of the above

24. Which unit of computer helps in communication between the memory and the arithmetic logical unit? **[IBPS RRB PO Mains 2017]**
(1) CMU (2) CCU
(3) UPS (4) CPU
(5) ALU

25. Which part of the computer is used for calculating and comparing?
(1) ALU (2) Control unit
(3) Disc unit (4) Modem

26. Pick the one that is used for logical operations or comparisons such as less than, equal to or greater than etc.
(1) ALU (2) CU (3) Input unit (4) MU

27. What does ALU in computing denote? **[UPSSSC 2016, IBPS Clerk 2014]**
(1) Application and Logic Unit
(2) Algorithm Logic Unit
(3) Arithmetic Layered Unit
(4) Arithmetic Legal Unit
(5) Arithmetic Logic Unit

28. How many types of arithmetic operations does the ALU of computer perform?
(1) 4 (2) 2 (3) 5 (4) 8

29. Processors contain a control unit and a/an **[SSC CGL 2016]**
(1) Control unit
(2) Primary storage unit
(3) Input unit
(4) Arithmetic logic unit

30. Which of the following executes the computer commands?
(1) Arithmetic unit (2) Logic unit
(3) Both (1) and (2) (4) Control unit

31. Which unit is a combinational digital electronic circuit that performs arithmetic and bitwise operations on integer binary numbers? **[IBPS RRB PO Mains 2017]**
(1) BOU (2) AEU (3) CPU (4) ALU
(5) UPS

32. Internal memory in a CPU is nothing but
(1) a set of registers (2) a set of ALU
(3) microprocessor (4) bus

33. Which among the following is a small set of data holding place that is a part of the computer processor and may hold an instruction, a storage address, or any kind of data? **[IBPS RRB PO Mains 2017]**
(1) Register (2) WAN
(3) Bus (4) Address
(5) Processor

34. The portion of the CPU that coordinates the activities of all the other computer components is the **[SBI PO 2015]**
(1) motherboard (2) coordination board
(3) control unit (4) arithmetic logic unit
(5) None of these

35. Which among the following is an important circuitry in a computer system that directs the operation of the processor? **[IBPS PO 2016]**
(1) Memory (2) Address Bus
(3) Accumulator (4) ALU
(5) Control unit

36. The part of a computer that coordinates all its functions, is called **[IBPS Clerk Mains 2017]**
(1) ROM program (2) System board
(3) Arithmetic logic unit (4) Control unit
(5) None of these

37. The control unit controls other units by generating
(1) control signal (2) timing signal
(3) transfer signal (4) command signal

38. Control unit of a digital computer is often called the
(1) clock (2) nerve centre
(3) Both (1) and (2) (4) IC

39. Memory unit that communicates directly with the CPU is called the
(1) main memory (2) secondary memory
(3) auxiliary memory (4) register

40. CPU retrieves its data and instructions from
(1) secondary memory (2) auxiliary memory
(3) main memory (4) All of these

41. Which computer memory is used for storing programs and data currently being processed by the CPU?
(1) Mass memory (2) Internal memory
(3) Non-volatile memory (4) PROM

42. The I/O processor has a direct access to ...... and contains a number of independent data channels.
(1) main memory (2) secondary memory
(3) cache (4) flash memory

43. The word 'computer' usually refers to the central processing unit plus
(1) external memory (2) internal memory
(3) input devices (4) output devices

44. Who invent the first microprocessor?
(1) Vint Cerf (2) Terence Percival
(3) John Mauchly (4) Ted Hoff

45. A microprocessor is the brain of the computer and is also called a **[RBI Grade B 2014]**
(1) microchip (2) macrochip
(3) macroprocessor (4) calculator
(5) software

46. Microprocessors can be used to make
(1) computer (2) digital system
(3) calculators (4) All of these

47. High power microprocessor is **[UPSSSC 2019]**
(1) Pentium, Pentium pro
(2) Pentium II and III
(3) Pentium II
(4) All of the above

48. The microprocessor of a computer
(1) does not understand machine language
(2) understands machine language and high level language
(3) understands only machine language
(4) understands only high level languages

49. The CPU and memory are located in which of the following devices? **[IBPS Clerk Mains 2017]**
(1) Motherboard (2) Expansion board
(3) Storage device (4) Output device
(5) System unit

50. Personal computers use a number of chips mounted on a main circuit board. What is the common name for such boards?
(1) Daughterboard
(2) Motherboard
(3) Broadboard
(4) None of the above

51. Which of the following are the components that reside on motherboard?
(1) CMOS battery (2) Fan
(3) PCI slot (4) All of these

52. A...... is the main Printed Circuit Board (PCB) in a computer. **[SSC CGL 2018]**
(1) ROM (Read Only Memory)
(2) CPU (Central Processing Unit)
(3) RAM (Random Access Memory)
(4) Motherboard

53. Which one among the following is a main system board of a computer? **[SSC CGL 2017]**
(1) CPU (2) Keyboard
(3) Microchip (4) Motherboard

54. The communication line between CPU, memory and peripherals is called a
(1) bus (2) line (3) media (4) All of these

55. A physical connection between the microprocessor memory and other parts of the micro computer is known as
(1) path (2) address bus
(3) route (4) All of these

56. The read/write line belongs to
(1) the data bus (2) the control bus
(3) the address bus (4) CPU bus

57. The name of the location of a particular piece of data is its
(1) address (2) memory name
(3) storage (4) data location

58. Which of the following is used to connect the different external devices?
(1) Address bus (2) Data bus
(3) Control bus (4) External bus

59. A computer executes program in the sequence of **[RRB NTPC 2016]**
A. Execute, Fetch, Decode
B. Store, Fetch, Execute
C. Fetch, Decode, Excecute
D. Decode, Fetch, Execute
(1) D (2) A
(3) C (4) B

60. Which is not an integral part of computer? **[SBI Clerk 2012]**
(1) CPU (2) Mouse
(3) Monitor (4) UPS
(5) None of these

61. A device that not only provides surge protection, but also furnishes the computer with battery backup power during a power outage is **[IBPS RRB PO Mains 2017]**
(1) battery strip
(2) UPS
(3) surge strip
(4) USB
(5) memory

62. What is a power strip? **[UPSSSC 2019]**
(1) It is an electrical device that is used to expand the capacity of a wall outlet which can accommodate the devices.
(2) It plugs multiple components into one power outlet.
(3) It provides power supply for electronic devices.
(4) It is used to increase the magnitude of voltage/current/power of an input signal.

ANSWERS

1. *(1)*	2. *(1)*	3. *(1)*	4. *(2)*	5. *(1)*	6. *(3)*	7. *(1)*	8. *(1)*	9. *(5)*	10. *(2)*
11. *(2)*	12. *(3)*	13. *(4)*	14. *(3)*	15. *(3)*	16. *(1)*	17. *(3)*	18. *(1)*	19. *(4)*	20. *(1)*
21. *(1)*	22. *(2)*	23. *(2)*	24. *(4)*	25. *(1)*	26. *(1)*	27. *(5)*	28. *(1)*	29. *(4)*	30. *(3)*
31. *(4)*	32. *(1)*	33. *(1)*	34. *(3)*	35. *(5)*	36. *(4)*	37. *(1)*	38. *(2)*	39. *(1)*	40. *(3)*
41. *(2)*	42. *(1)*	43. *(1)*	44. *(4)*	45. *(1)*	46. *(4)*	47. *(4)*	48. *(3)*	49. *(1)*	50. *(2)*
51. *(4)*	52. *(4)*	53. *(4)*	54. *(1)*	55. *(2)*	56. *(2)*	57. *(1)*	58. *(4)*	59. *(3)*	60. *(4)*
61. *(2)*	62. *(1)*								

CHAPTER

03

COMPUTER HARDWARE

Computer hardware refers to the physical components of a computer that can be seen and touched by the user. The hardware component could be an electronic, electrical and mechanical devices used in the computer system.

Input Devices

An input device can be defined as an electro-mechanical device that allows the user to feed data into the computer. This data is useful for analysis and storage and to give commands to the computer.

The data is entered into the main memory through these input devices. They accept instructions from the user and convert these accepted instructions into machine language.

Some of the commonly used input devices are described below

Keyboard

Keyboard is used to enter data or information in a computer system, which may be in numeric form or alphabetic form. When key is pressed, keyboard interacts with a keyboard controller and keyboard buffer. Keyboard controller stores the code of pressed key in keyboard buffer. The user can type text and command using this device. The layout of the keyboard was borrowed from the regular typewriter with some additional keys.

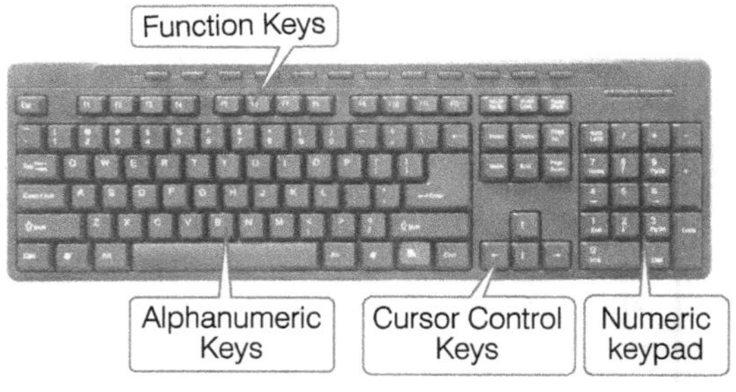

Keyboard

There are different types of keyboard such as QWERTY, DVORAK and AZERTY.

Types of Keys

1. **Alphanumeric Keys** include the alphabet keys (A, B, C, ..., Z) and number keys (0, 1, 2, 3, ..., 9).
2. **Numeric Keys** are located at the right hand side of the keyboard. They consist of digits and mathematical operators.
3. **Function Keys** are the programmable keys, i.e. the programs can assign some specific actions. They are numbered from F1 to F12.
4. **Cursor Control Keys** include four directional (left, right, up, down) arrow keys that are arranged in a inverted T formation between the alphanumeric and numeric keypad. Apart from the above arrow keys, there are four more keys to control the cursor.

   These are as follows

   (i) **Home** It is used to return the cursor to the beginning of the line or the beginning of a document.

   (ii) **End** It moves the cursor to the end of line.

   (iii) **Page Up** When it is pressed, the page view will move up one page and cursor goes to the previous page.

   (iv) **Page Down** When it is pressed, the page view will move down one page and cursor goes to the next page.
5. **Other Keys** *A keyboard contains some other keys such as follows*

   (i) **Control Key** It performs a special operation as the combination with other keys. *For example,* Ctrl + C is used for copying.

   (ii) **Enter Key** It is used to finish an entry and begin a new entry in the document. Enter key is an alternative to press OK button.

   (iii) **Shift Key** Some keys on the keyboard like numeric keys have a symbol printed on their upper portion. Shift key is used to print these symbols. This key is also called combination key, because it is always used with other keys. *For example,* Shift + a, converts small 'a' into capital 'A'.

   (iv) **Escape Key** (Esc) It allows a user to cancel or abort operations, which are executing at present. It opens Start menu with the combination of Ctrl key.

   (v) **Backspace Key** It is used to erase anything typed.

   (vi) **Delete Key** It is used to erase information from the computer's memory and characters on the screen.

   (vii) **Caps Lock Key** It is used to type the alphabet in capital letters. It enables or disables all the letters from being typed in capital letters.

   (viii) **Num Lock Key** It is used to enable and disable the numeric keypad.

   (ix) **Windows Key** It is used to open the Start menu.

   (x) **Spacebar Key** It provides space between two words. It is the longest key on the keyboard.

   (xi) **Tab Key** It is used to move the cursor over the right to a pre-set point. In Word document, tab is used to indent a paragraph.

Note **QWERTY** keyboard contains total 104 keys.
Caps Lock and Num Lock keys are called as '**toggle keys**' because when they are pressed, they toggle or change their status from one state to another. Shift, Ctrl and Alt keys are also known as **modifier keys**.

Pointing Device

A **pointing device** is used to communicate with the computer by pointing to the location on the monitor. Movements of the pointing device are echoed on the screen by movements of the pointer.

Some commonly used pointing devices are described below

Mouse

Mouse is a small handheld pointing device having two buttons on its upper side and also has a small wheel between these buttons. It was invented by Douglas Engelbart at Stanford Research Centre in 1963.

It provides to input data and commands in graphic form through moving an arrow called pointer on monitor.

The mouse may be used to position the cursor on screen, move an object by dragging or select an object by clicking.

Three types of mouse are as follows

(i) Wireless mouse
(ii) Mechanical mouse
(iii) Optical mouse

Four actions of mouse are as follows

1. **Click or Left Click** It selects an item on the screen.
2. **Double Click** It is used to open a document or program.
3. **Right Click** It displays a list of commands on the screen. Right click is used to access the properties of the selected object.
4. **Drag and Drop** It is used to move an item on the screen.

Trackball

Trackball is another pointing device which is an alternative to a mouse. Trackball is also used to control cursor movements and actions on a computer screen.

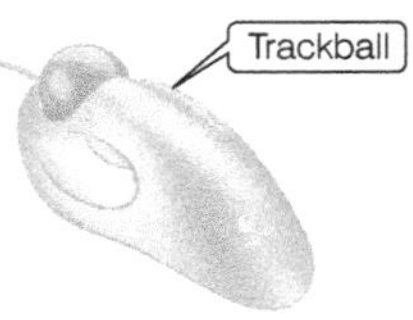

It is used on CAD/CAM workstations and sometimes seen on computerised special purpose workstations such as radar consoles in an air-traffic control room and sonar equipment on a ship or submarine.

Joystick

Joystick is a device that moves in all directions and controls the movement of the cursor. Joysticks are used in flight simulators, Computer Aided Design/Computer Aided Manufacturing (CAD/CAM) system, etc.

Joystick

A joystick is similar to a mouse except that the movement of the cursor on screen stops as soon as the user stops moving the mouse. But with a joystick, the pointer continues moving in the previously pointing direction. Joystick allows movements in all directions (360°).

Light Pen

Light pen is a handheld electro-optical pointing device. It is used for making drawings, graphics and menu selection.

The pen contains a photocell in a small tube. It senses the light from the screen when it becomes closer and generates a pulse.

Light pen is used especially in Personal Digital Assistants (PDA). It is very useful in identifying a specific location on the screen. However, it does not provide any information when held over a blank part of the screen.

Touch Screen

Touch screen is an input device that accepts input when the user places a fingertip on the computer screen. Touch screens have an infrared beam that criss-cross the surface of screen. Touch screen is generally used in applications like ATM, hospitals, airline reservation, supermarkets, etc.

Barcode Reader

Barcode reader is an input device used for reading printed barcodes (Universal Product Code) available on products to be sold. A light sensitive detector in the barcode reader identifies the barcode image by recognising special bars at both the ends of the image.

Barcode Reader

A perfect example of a barcode reader is, to use it in a super market where barcode scanner reads the price of a product which is in the form of barcode. A barcode is a machine readable representation of information in the form of stripes of dark and light ink.

Barcode

Optical Mark Reader (OMR)

OMR is also known as Optical Mark Recognition. It is the process of detecting the presence of intended marked responses.

OMR is mainly used to detect marks on a paper. It uses a beam of light that is reflected on the paper with marks, to capture presence and absence of data (marks).

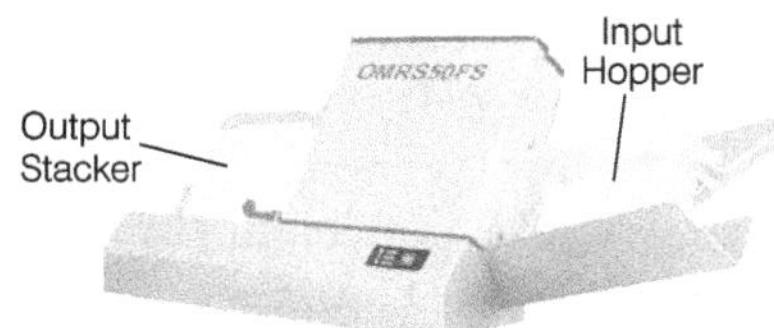

Optical Mark Reader

The OMR interprets the pattern of marks into a data record and sends this to the computer for storage, analysis and reporting. OMR is widely used to read the answer of objective type tests, voting applications and other evaluation studies.

Optical Character Recognition (OCR)

OCR is a technique for scanning a printed page, translating it and then using the OCR software to recognise the image as **ASCII** text that is editable. It translates the array of dots into text that the computer can interpret as words and letters.

OCR is a widely used technique for acquiring textual data from image. It is used in many applications such as telephone bills, electricity bills, insurance premium, etc.

OCR technology is being developed for greater accurate recognition and is also known as Intelligent Character Recognition (ICR).

Magnetic Ink Character Recognition (MICR)

MICR reads the characters by examining their shapes in a matrix form and the information is then passed on to the computer. The characters are printed using a special ink (contains iron oxide) that can be magnetised.

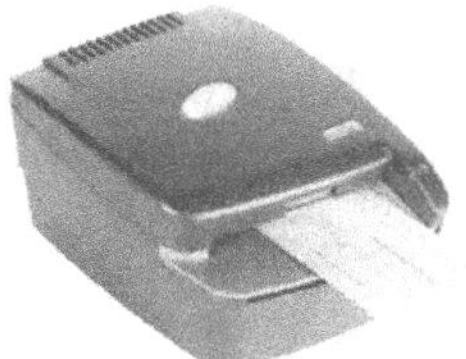

Format of a Cheque

It is generally used in banks to process the cheques for recognising the magnetic encoding numbers printed at the bottom of a cheque.

Smart Card Reader

It is a device which is used to access the microprocessor of a **smart card**.

There are two kinds of smart card reader which are as follows

- Memory cards are the cards which contain only non-volatile memory storage components and some specific security logic.
- **Microprocessor cards** contain volatile memory and microprocessor components.

The card is made-up of plastic, generally PVC. Smart cards are used in large companies and organisations for stronger security authentication.

Biometric Sensor

Biometric Sensor is a device which recognises physical traits of the individual. Biometric sensors are used for marking attendance of employees/ students in organisations/ institutions.

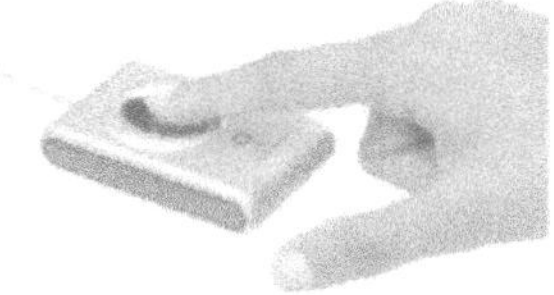

Biometric Sensor

Scanner

Scanner is an optical input device which uses light as an input source to convert an image into an electronic form that can be stored on the computer.

It is used to convert the data and image on paper into the digital form. Scanners can be used for storing the documents in their original form that can be modified and manipulated later on.

Scanner stores images in both gray scale and color mode. *The most common types of scanners are as follows*

(i) Handheld scanners
(ii) Flatbed scanners
(iii) Drum scanners

Microphone (Mic)

We can send input to the computer through a special manual input device called **microphone** or **mic**. A mic converts the received sound into computer's format, which is called **Digitised Sound** or **Digital Audio**.

To convert a voice into digital form, you need an additional hardware known as **Sound Card**. Sound is used most often in multimedia. *For example,* we can make our presentations more attractive using recorded narration, music or sound effects.

Now-a-days, microphones are also used with speech recognition software. This means that we do not have to type, rather just have to speak and the spoken words appear in our document.

Webcam (Web Camera)

It is a video capturing device. Webcam is a digital camera attached to computer and can be used for video conferencing, online chatting, etc.

Webcam with Computer

Webcam

Now-a-days, webcams are either embedded into the display with laptop/computer or connected *via* USB or firewire port or Wi-Fi to the computer.

Output Devices

An output device is a piece of computer hardware that receives data from a computer and then translates that data into another form. That form may be audio, visual, textual or hard copy such as printed document.

Some of the commonly used output devices are described below

Monitor

It is also known as Visual Display Unit (VDU). The monitor is provided alongwith the computer to view display the result.

An image on the monitor is created by a configuration of dots, also known as **pixels.**

A monitor is of two kinds; *monochrome display monitor* and *colour display monitor.*

A monochrome display monitor uses only one colour to display text and colour display monitor can display 256 colours at a time.

The clarity of image depends on three factors which are as follows

1. **Resolution of Screen** Resolution refers to the number of pixels in horizontal and vertical directions. The resolution of a monitor is higher when the pixels are closer together.
2. **Dot Pitch** It refers to the diagonal distance between two coloured pixels. The smaller the dot pitch, the better the resolution.
3. **Refresh Rate** The refresh rate of your display refers to how many times per second the display is able to draw a new image. The higher the refresh rate, the more solid the image looks on the screen. The refresh rate of monitor is measured in Hertz (Hz).

The popular types of monitor are as follows

1. **Cathode Ray Tube** (CRT) It is a typical rectangular shaped monitor that you see on a desktop computer. The CRT works in a same way as a television. CRT has a vacuum tube. The screen of CRT is covered with a fine layer of phosphorescent elements, called *phosphores.*
2. **Liquid Crystal Display** (LCD) These screens are used in laptops and notebook sized PCs. A special type of liquid is sandwiched between two plates. It is a thin, flat and light weight screen made up of any number of color or monochrome pixels arranged in front of a light source.
3. **Light Emitting Diode** (LED) It is an electronic device that emits light when electrical current

is passed through it. LEDs usually produce red light, but today's LEDs can produce RGB (Red, Green and Blue) light, and white light as well.

4. **3-D Monitor** It is a television that conveys depth perception to the viewer. When 3-D images are made interactive then user feels involved with the scene and this experience is called **virtual reality**.
5. **Thin Film Transistor** (TFT) It is a type of field effect transistor that is usually used in a LCD. This type of display features a TFT for each individual pixel.

   These TFTs act as individual switches that allow the pixels to change state rapidly, making them turn ON and OFF much more quickly.

Printers

A printer prints information and data from the computer onto a paper. It can print documents in colour as well as in black and white. The quality of a printer is determined by the clarity of the print.

The speed of a printer is measured in Characters Per Second (CPS), Lines Per Minute (LPM) and Pages Per Minute (PPM). Printer resolution is a numerical measure of print quality that is measured in Dots Per Inch (DPI).

Printers are divided into two basic categories which are as follows

Impact Printer

This type of printer strikes paper and ribbon together to form a character, like a typewriter. Impact printer can print a character or an entire line at a time. They use pins or hammers that pressed an inked ribbon against the paper. They are less expensive, fast and can make multiple copies with multipart paper.

There are four types of impact printer which are described below

1. **Dot Matrix Printer** It forms characters using rows of pins which impact the ribbon on top of the paper therefore also called pin printers. Dot matrix printer prints one character at a time. It prints characters and images as a pattern of dots. Many dot matrix printers are bi-directional, that is they can print the characters from either direction, i.e. left or right.
2. **Daisy Wheel Printer** In daisy wheel printers, characters are fully formed on the petals, like typewriter keys. These printers produce high resolution output and are more reliable than dot matrix.
3. **Line Printer** It is a high-speed printer capable of printing an entire line of a text at once instead of one or more characters at a time. Print quality of line printer is not high.
4. **Drum Printer** It uses a drum to hold paper in place. It receives an image from the laser and transfers it onto the paper. The drum is coated with photoreceptor materials.

Non-Impact Printer

This type of printer uses electrostatic chemicals and inkjet technologies. They do not hit or impact a ribbon to print. It can produce high quality graphics and often a wide variety of fonts than impact printer.

The types of non-impact printer are as follows

1. **Inkjet Printer** It is a printer that places extremely small droplets of ink onto paper to create an image. It sprays ink onto paper to form characters and prints high quality text and graphics.
2. **Thermal Printer** It uses heat on chemically treated paper to form characters.
3. **Laser Printer** They can print in different fonts that is, type, styles and sizes. Laser printer uses laser beam onto photo sensitive surface for printing. It prints high quality graphics.
4. **Electromagnetic Printer** These printers are also known as Electrographic or electro-photographic printers. These are very fast printers and fall under the category of page printers. The electrographic technology have developed from the paper copier technology.
5. **Electrostatic Printer** These printers are generally used for large format printing. They are favoured by large printing shops because of their ability to print fast and making low cost.

Note Chuck Hull, the engineer designed and created the first **3D printer** in 1984. These printers can be used to print almost anything into a real life model.

Plotter

A plotter is a special kind of output channel like a printer, that produces images on paper. It uses a pen, pencil, marker or other writing tools for making vector graphics.

They are mainly used to produce large drawings or images such as construction plans, blueprints for mechanical objects, AUTOCAD, CAD/CAM, etc.

Plotters usually come in two forms as follows

1. Flatbed plotter
2. Drum plotter

Speaker

It is an output device that receives sound in the form of electric current. It needs a sound card connected to a CPU, that generates sound.

These are attached internally or externally to a computer system.

These are used for listening music, for being audible in seminars during presentations, etc.

Headphones

These are a pair of small loudspeakers or less commonly a single speaker, held close to a user's ears and connected to a signal source such as an audio amplifier, radio, CD player or portable media player. They are also known as stereo phones, headsets or cans.

Projector

It is an output device which is used to project information from a computer onto a large screen, so it can be viewed by a large group of people simultaneously.

Projectors are widely used for classroom training or conference halls with a large audience. It provides a temporary output display.

There are mainly two types of projectors; LCD (Liquid Crystal Display) projector and DLP (Digital Light Processing) projector.

Input/Output (I/O)Port

Input/Output ports are the external interfaces that are used to connect input and output devices like printer, monitor and joystick to computer.

The I/O devices are connected to the computer *via* different ports which describe below

1. **Parallel Port** It is an interface for connecting eight or more data wires. The data flows through the wires simultaneously. They can transmit eight bits of data in parallel.

   As a result, parallel ports provide high speed data transmission. Parallel port is used to connect printer to the computer.
2. **Serial Port** It transmits one bit of data through a single wire. Since, data is transmitted serially as single bit. It provides slow speed data transmission. It is used to connect external modems, plotters, barcode reader, etc.
3. **Universal Serial Bus** (USB) It is a common and popular external port available with computers. Normally, two to four USB ports are provided on a PC. USB also has the plug and play feature, which allows devices ready to be run.
4. **Firewire** It is used to connect audio and video multimedia devices like video camera. Firewire is an expensive technology used for large data movement. Hard disk drive and new DVD drives connect through firewire. It has data transfer rate of upto 400 MB/second.

Tit-Bits

- **MP3** is an audio coding format for digital audio, which uses a form of lossy data compression.
- The I/O devices that are attached, externally to the computer machine are also called **peripheral devices**.
- **Speech recognition software** can interpret voice data into words that can be understood by the computer.
- A **dumb terminal** is simply an output device that accepts data from the CPU.

QUESTION BANK

1. Any component of the computer you can see and touch is **[IBPS Clerk 2015]**
   (1) software (2) peripheral
   (3) storage (4) CPU
   (5) hardware
2. Which of the following is not a hardware? **[SSC FCI 2012]**
   (1) Processor chip (2) Printer
   (3) Mouse (4) Java
3. A(n) ...... device is any hardware component that allows you to enter data and instructions into a computer. **[SBI Clerk 2014]**
   (1) interaction (2) input
   (3) communication (4) output
   (5) terminal
4. Computer gets ...... with the help of mouse, joystick or keyboard.
   (1) insert (2) delete
   (3) input (4) output
5. Computer keyboard is an example of
   (1) memory device
   (2) input device
   (3) output device
   (4) Both (2) and (3)
6. The most common method of entering text and numerical data into a computer system is through the use of a **[SBI PO 2015]**
   (1) plotter (2) scanner
   (3) printer (4) keyboard
   (5) None of these
7. Which key is also known as toggle keys?
   (1) Caps lock (2) Num lock
   (3) Both (1) and (2) (4) None of these
8. You can use the Tab key to **[SBI Clerk 2013]**
   (1) move a cursor across the screen
   (2) indent a paragraph
   (3) move the cursor down the screen
   (4) Both (1) and (2)
   (5) None of the above
9. To move to the beginning of a line of text, press the ...... key.
   (1) Page up (2) Shift
   (3) Home (4) Enter
10. In a keyboard, left-right-up-down set of keys facilitates which among the following functions? **[IBPS RRB PO Mains 2017]**
    (1) Deleting data or modification
    (2) Page scrolling to view a document
    (3) Launching Start Menu
    (4) Initiating Search and Help
    (5) Controlling RAM or process execution
11. Shift, Ctrl, Alt are examples of which among the following category? **[IBPS RRB PO Mains 2017]**
    (1) Modifier keys (2) Primary keys
    (3) Function keys (4) Alternate keys
    (5) Candidate keys
12. Pointing device includes the following except
    (1) mouse (2) joystick
    (3) trackball (4) keyboard
13. What type of device is a computer mouse? **[IBPS Clerk 2013]**
    (1) Storage (2) Output
    (3) Input (4) Input/output
    (5) Software
14. Which of these is a pointing and draw device? **[IBPS Clerk 2013]**
    (1) Mouse (2) Scanner
    (3) Printer (4) CD-ROM
    (5) Keyboard
15. First computer mouse was built by **[SSC CGL 2016, RRB NTPC 2016]**
    (1) Douglas Engelbart (2) William English
    (3) Oaniel Coogher (4) Robert Zawacki
16. Keyboard and ...... are the examples of input device. **[SBI Clerk 2014]**
    (1) monitor (2) modem
    (3) printer (4) mouse
    (5) CPU

17. Which is the best position for operating the mouse?
(1) Tail away from the user
(2) Tail towards the user
(3) Tail facing the right
(4) Tail facing the left

18. Which button is called as middle button used as third mouse button by pressing on it? **[IBPS RRB PO Mains 2017]**
(1) Right button (2) Scroll wheel
(3) Touch bar (4) Light bar
(5) Left button

19. Trackball is an example of a/an
(1) programming device (2) pointing device
(3) output device (4) software device

20. Which of the following is an input device used to enter motion data into computers or other electronic devices? **[SSC CHSL 2019]**
(1) Plotter (2) Trackball
(3) Monitor (4) Joystick

21. A joystick is primarily used to/for .... **[SBI PO 2013]**
(1) control sound on the screen
(2) computer gaming
(3) enter text
(4) draw pictures
(5) print text

22. Which of the following is a lever that can be moved in several directions to control the movement of an image on a computer monitor or similar display screen? **[SSC CHSL 2019]**
(1) MIDI devices (2) Optical mark reader
(3) Visual display unit (4) Joystick

23. Which one of the following is not an output device? **[SSC CGL 2018]**
(1) Projector (2) Headphones
(3) Plotter (4) Joystick

24. CAD stands for **[SSC CGL 2014]**
(1) Computer Automatic Design
(2) Computer Aided Decode
(3) Computer Automatic Decode
(4) Computer Aided Design

25. .... is generally used in applications like ATM, hospitals, airline reservation, etc.
(1) Light pen (2) Touch screen
(3) Joystick (4) Trackball

26. Which one does not related to mobile phone touch panel sensing methods? **[RRB NTPC 2016]**
A. Finger touch
B. Voice recognition
C. Gloved touch
D. Light transmittance
(1) B (2) A
(3) D (4) C

27. The pattern of printed lines on most products are called
(1) prices (2) OCR
(3) scanners (4) barcodes

28. A barcode reader is an example of
(1) processing device (2) storage device
(3) input device (4) output device

29. An optical input device that interprets pencil marks on paper media is .... **[IBPS RRB PO Mains 2017]**
(1) OMR (2) punch card reader
(3) optical scanners (4) magnetic tapes
(5) stylus

30. The OCR is used for the preparation of **[IBPS Clerk 2013]**
(1) electricity bills (2) insurance premium
(3) telephone bills (4) All of these
(5) None of these

31. The OCR recognises the ...... of the characters with the help of light source.
(1) size (2) shape
(3) colour (4) used ink

32. What does MICR stand for? **[IBPS Clerk 2014, RBI Grade B 2014]**
(1) Magnetic Ink Character Register
(2) Magnetic Ink Code Reader
(3) Magnetic Ink Code Register
(4) Magnetic Ink Character Recognition
(5) Magnetic Ink Cases Reader

33. Large amounts of cheques are processed by using
(1) OCR (2) MICR
(3) OMR (4) All of these

34. Which of the following device recognises physical traits of an individual?
(1) Smart card (2) Biometric sensor
(3) Barcode (4) MICR

35. Which of the following consists of an electronic writing area and a special pen that works with it? **[SSC CHSL 2019]**
(1) Trackball (2) Plotters
(3) Abacus (4) Graphics tablet

36. Which of the following converts analog information into digital form?
(1) Barcode reader **[SSC CHSL 2019]**
(2) Optical mark reading
(3) Digitizer
(4) Gamepad

37. A........ is used to read handwritten or printed text to make a digital image that is stored in memory.
(1) printer (2) laser beam
(3) scanner (4) touchpad

38. The input device to be used to get a printed diagram into a computer is the
[IBPS Clerk 2013, IBPS Clerk 2015]
(1) printer (2) mouse
(3) keyboard (4) touchpad
(5) scanner

39. A scanner scans **[SBI PO 2015]**
(1) pictures
(2) text
(3) both pictures and text
(4) neither pictures nor text
(5) None of the above

40. It is a video capturing device
(1) webcam (2) microphone
(3) monitor (4) mouse

41. An example of an input device is
[SSC CGL 2018]
(1) soundcard (2) headphones
(3) projector (4) webcam

42. Which of the following could be digital input devices for computers?
[RBI Grade B 2014]
(1) Digital camcorder
(2) Microphone
(3) Scanner
(4) All of the above
(5) None of the above

43. Which of the following groups consists of only input devices?
(1) Mouse, Keyboard, Monitor
(2) Mouse, Keyboard, Printer
(3) Mouse, Keyboard, Plotter
(4) Mouse, Keyboard, Scanner

44. Results are obtained from computer through its
(1) input unit (2) ALU unit
(3) CU unit (4) output unit

45. After a picture has been taken with a digital camera and processed appropriately, the actual print of the picture is considered as
(1) data (2) output
(3) input (4) the process

46. Using output device one can ....
[IBPS RRB PO Mains 2017]
(1) view or print data (2) modify data
(3) store data (4) replicate data
(5) enter data

47. Which among the following is the smallest unit in an image in a computer screen?
[IBPS RRB PO Mains 2017]
(1) Unit (2) Pixel
(3) Array (4) Resolution
(5) Clip

48. What type of device is a computer monitor?
[SBI Clerk 2014]
(1) Software (2) Processing
(3) Storage (4) Input
(5) Output

49. Soft copy refers to .... **[IBPS Clerk 2013]**
(1) printed output (2) digitising
(3) music sounds (4) screen output
(5) None of these

50. The higher the resolution of a monitor, the
(1) larger the pixels
(2) less clear the screen is
(3) further apart the pixels
(4) closer together the pixels

51. Screen or monitor device is **[UPSSSC 2016]**
(1) hard copy (2) soft copy
(3) input device (4) display device

52. The CRT is .... in shape. **[RBI Grade B 2013]**
(1) circular (2) rectangular
(3) eclipse (4) conical
(5) None of these

53. CRT has a **[RBI Grade B 2013]**
(1) hollow tube (2) vacuum tube
(3) long tube (4) round tube
(5) None of these

54. The rate at which scanning is repeated in a CRT is called
(1) refresh rate (2) resolution
(3) pitch (4) bandwidth

55. ...... provides hard copy output on paper. **[SBI Clerk 2015]**
(1) Mouse (2) Keyboard
(3) LCD monitor (4) Scanner
(5) Printer

56. Printer is an example of **[SBI Clerk 2014]**
(1) output device (2) input device
(3) processing device (4) storage device
(5) None of the above

57. What are the units used to count the speed of a printer? **[IBPS Clerk 2013]**
(1) CPM (2) DPI (3) PPM (4) BIT
(5) None of these

58. ...... printer cannot print more than one character at a time. **[SSC CHSL 2013]**
(1) Line (2) Daisy wheel
(3) Laser (4) Dot matrix

59. Speed of line printer is limited by the speed of **[Clerk 2013]**
(1) paper movements (2) cartridge used
(3) length of paper (4) All of these
(5) None of these

60. An example of peripheral equipment is
(1) printer
(2) CPU
(3) spreadsheet
(4) microcomputer

61. Dot matrix printer is
(1) unidirectional (2) bi-directional
(3) sequential (4) random

62. The impact printers are
(1) dot matrix (2) drum
(3) inkjet (4) Both (1) and (2)

63. Drum printer is an example of
(1) input (2) output
(3) processing (4) storage

64. The example of non-impact printers are **[RBI Grade B 2013]**
(1) Laser-Dot matrix (2) Inkjet-Laser
(3) Inkjet-Dot matrix (4) Dot matrix
(5) None of these

65. Line printer speed is specified in terms of **[RBI Grade B 2013]**
(1) LPM (Lines Per Minute)
(2) CPM (Characters Per Minute)
(3) DPM
(4) Any of the above
(5) None of the above

66. In laser printers, printing is achieved by deflecting laser beam on to ...... surface of a drum. **[SBI PO 2013]**
(1) magnetised (2) photosensitive
(3) magnetic (4) Either (1) or (2)
(5) None of these

67. Which of the following printers, are you sure, will not to use if your objective is to print on multi carbon forms?
(1) Daisy wheel (2) Dot matrix
(3) Laser (4) Thermal

68. Laser printers belong to
(1) line printer (2) page printer
(3) band printer (4) dot matrix printer

69. A hard copy would prepared on a **[SBI Clerk 2013]**
(1) line printer (2) dot matrix printer
(3) plotter (4) type writer terminal
(5) All of these

70. Who invented the 3D printer? **[SSC CGL 2016]**
(1) Nick Holonyak
(2) Elias Howe
(3) Chuck Hull
(4) Christian Huygens

71. It is used to produce large drawings or images such as construction plans, blueprints for mechnanical object, etc.
(1) Printer (2) Plotter
(3) MICR (4) OCR

72. What type of devices are computer speakers or headphones? **[IBPS Clerk 2015]**
(1) Input (2) Input/Output
(3) Software (4) Storage
(5) Output

73. Which is not an item of hardware? **[IBPS Clerk 2013]**
(1) An MP3 file (2) A keyboard
(3) A mouse (4) Printer
(5) None of these

74. The transfer of data from a CPU to peripheral devices of computer is achieved through **[SSC CGL 2012]**
(1) interfaces (2) buffer memory
(3) modems (4) I/O ports

75. A parallel port is most often used by a **[SSC CPO 2011]**
(1) printer
(2) monitor
(3) mouse
(4) external storage device

76. USB in data cables stands for
(1) Unicode Smart Bus **[IBPS Clerk 2014]**
(2) Universal Structural Bus
(3) Unicode Serial Bus
(4) Universal Smart Bus
(5) Universal Serial Bus

77. USB refers to **[SSC MTS 2013]**
(1) a storage device
(2) a processor
(3) a port type
(4) a serial bus standard

78. Which of the following are properties of USB? **[IBPS Clerk Mains 2017]**
(1) Platform independent
(2) Platform dependent
(3) Source dependent
(4) Software dependent
(5) Software Independent

79. The ...... format reduces an audio file to about one-tenth of its original size, while preserving much of the original quality of the sound. **[SBI Clerk 2014]**
(1) DOC (2) PNG (3) GIF (4) MP3
(5) VMEG

80. Peripheral devices such as printers and monitors are considered to be .... **[IBPS Clerk 2013]**
(1) hardware (2) software
(3) data (4) information
(5) source code

81. External devices such as printers, keyboards and modems are known as **[IBPS Clerk 2015]**
(1) add-on devices
(2) peripherals
(3) extra software devices
(4) PC expansion slot add-ons
(5) special buys

82. ...... can interpret voice data into words that can be understood by the computer. **[IBPS Clerk 2014]**
(1) Speech input hardware
(2) Speech recognition software
(3) Word recognition software
(4) Talking software
(5) Other than those given as options

83. Dumb terminals have terminals and **[SBI PO 2015]**
(1) mouse (2) speakers
(3) keyboard (4) mouse or speakers
(5) None of these

84. Which one of the following input device is user-programmable? **[IBPS Clerk 2015]**
(1) Dumb terminal (2) Smart terminal
(3) VDT (4) Intelligent terminal
(5) All of these

85. Input devices are used to provide the steps and tasks the computer needs to process data and these steps and tasks are called **[IBPS Clerk 2015]**

(1) program (2) design
(3) information (4) instructions
(5) flow chart

86. For printing MICR characters, the ink used contains **[RRB NTPC 2016]**

A. Lead oxide B. Graphite
C. Cuprous oxide D. Iron oxide

(1) B (2) C
(3) D (4) A

ANSWERS

1. *(5)*	2. *(4)*	3. *(2)*	4. *(3)*	5. *(2)*	6. *(4)*	7. *(3)*	8. *(2)*	9. *(3)*	10. *(2)*
11. *(1)*	12. *(4)*	13. *(3)*	14. *(1)*	15. *(1)*	16. *(4)*	17. *(2)*	18. *(2)*	19. *(2)*	20. *(2)*
21. *(2)*	22. *(4)*	23. *(4)*	24. *(4)*	25. *(2)*	26. *(1)*	27. *(4)*	28. *(3)*	29. *(1)*	30. *(4)*
31. *(2)*	32. *(4)*	33. *(2)*	34. *(2)*	35. *(4)*	36. *(3)*	37. *(3)*	38. *(5)*	39. *(3)*	40. *(1)*
41. *(4)*	42. *(4)*	43. *(4)*	44. *(4)*	45. *(2)*	46. *(1)*	47. *(2)*	48. *(5)*	49. *(4)*	50. *(4)*
51. *(4)*	52. *(2)*	53. *(2)*	54. *(1)*	55. *(5)*	56. *(1)*	57. *(2)*	58. *(4)*	59. *(1)*	60. *(1)*
61. *(2)*	62. *(4)*	63. *(2)*	64. *(2)*	65. *(2)*	66. *(2)*	67. *(3)*	68. *(2)*	69. *(5)*	70. *(3)*
71. *(2)*	72. *(5)*	73. *(1)*	74. *(4)*	75. *(1)*	76. *(5)*	77. *(3)*	78. *(1)*	79. *(4)*	80. *(1)*
81. *(2)*	82. *(2)*	83. *(4)*	84. *(4)*	85. *(4)*	86. *(3)*				

CHAPTER

04

COMPUTER MEMORY

Computer memory stores data and instructions required during the processing of data and output results. It also relates to many devices that are responsible for storing data on a temporary or a permanent basis.

Types of Memory

Primary Memory

The memory unit that communicates directly with the CPU is called main memory or internal memory or primary memory.

The primary memory allows the computer to store data for immediate manipulation and to keep track of what is currently being processed. It has limited storage capacity.

Main memory is volatile in nature, it means that when the power is turned OFF, the contents of this memory are lost forever.

Primary memory can be further classified in two types which are as follows

1. **Random Access Memory** (RAM) It is also known as read/write memory, that allows CPU to read as well as write data and instructions into it.

   RAM is used for the temporary storage of input data, output data and intermediate results.

   The two categories of RAM are as follows

   (i) **Dynamic RAM** (DRAM) It is made up of memory cells where each cell is composed of one capacitor and one transistor.

   DRAM must be refreshed continually to store information. DRAM is slower, less expensive and occupies less space on the computer's motherboard.

   (ii) **Static RAM** (SRAM) It retains the data as long as power is provided to the memory chip.

   SRAM needs not be refreshed periodically. It uses multiple transistors for each memory cell. It does not use capacitor. SRAM is often used cache memory due to its high speed. SRAM is more expensive and faster than DRAM.

2. **Read Only Memory** (ROM) It is also known as non-volatile memory or permanent storage. It does not lose its contents when the power is switched OFF.

   ROM can written data and instructions to it only one time. Once a ROM chip is programmed at the time of manufacturing, it cannot be reprogrammed or rewritten. So, it has only read capability, not write.

The three categories of ROM are as follows

(i) **Programmable ROM** (PROM) It is also non-volatile in nature. Once a PROM has been programmed, its content can never be changed. It is one-time programmable device. This type of memory is found in video game consoles, mobile phones, implantable medical devices and high definition multimedia interfaces.

(ii) **Erasable Programmable ROM** (EPROM) It is similar to PROM, but it can be erased by exposure to strong ultraviolet light, then rewritten. So, it is also known as Ultraviolet Erasable Programmable ROM (UVEPROM).

(iii) **Electrically Erasable Programmable ROM** (EEPROM) It is similar to EPROM, but it can be erased electrically, then rewritten electrically and the burning process is reversible by exposure to electric pulses. It is the most flexible type of ROM and is now commonly used for holding BIOS.

Note *BIOS stands for Basic Input/Output System.*

Some Special Memories

Apart from above memories, there are also some other memories that help to primary memory, *which are as follows*

Cache Memory

It is a storage buffer that stores the data which is used more often, temporarily and makes it available to CPU at a fast rate. Cache memory is a very high speed memory placed in between RAM and CPU. It increases the speed of processing.

Flash Memory

It is a kind of semiconductor based non-volatile rewritable memory, used in digital camera, mobile phone, printer, etc.

Virtual Memory

It is a technique that allows the execution of processes that are not completely in main memory. One major advantage of this memory is that programs can be larger than main memory.

Secondary Memory/ Storage

This memory stores much larger amount of data and information for extended periods of time. Data in secondary memory cannot be processed directly by the CPU, it must first be copied into primary memory, i.e. RAM. It is the slower and cheaper form of memory than primary memory.

Secondary storage is used to store data and programs when they are not being processed. It is also non-volatile in nature. Due to this, the data remain in the secondary storage as long as it is not overwritten or deleted by the user. It is a permanent storage.

Secondary memory devices include following types of memory

1. **Magnetic Storage** It is the manipulation of magnetic fields on a medium in order to record audio, video or other data. It includes hard disk drive, floppy disk and magnetic tape, *which are described below*

   (i) **Hard Disk Drive** (HDD) It is a non-volatile and random access digital data storage device. HDD is a data storage device used for storing and retrieving digital information using rotating disks (platters) coated with magnetic material.

   All programs of a computer are installed in hard disk. It is a fixed disk, i.e. cannot be removed from the drive. It consists of a **spindle** that holds non-magnetic flat circular disks called **platters**, which hold the recorded data. Each platter requires two read/write heads, that are used to write and read information from a platter.

   All the read/write heads are attached to a single access arm so that they cannot move independently.

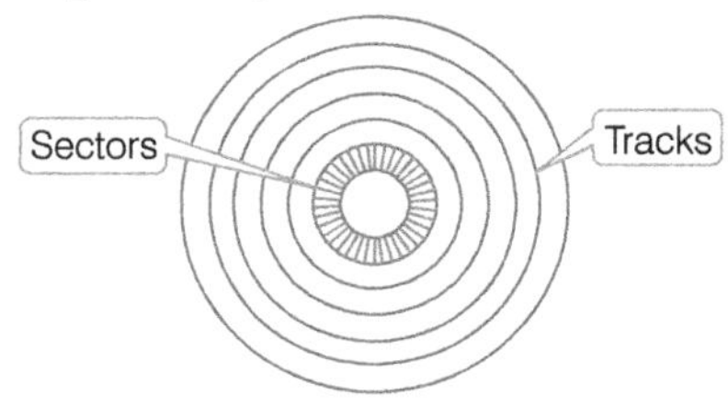

Tracks and Sectors

The information is recorded in bands; each band of information is called a **track**. Each platter has the same number of tracks and a track location that cuts across all platters is called a **cylinder.** The tracks are divided into pie-shaped sections known as **sectors.**

(ii) **Floppy Disk** (Diskette) Floppy disk is round in shape and a thin plastic disk coated with iron oxide. It is used to store data but it can store small amount of data and it is slower to access than hard disks.

Data is retrieved or recorded on the surface of the disk through a slot on the envelope. Floppy disk is removable from the drive. Floppy disk is available in three sizes; 8 inch, $5\frac{1}{4}$ inch and $3\frac{1}{2}$ inch.

(iii) **Magnetic Tape** These tapes are made of a plastic film-type material coated with magnetic materials to store data permanently. Data can be read as well as write. It is usually 12.5 mm to 25 mm wide and 500 m to 1200 m long.

Magnetic tapes hold the maximum data, which can be accessed sequentially. They are generally used to store backup data or that type of data, which is not frequently used or to transfer data from one system to another.

2. **Optical Storage** It is any storage type in which data is written and read with a laser. It includes CD, DVD and Blu-ray disc, *which are described below*

(i) **Compact Disc** (CD) It is the most popular and the least expensive type of optical disc. A CD is capable of being used as a data storage device alongwith storing of digital audio.

CD is categorised into three main types as follows

- CD-ROM (Compact Disc-Read Only Memory)
- CD-R (Compact Disc- Recordable)
- CD-RW (Compact Disc- Re-Writable)

(ii) **Digital Video Disc** (DVD) It is also known as Super Density Disc (SDD) or Digital Versatile Disc (DVD). It is an optical disc storage device. DVDs offer higher storage capacity than CDs while having the same dimensions.

Depending upon the disc type, DVD can store several gigabytes of data (4.7 GB-17.08 GB). DVDs are primarily used to store music or movies and can be played back on your television or computer too. They are not rewritable storage device.

DVDs come in three varieties are as follows

- DVD-ROM (Digital Video Disc-Read Only Memory)
- DVD-R (DVD-Recordable)
- DVD-RW (DVD-Re-Writable)

(iii) **Blu-ray Disc** It is an optical disc storage medium designed to re-capture the data normally in DVD format. Blu-ray disc (BD) contains 25 GB (23.31 GB) per layer space.

The name Blu-ray disc refers to the blue laser used to read the disc, which allows information to be stored at a greater density than the longer- wavelength red laser used in DVDs.

Blu-ray can hold almost 5 times more data than a single layer DVD.

The variations in the formats are as follows

- BD-ROM (Read only)
- BD-R (Recordable)
- BD-RW (Rewritable)
- BD-RE (Rewritable)

3. **Solid State Storage** It is a type of storage technique that employs storage devices built using silicon microchip based storage architecture. It includes pen/flash drive, memory card, *which are described below*

(i) **Pen/Thumb Drive** It is also known as flash drive. A flash drive is a data storage device that consists of flash memory (key memory) with a portable USB (Universal Serial Bus) interface. USB flash drives are typically removable, rewritable and much smaller than a floppy disk.

Today, **flash drives** are available in various storage capacities as 256MB, 512MB, 1GB, 4GB, 16GB upto 64 GB. They are widely used as an easy and small medium to transfer and store the information from the computers.

(ii) **Memory Cards** These are the data storage devices in chip shaped. They are commonly used in many electronic devices, including digital cameras, mobile phones, laptop, computers. They are small, re-recordable, easily portable and very light weighted.

Basic Units of Memory Measurements

1 Bit	=	Binary Digit (0 or 1)
4 Bits	=	1 Nibble
8 Bits	=	1 Byte = 2 Nibble
1024 Bytes	=	1 KB (KiloByte)
1024 KB	=	1 MB (MegaByte)
1024 MB	=	1 GB(GigaByte)
1024 GB	=	1 TB(TeraByte)
1024 TB	=	1 PB(PetaByte)
1024 PB	=	1 EB(ExaByte)
1024 EB	=	1 ZB(ZettaByte)
1024 ZB	=	1 YB (YottaByte)
1024 YB	=	1 (BrontoByte)
1024 BB	=	1 (GeopByte)

Note *Bit is the smallest memory measurement unit. GeopByte is the highest memory measurement unit. A byte can represent* 256 (0-255 or 2^8) *distinct values.*

Cloud Computing

It is a general term for anything that involves hosted services over the internet. The name comes from the use of clouds as an abstraction for the complex infrastructure it contains in system diagrams.

It entrusts services with a user's data, software and computation over a network. It has considerable overlap with Software as a Service (SaaS).

Types of Cloud Deployments

The three types of cloud deployments categorised based on an organisation's ability to manage and secure assets are as follows

1. **Public Cloud** These are managed by third party which provides cloud services over the Internet to public. They offer solutions for minimising IT infrastructure costs and act as a good option for handling peak loads on the local infrastructure. A public cloud is meant to serve multiple users, not a single customer.
2. **Private Cloud** These are distributed systems that work on a private infrastructure and providing the users with dynamic provisioning of computing resources.
3. **Hybrid Cloud** It is a heterogeneous distributed system resulted by combining facilities of public cloud and private cloud. For this reason, they are also called heterogeneous clouds.

Cloud Computing Services

1. **Infrastructure as a Service** (IaaS) It is a cloud computing model where virtualised infrastructure is offered to and managed for business by external cloud providers. Some examples of the wide usage of IaaS are automated policy-driven operations such as backup, recovery, etc.
2. **Software as a Service** (SaaS) It is a method for delivering software applications over the Internet as per the demand and on a subscription basis. Most common examples of SaaS are Microsoft Office 360, Oracle CRM, Marketo, etc.
3. **Platform as a Service** (PaaS) It refers to the supply an on-demand environment for developing, testing, delivering and managing software applications. Some key players offering PaaS are Bluemix, CloudBees, Salesforce.com, etc.

Several Next Generation Memories

- **FeFET or FeRAM** A next generation ferroelectric memory.
- **Nanotube RAM** In R & D for years, nanotube RAM is targeted to displace DRAM. Others are developing carbon nanotubes and next generation memories on the same device.
- **Phase Change Memory** After shipping the first

PCM devices, Intel is readying a new version. Others may enter the PCM market.

- **ReRAM** Future versions are positioned for AI apps.
- **Spin Orbit Torque-MRAM** (SOT-MRAM) A next generation MRAM targeted to replace SRAM.

Tit-Bits

- The rate at which data is written to disc or read from disc is called **data transfer rate**.
- **Root directory** is the main folder of disk. It contains information about all folders on the disk.

QUESTION BANK

1. ...... stores data and instructions required during the processing of data and output results.
(1) Memory (2) Architecture
(3) Input (4) Output

2. Where is data saved permanently?
(1) Memory (2) Storage
(3) CPU (4) Printer

3. Where are programs and data to be used by the computer available? **[SSC FCI 2012]**
(1) Processing unit (2) Output
(3) Storage (4) Input

4. How many types of memory does a computer have?
(1) Four (2) Eight
(3) One (4) Two

5. Primary storage is .... as compared to secondary storage.
(1) slow and inexpensive
(2) fast and inexpensive
(3) fast and expensive
(4) slow and expensive

6. The key feature(s) of internal memory is/are
(1) limited storage capacity
(2) temporary storage
(3) fast access and high cost
(4) All of the above

7. The two kinds of main memory are
(1) ROM and RAM
(2) primary and secondary
(3) floppy disk and hard disk
(4) direct and sequential

8. Which of the following is a correct definition of volatile memory?
(1) It does retain its contents at high temperature
(2) It is to be kept in air-tight box
(3) It loses its content on failure of power supply
(4) It does not lose its content on failure of power supply

9. Cache and main memory will not be able to hold their contents when the power is OFF. They are
(1) dynamic (2) static
(3) volatile (4) non-volatile

10. In computer terminology, what is the full form of RAM? **[SSC CGL 2018]**
(1) Random Access Memory
(2) Repeated Access Memory
(3) Rapid Access Memory
(4) Regular Access Memory

11. ...... memory in a computer is where information is temporarily stored while it is being accessed or worked on by the processor. **[IBPS RRB PO 2017]**
(1) Logical (2) Secondary
(3) ROM (4) RAM
(5) Cache

12. Why RAM is so called? **[IBPS Clerk 2015]**
(1) Because it is read and write memory
(2) Because it is a volatile memory
(3) Because it can be selected directly for storing and retrieving data and instructions of any location of chip
(4) Because it is a non-volatile memory
(5) None of the above

13. Which of the following is not true about RAM? **[IBPS PO 2015, IBPS Clerk 2014]**
(1) RAM is the same as hard disk storage
(2) RAM is a temporary storage area
(3) RAM is volatile
(4) RAM is a primary memory
(5) Other than those given as options

14. Virtual memory allocates hard disk space to supplement the immediate, functional memory capacity of **[SBI PO 2014]**
(1) ROM (2) EPROM
(3) the registers (4) extended memory
(5) RAM

15. Storage that retains its data after the power is turned OFF is referred to as **[SBI Clerk 2009]**
(1) volatile storage (2) non-volatile storage
(3) sequential storage (4) direct storage

16. The advantage of DRAM is
(1) it is cheaper than SRAM
(2) it can store data more than that of SRAM
(3) it is faster than SRAM
(4) data can be erased easily from it as compared to SRAM

17. Which of the following stores data permanently in a computer? **[SSC CGL 2017]**
(1) ALU (2) Cache memory
(3) RAM (4) ROM

18. Permanent instructions that the computer use when it is turned ON and that cannot be changed by other instructions are contained in **[UPSSSC 2016]**
(1) ROM (2) RAM (3) ALU (4) SRAM

19. When you first turn on a computer, the CPU is preset to execute instructions stored in the **[IBPS PO 2015]**
(1) RAM (2) flash memory
(3) ROM (4) CD-ROM
(5) ALU

20. What is the full form of PROM? **[SSC CHSL 2019]**
(1) Programmable Read Only Memory
(2) Program Read Output Memory
(3) Program Read Only Memory
(4) Primary Read Only Memory

21. A disc's content that is recorded at the time of manufacture and cannot be changed or erased by the user is **[IBPS Clerk 2013]**
(1) memory only (2) write only
(3) once only (4) run only
(5) read only

22. In the field of Information and Communication Technology (ICT), what is the full form of EEPROM? **[SSC CGL 2018]**
(1) Electrically Erasable Programmable Read Only Memory
(2) Electrically Efficient Portable Read Only Memory
(3) Electrically Efficient Programmable Read Only Memory
(4) Enhanced Electrical Portable Read Only Memory

23. The difference between memory and storage is that memory is ...... and storage is .... **[IBPS Clerk 2015]**
(1) temporary; permanent
(2) permanent; temporary
(3) slow; fast
(4) non-volatile; volatile
(5) None of the above

24. The ...... acts as a buffer between the CPU and the main memory. **[UPSSSC 2018]**
(1) primary memory (2) cache memory
(3) secondary memory (4) RAM

25. Which of the following is a very high speed semiconductor memory which can speed up the CPU? **[SSC CHSL 2019]**
(1) Secondary memory (2) Main memory
(3) Primary memory (4) Cache memory

26. What is the term used for temporarily stored data? **[UPSSSC 2019]**
(1) Miscellaneous data (2) Cache data
(3) Picked data (4) Tempo data

27. .... is having more memory addresses than are physically available. **[SBI PO 2014]**
(1) Virtual memory
(2) System software
(3) Application software
(4) RAM
(5) Vertical memory

28. .... is the ability of a device to 'jump' directly to the requested data.
(1) Sequential access
(2) Random access
(3) Quick access
(4) All of the above

29. The .... is the amount of data that a storage device can move from the storage to the computer per second.
(1) data migration rate
(2) data digitising rate
(3) data transfer rate
(4) data access rate

30. The main directory of a disk is called the .... directory. **[IBPS PO 2015]**
(1) network
(2) folder
(3) root
(4) other than those given as options
(5) program

31. The ...... indicates how much data a particular storage medium can hold. **[IBPS Clerk 2013]**
(1) storage (2) access
(3) capacity (4) memory
(5) None of these

32. The secondary storage devices can only store data but they cannot perform
(1) arithmetic operations
(2) logic operations
(3) fetch operations
(4) All of the above

33. Where do you save the data that, your data will remain intact even when the computer is turned OFF?
(1) RAM
(2) Motherboard
(3) Secondary storage device
(4) Primary storage device

34. The term .... refers to data storage systems that make it possible for a computer or electronic device to store and retrieve data.
(1) retrieval technology
(2) input technology
(3) output technology
(4) storage technology

35. The storage device used to compensate for the difference in rates of flow of data from one device to another is termed as
(1) chip (2) channel
(3) floppy (4) buffer

36. Which of the following is the magnetic storage device?
(1) Hard disk (2) Compact disc
(3) Audio tapes (4) All of these

37. Hard disk devices are considered ...... storage. **[SBI Clerk 2014]**
(1) flash (2) temporary
(3) worthless (4) non-volatile
(5) non-permanent

38. The thick, rigid metal plotters that are capable of retrieving information at a high rate of speed are known as **[SBI Clerk 2014]**
(1) hard disk (2) SAN
(3) soft disk (4) flash memory
(5) None of these

39. Hard drive is used to store **[IBPS Clerk Mains 2017]**
(1) volatile data (2) non-volatile data
(3) permanent data (4) temporary data
(5) intermediate data

40. The hard drive is normally located
(1) next to the printer **[SBI PO 2014]**
(2) plugged into the back of the computer
(3) underneath the monitor
(4) on top of the CD-ROM
(5) inside the system base unit

41. Data on a floppy disk is recorded in rings called
(1) sectors (2) ringers
(3) rounders (4) tracks

42. Which of the following is/are example(s) of magnetic storage media?
(1) Zip disk (2) CD-ROM
(3) Floppy disk (4) DVD
(5) Both (1) and (3)

43. Floppy disks are organised as
(1) files
(2) heads and folders
(3) tracks and sectors
(4) All of the above

44. The capacity of 3.5 inch floppy disk is
(1) 1.40 MB (2) 1.44 GB
(3) 1.40 GB (4) 1.44 MB

45. The most common storage device for the personal computer is the **[SBI Clerk 2014]**
(1) floppy disk
(2) USB personal computer
(3) mainframe
(4) a laptop
(5) None of these

46. Which of the following has the smallest storage capacity? **[IBPS Clerk 2015]**
(1) Zip disk (2) Hard disk
(3) Floppy disk (4) Data cartridge
(5) CD

47. FDD stands for **[SSC, CGL 2018, IBPS Clerk 2015]**
(1) Floppy Drive Detector
(2) Floppy Drive Demodulator
(3) Floppy Disk Drive
(4) Floppy Demodulator Disc
(5) None of the above

48. .... is the process of dividing the disc into tracks and sectors. **[SBI PO 2015, IBPS Clerk Mains 2017]**
(1) Tracking (2) Formatting
(3) Crashing (4) Allotting
(5) None of these

49. Data on a floppy disk was recorded in rings called **[IBPS RRB PO 2017]**
(1) flip (2) ringers
(3) rounders (4) fields
(5) segments

50. Magnetic tape is not practical for applications where data must be quickly recalled because tape is
(1) a random access medium
(2) a sequential access medium
(3) a read only medium
(4) fragile and easily damaged

51. Which of the following can hold maximum data?
(1) Optical disc (2) Floppy disk
(3) Magnetic disk (4) Magnetic tape

52. On a CD-RW, you can
(1) read and write information
(2) only read information
(3) only write information
(4) read, write and rewrite information

53. Which of the following are advantages of CD-ROM as a storage media? **[RBI Grade B 2014]**
(1) CD-ROM is an inexpensive way to store large amount of data and information
(2) CD-ROM discs retrieve data and information more quickly than magnetic disks
(3) CD-ROMs make less errors than magnetic media
(4) All of the above
(5) None of the above

54. Which media has the ability to have data/information stored (written) on them by users more than once? **[RBI Grade B 2014]**
(1) CD-R discs
(2) CD-RW discs
(3) Zip discs
(4) Optical discs
(5) CD-RW discs and Zip discs

55. What is the difference between a CD-ROM and CD-RW? **[IBPS PO 2015]**
(1) They are the same—just two different terms used by different manufactures.
(2) A CD-ROM can be written to and a CD-RW cannot.
(3) Other than those given as options
(4) A CD-ROM holds more information than a CD-RW.
(5) A CD-RW can be written to but a CD-ROM can only be read from.

56. Compact discs that can store approximately 650-800 MB of data or 74-80 min of music are **[SBI Clerk 2015]**
(1) zip discs (2) CD-ROM
(3) video cards (4) pressing machines
(5) floppy diskettes

57. A flat metallic disk that contains a large amount of permanently stored information read optically, is called a
(1) monitor (2) ALU
(3) CD-ROM (4) RAM

58. CD-ROM is an example of **[RBI Grade B 2014]**
(1) input device
(2) output device
(3) Both input & output devices
(4) Memory device
(5) None of the above

59. DVD refers to **[SSC MTS 2013]**
(1) Digital Video Developer
(2) Digital Video Device
(3) Digital Video Disc
(4) None of the above

60. A DVD is an example of a(n) **[SBI Clerk 2014]**
(1) optical device
(2) output device
(3) hard disk
(4) solid state storage device
(5) None of the above

61. Which of the following discs can be read only? **[IBPS Clerk 2015]**
(1) DVD-R (2) DVD-ROM
(3) DVR-RW (4) CD-R
(5) None of these

62. Which is not an external storage device? **[SSC CGL 2016]**
(1) CD-ROM (2) DVD-ROM
(3) Pen drive (4) RAM

63. ...... is the smallest unit of data in a computer. **[SSC CGL 2018]**
(1) Gigabyte (2) Bit
(3) Byte (4) Terabyte

64. The term Bit is short for **[SBI Clerk 2009]**
(1) megabyte
(2) binary language
(3) binary digit
(4) binary number
(5) None of the above

65. Which among the following is another name for a group of 4 bits? **[IBPS Clerk 2015, IBPS PO 2016]**
(1) Nibble (2) Byte
(3) KiloByte (3) MegaByte
(5) PetaByte

66. Which of the following is the smallest measure of storage? **[UPSSSC 2015]**
(1) Tera byte (2) Gigabyte
(3) Kilobyte (4) Byte

67. .... are used to measure both computer memory (RAM) and storage capacity of Floppy disks, CD-ROM drives and Hard drives. **[SBI Clerk 2015]**
(1) Bytes
(2) Bits
(3) Octal numbers
(4) Hexadecimal numbers
(5) Binary numbers

68. How many bits are equal to one byte ? **[SSC CGL 2016]**
(1) 8 (2) 6 (3) 7 (4) 2

69. Instructions and memory address are represented by **[IBPS Clerk 2015]**
(1) character code (2) binary codes
(3) binary word (4) parity bit
(5) None of these

70. Kilo Byte equals to how many bytes? **[SBI Clerk 2012]**
(1) 1000 (2) 1035 (3) 100 (4) 1008
(5) 1024

71. A ...... is approximately a million bytes. **[SBI PO 2014]**
(1) giga byte (2) kilo byte
(3) mega byte (4) tera byte
(5) None of these

72. What does the computer abbreviation 'MB' used for? **[IBPS Clerk 2014]**
(1) Megabit (2) Millionbytes
(3) Megabytes (4) Millionbit
(5) Microbytes

73. The amount of memory (RAM or ROM) is measured in **[SBI PO 2014]**
(1) bytes (2) bits
(3) megabytes (4) megabits
(5) hertz

74. How many kilobytes make a megabyte? **[UPSSSC 2016, IBPS Clerk 2015]**
(1) 128 (2) 1024 (3) 256 (4) 512
(5) 64

75. A ... is approximately one billion bytes. **[IBPS Clerk 2014, SBI PO 2015]**
(1) kilobyte (2) bit
(3) gigabyte (4) megabyte
(5) None of these

76. The term 'gigabyte' refers to **[IBPS PO 2012]**
(1) 1024 byte
(2) 1024 kilobyte
(3) 1024 megabyte
(4) 1024 gigabyte
(5) None of the above

77. Which of the following is the largest unit of storage? **[SBI PO 2015]**
(1) GB (2) KB
(3) MB (4) TB
(5) None of these

78. Which of the following is correct sequence of smallest to largest units of storage size? **[SBI PO 2014]**
(1) Petabyte, Kilobyte, Megabyte, Gigabyte, Terabyte
(2) Kilobyte, Megabyte, Terabyte, Petabyte, Gigabyte
(3) Megabyte, Terabyte, Gigabyte, Kilobyte, Petabyte
(4) Kilobyte, Megabyte, Petabyte, Terabyte, Gigabyte
(5) Kilobyte, Megabyte, Gigabyte, Terabyte, Petabyte

79. How many gigabytes is equal to 1 petabyte? **[SSC CGL 2016]**
(1) 256 (2) 512
(3) 1024 (4) 1024×1024

80. ...... (HHDD) is a technology where the conventional disk drive is combined with non-volatile flash memory, of typically 128 MB or more to cache data during normal use. **[SSC CGL 2017]**
(1) Hyper Hard Disk Drive
(2) Hybrid Hard Disk Drive
(3) Hybrid Helium Disk Drive
(4) Hyper Helium Disk Drive

81. Which of the following provides computing and storage capacity services to heterogeneous community of end recipients?
(1) Cloud computing (2) Big data
(3) FutureSkills (4) Robotics

82. What is/are characteristics of cloud computing?
(1) On demand self services
(2) Broad network access
(3) Resource pooling
(4) All of the above

83. Which type of cloud deployments is used to serve multiple users, not a single customer?
(1) Private cloud (2) Public cloud
(3) Hybrid cloud (4) None of these

84. Which cloud computing services refers to supply on demand environment for developing software applications?
(1) SaaS (2) AaaS
(3) PaaS (4) IaaS

ANSWERS

1. (1)	2. (2)	3. (3)	4. (4)	5. (5)	6. (4)	7. (1)	8. (3)	9. (3)	10. (1)
11. (4)	12. (3)	13. (1)	14. (5)	15. (2)	16. (1)	17. (4)	18. (1)	19. (3)	20. (1)
21. (5)	22. (1)	23. (1)	24. (2)	25. (4)	26. (2)	27. (1)	28. (2)	29. (2)	30. (3)
31. (3)	32. (4)	33. (3)	34. (4)	35. (4)	36. (1)	37. (4)	38. (1)	39. (3)	40. (5)
41. (4)	42. (5)	43. (3)	44. (4)	45. (1)	46. (3)	47. (3)	48. (2)	49. (5)	50. (2)
51. (4)	52. (4)	53. (1)	54. (2)	55. (1)	56. (2)	57. (3)	58. (4)	59. (3)	60. (1)
61. (2)	62. (4)	63. (2)	64. (3)	65. (1)	66. (4)	67. (1)	68. (1)	69. (2)	70. (5)
71. (3)	72. (3)	73. (3)	74. (2)	75. (3)	76. (3)	77. (4)	78. (5)	79. (4)	80. (2)
81. (1)	82. (4)	83. (2)	84. (3)						

CHAPTER

05

DATA REPRESENTATION

Data representation refers those methods which are used internally to represent information stored in a computer. Computer store lots of different types of information as numbers, text, graphics, sounds, etc.

Number System

It is a technique to represent numbers in the computer system architecture, every value that you are saving into/from computer memory has a defined number system.

Types of Number System

Binary Number System

This system is very efficient for computers, but not for humans. It contains only two unique digits 0's and 1's.

It is also known as Base 2 system. A string, which has any combination of these two digits (0 and 1 are called bit) is called a binary number. The computer always calculates the input in binary form and digital computers internally use the binary number system to represent data and perform arithmetic calculations.

For example, $(10101)_2$

Here, 2 represents the base of binary number.

Decimal Number System

The number system that we use in our day-to-day life is decimal number system.

It consists of 10 digits from 0 to 9. These digits can be used to represent any numeric value. It is also known as Base 10 system or positional number system. *For example,* $(1275)_{10}$

Here, 10 represents the base of decimal number.

Octal Number System

It consists of 8 digits from 0 to 7. It is also known as Base 8 system. Each position of the octal number represents a successive power of eight.

For example, $(234)_8$

Here, 8 represents the base of octal number.

Hexadecimal Number System

It provides us with a shorthand method of working with binary numbers. There are 16 unique digits available in this system.

These are 0 to 9 and A to F, where A denotes 10, B denotes 11, ..., F denotes 15.

It is also known as Base 16 system or simply Hex.

So, each position of the hexadecimal number represents a successive power of 16.

For example, $(\text{F9D})_{16}$

Here, 16 represents the base of hexadecimal number.

Decimal, Binary, Octal and Hexadecimal Equivalents

Decimal	Binary	Octal	Hexadecimal
0	0000	0	0
1	0001	1	1
2	0010	2	2
3	0011	3	3
4	0100	4	4
5	0101	5	5
6	0110	6	6
7	0111	7	7
8	1000	—	8
9	1001	—	9
10	1010	—	A
11	1011	—	B
12	1100	—	C
13	1101	—	D
14	1110	—	E
15	1111	—	F

Conversion between the Number Systems

Decimal to Binary

To convert decimal to binary, following steps are involved

Step 1 Divide the given number by 2.

Step 2 Note the quotient and remainder. Remainder should be 0 or 1.

Step 3 If quotient $\neq 0$, then again divide the quotient by 2 and back to step 2.
If quotient $= 0$, then stop the process.

Step 4 First remainder is called as **Least Significant Bit** (LSB) and last remainder is called as **Most Significant Bit** (MSB).

Step 5 Arrange all remainders from MSB to LSB.

Example $(43)_{10} \rightarrow (?)_2$

		Remainder
2	43	$1 \rightarrow$ LSB
2	21	1
2	10	0
2	5	1
2	2	0
2	1	$1 \rightarrow$ MSB
	0	

Then, $(43)_{10} \rightarrow (101011)_2$

Binary to Decimal

To convert binary to decimal, following steps are involved

Step 1 Multiply the all binary digits by powers of 2.

Step 2 The power for integral part will be positive and for fractional part will be negative.

Step 3 Add all the multiplying digits.

Example $(1101.10)_2 \rightarrow (?)_{10}$

$$(1101.10)_2 = 1\times 2^3 + 1\times 2^2 + 0\times 2^1 + 1\times 2^0 + 1\times 2^{-1} + 0\times 2^{-2}$$
$$= 8 + 4 + 0 + 1 + 0.5 + 0 = 13.5$$

Then, $(1101.10)_2 \rightarrow (13.5)_{10}$

Binary to Octal

To convert binary to octal, following steps are involved

Step 1 Make the group of 3 bits from right to left. If the left most group has less than 3 bits, put in the necessary number of leading zeroes on the left.

Step 2 Now, convert each group to decimal number.

Example $(110110100)_2 \rightarrow (?)_8$

110 110 100
↓ ↓ ↓
6 6 4

Then, $(110110100)_2 \rightarrow (664)_8$

Octal to Binary

Convert every digit of the number from octal to binary in the group of 3 bits.

Example $(1034.5)_8 \rightarrow (?)_2$

1 0 3 4 5
↓ ↓ ↓ ↓ ↓
001 000 011 100 101

Then, $(1034.5)_8 \rightarrow (001000011100.101)_2$

Binary to Hexadecimal

To convert a binary number to its hexadecimal equivalent, follow these steps

Step 1 Start making the group of 4 bits each from right to left from the given binary number. If the left most group has less than 4 bits, put in the necessary number of leading 0's on the left.

Step 2 Now, each group will be converted to decimal number.

Example $(11110101111011)_2 \rightarrow (?)_{16}$

0011	1101	0111	1011
↓	↓	↓	↓
3	13	7	11
	D		B

Then, $(11110101111011)_2 \rightarrow (3D7B)_{16}$

Hexadecimal to Binary

For this type of conversion, convert each hexadecimal digit to 4 bits binary equivalent.

Example $(BA81)_{16} \rightarrow (?)_2$

B = 11	A = 10	8	1
↓	↓	↓	↓
1011	1010	1000	0001

Then, $(BA81)_{16} \rightarrow (1011101010000001)_2$

Decimal to Octal

To convert decimal to octal, following steps are involved

***Step* 1** Divide the given number by 8.

***Step* 2** Note the quotient and remainder. Digits of remainder will be from 0 to 7.

***Step* 3** If quotient ≠ 0, then again divide the quotient by 8 and go back to step 2.

***Step* 4** If quotient = 0 or less than 8 then stop the process.

***Step* 5** Write each remainder from left to right starting from MSD (Most Significant Digit) to LSD (Least Significant Digit).

Example $(97647)_{10} \rightarrow (?)_8$

8	97647	7 LSD
8	12205	5 ↑
8	1525	5
8	190	6
8	23	7
8	2	2 MSD
	0	

Then, $(97647)_{10} \rightarrow (276557)_8$

Octal to Decimal

To convert octal to decimal, following steps are involved

***Step* 1** Multiply each digit of octal number with powers of 8.

***Step* 2** These powers should be positive for integral part and negative for fractional part.

***Step* 3** Add the all multiplying digits.

Example $(327.4)_8 \rightarrow (?)_{10}$

$$(327.4)_8 = 3\times 8^2 + 2\times 8^1 + 7\times 8^0 + 4\times 8^{-1}$$
$$= 3\times 64 + 2\times 8 + 7\times 1 + \frac{4}{8}$$
$$= 192 + 16 + 7 + 0.5$$
$$= 215.5$$

Then, $(327.4)_8 \rightarrow (215.5)_{10}$

Decimal to Hexadecimal

To convert decimal to hexadecimal, following steps are involved

***Step* 1** Divide the given number by 16.

***Step* 2** Note the quotient and remainder. Digits of remainder will be 0 to 9 or A to F.

***Step* 3** If quotient ≠ 0, then again divide the quotient by 16 and go back to step 2.

***Step* 4** If quotient = 0 or less than 16, then stop the process.

***Step* 5** Write each remainder from left to right starting from MSD (Most Singnificaut Digit) to LSD (Least Singnificaut Digit).

Example $(929987)_{10} \rightarrow (?)_{16}$

16	929987	3 LSD
16	58124	12 → C ↑
16	3632	0
16	227	3
16	14	14 → E MSD
	0	

Then, $(929987)_{10} \rightarrow (E30C3)_{16}$

Hexadecimal to Decimal

To convert hexadecimal to decimal, following steps are involved

***Step* 1** Multiply each digit of hexadecimal number with powers of 16.

***Step* 2** These powers should be positive for integral part and negative for fractional part.

***Step* 3** Add the all multiplying digits.

Example $(BC9.8)_{16} \rightarrow (?)_{10}$

$$(BC\ 9.\ 8)_{16} = B \times 16^2 + C \times 16^1 + 9 \times 16^0 + 8 \times 16^{-1}$$
$$= 11 \times 256 + 12 \times 16 + 9 \times 1 + \frac{8}{16}$$
$$= 2816 + 192 + 9 + 0.5 = 3017.5$$

Then, $(BC9.8)_{16} \rightarrow (3017.5)_{10}$

Octal to Hexadecimal

To convert octal to hexadecimal, following steps are involved

***Step* 1** Convert each digit of octal number to binary number.

***Step* 2** Again, convert each binary digit to hexadecimal number.

Example $(7632)_8 \rightarrow (?)_{16}$

Now,

7	6	3	2
↓	↓	↓	↓
111	110	011	010

$(7632)_8 \rightarrow (111110011010)_2$

1111	1001	1010
↓	↓	↓
15	9	10
F		A

Then, $(7632)_8 \rightarrow (F9A)_{16}$

Hexadecimal to Octal

To convert hexadecimal to octal, following steps are involved

***Step* 1** Convert each digit of the hexadecimal number to binary number.

***Step* 2** Again, convert each binary digit to octal number.

Example $(AC2D)_{16} \rightarrow (?)_8$

A	C	2	D
↓	↓	↓	↓
1010	1100	0010	1101

Now, $(AC2D)_{16} \rightarrow (1010110000101101)_2$

001	010	110	000	101	101
↓	↓	↓	↓	↓	↓
1	2	6	0	5	5

Then, $(AC2D)_{16} \rightarrow (126055)_8$

Computer Codes

In computer, any character like alphabet, digit or special character is represented by collection of 1's and 0's in a unique coded pattern.

In computers, the code is made up of fixed size groups of binary positions.

The binary coding schemes that are most commonly used are as follows

Binary Coded Decimal (BCD)

This system was developed by IBM. It is a number system where four bits are used to represent each decimal digits.

BCD is a method of using binary digits to represent the decimal digits (0-9). In BCD system, there is no limit on size of a number.

American Standard Code for Information Interchange (ASCII)

These are standard character codes used to store data so that it may be used by other software programs.

Basically, ASCII codes are of two types, which are as follows

(i) **ASCII-7** It is a 7-bit standard ASCII code. It allows $2^7 = 128$ (from 0 to 127) unique symbols or characters.

(ii) **ASCII-8** It is an extended version of ASCII-7. It is an 8-bit code, allows $2^8 = 256$ (0 to 255) unique symbols or characters.

Extended Binary Coded Decimal Interchange (EBCDIC)

In EBCDIC, characters are represented by eight bits. These codes store information which is readable by other computers. It allows $2^8 = 256$ combination of bits.

Logic Gate

It is a basic building block of a digital circuit that has two inputs and one output. The relationship between the input and the output is based on a certain logic. These gates are implemented using electronic switches like transistors, diodes.

There are various types of logic gate as follows

1. **AND Gate** This gate is also represented by $(\cdot)$, i.e. $(A \cdot B)$. It returns True only if both the conditions or inputs are True otherwise it returns False.

Truth Table of AND Gate

A	B	X
0	0	0
0	1	0
1	0	0
1	1	1

$\therefore \quad X = A \cdot B$

2. **OR Gate** This is represented by (+), i.e. $(A + B)$. It returns True if any one of the conditions or inputs is True and if both conditions are False, then it returns False.

Truth Table of OR Gate

A	B	X
0	0	0
0	1	1
1	0	1
1	1	1

$\therefore \quad X = A + B$

3. **Inverter or NOT Gate** This gate is also represented by ($'$), i.e. A'. It returns True if the input is false and *vice-versa.*

Truth Table of NOT Gate

A	X = A′
0	1
1	0

4. **NAND Gate** It is basically the inverse of the AND gate. This gate is designed by combining the AND and NOT gates.

   It returns False only if the both conditions or inputs are True otherwise it returns True.

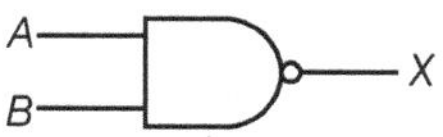

Truth Table of NAND Gate

A	B	X
0	0	1
0	1	1
1	0	1
1	1	0

$$X = (\overline{A \cdot B}) = \overline{A} + \overline{B}$$

5. **NOR Gate** It is inverse of the OR gate. This gate is designed by combining the OR and NOT gates. It returns True only if both the conditions or inputs are False otherwise it returns False.

Truth Table of NOR Gate

A	B	X
0	0	1
0	1	0
1	0	0
1	1	0

$$X = (\overline{A + B}) = \overline{A} \cdot \overline{B}$$

Note *NAND and NOR gates are also called universal gates.*

6. **Exclusive-OR or XOR Gate** It performs based on the operation of OR gate.

   It returns True only if one condition is true from both the conditions otherwise it returns False.

Truth Table of XOR Gate

A	B	X
0	0	0
0	1	1
1	0	1
1	1	0

$X = A \oplus B$

$X = \overline{A}B + A\overline{B}$

Tit-Bits

- **UNICODE** uses 16-bits to represent a symbol in the data. It represents any non-english character, scientific symbol in any language like Chinese, Japanese.
- One's complement of binary number is defined as the value obtained by inverting all the bits
  For example, 110100
  One's complement is
  001011

QUESTION BANK

1. There are how many types of number system?
(1) One (2) Two (3) Three (4) Four

2. Modern computers represent characters and numbers internally using one of the following number systems.
(1) Penta (2) Octal
(3) Hexa (4) Septa
(5) Binary

3. In the binary language, each letter of the alphabet, each number and each special character is made up of a unique combination of
(1) 8 bytes (2) 8 KB
(3) 8 characters (4) 8 bits

4. To perform calculation on stored data computer, uses .... number system.
(1) decimal (2) hexadecimal
(3) octal (4) binary

5. Which of the following is not a binary number?
(1) 001 (2) 101
(3) 202 (4) 110

6. The number system based on '0' and '1' only, is known as
(1) binary system (2) barter system
(3) number system (4) hexadecimal system

7. Binary system is also called
(1) base one system (2) base two system
(3) base system (4) binary system

8. Which of the following is an example of binary number?
(1) 6AH1 (2) 100101
(3) 005 (4) ABCD

9. Numbers that are written with base 10 are classified as
(1) decimal number
(2) whole number
(3) hexadecimal number
(4) exponential integers
(5) mantissa

10. Decimal number system is the group of .... numbers.
(1) 0 or 1 (2) 0 to 9
(3) 0 to 7 (4) 0 to 9 and A to F

11. The octal system
(1) needs less digits to represent a number than in the binary system
(2) needs more digits to represent a number than in the binary system
(3) needs the same number of digits to represent a number as in the binary system
(4) needs the same number of digits to represent a number as in the decimal system

12. A hexadecimal number is represented by
(1) three digits (2) four binary digits
(3) four digits (4) All of these

13. Hexadecimal number system has .... base.
(1) 2 (2) 8 (3) 10 (4) 16

14. Hexadecimal number system consists of
(1) 0 to 9 (2) A to F
(3) Both (1) and (2) (4) Either (1) or (2)

15. A hexadigit can be represented by **[IBPS Clerk 2012]**
(1) three binary (consecutive) bits
(2) four binary (consecutive) bits
(3) eight binary (consecutive) bits
(4) sixteen binary (consecutive) bits
(5) None of the above

16. Which of the following is invalid hexadecimal number?
(1) A0XB (2) A0F6
(3) 4568 (4) ACDB

17. What type of information system would be recognised by digital circuits?
(1) Hexadecimal system
(2) Binary system
(3) Both (1) and (2)
(4) Only roman system

18. The binary equivalent of decimal number 98 is **[IBPS Clerk 2012]**
(1) 1110001 (2) 1110100
(3) 1100010 (4) 1111001
(5) None of these

19. Conversion of decimal number $(71)_{10}$ to its binary number equivalent is **[IBPS Clerk 2012]**
(1) $(110011)_2$ (2) $(1110011)_2$
(3) $(0110011)_2$ (4) $(1000111)_2$
(5) None of these

20. What is the value of the binary number 101?
(1) 3 (2) 5 (3) 6 (4) 101

21. Decimal equivalent of $(1111)_2$ is **[IBPS Clerk 2012]**
(1) 11 (2) 10 (3) 1 (4) 15
(5) 13

22. The decimal equivalent of binary number $(1010)_2$ is
(1) 8 (2) 9 (3) 10 (4) 11

23. The binary number 10101 is equivalent to decimal number ....
(1) 19 (2) 12 (3) 27 (4) 21

24. Which of the following is octal number equivalent to binary number $(110101)_2$?
(1) 12 (2) 65
(3) 56 (4) 1111

25. Which of the following is a binary number equivalent to octal number $(.431)_8$?
(1) $(100011001)_2$ (2) $(.100011001)_2$
(3) $(100110100)_2$ (4) $(.100110001)_2$

26. To convert binary number to decimal, multiply the all binary digits by power of
(1) 0 (2) 2
(3) 4 (4) 6

27. Which of the following is hexadecimal number equivalent to binary number $(1111\ 1001)_2$?
(1) 9F (2) FF
(3) 99 (4) F9

28. Conversion of binary number $(1001001)_2$ to hexadecimal is
(1) $(40)_{16}$ (2) $(39)_{16}$
(3) $(49)_{16}$ (4) $(42)_{16}$

29. Which of the following is the correct binary form of $(4A2.8D)_{16}$? **[IBPS PO Mains 2017]**
(1) $(010010100010.10001101)_2$
(2) $(010110100010.11101101)_2$
(3) $(011110100010.10001101)_2$
(4) $(010010111110.10001101)_2$
(5) None of the above

30. Which of the following is an octal number equal to decimal number $(896)_{10}$?
(1) 0061 (2) 6001
(3) 1006 (4) 1600

31. Conversion of decimal number $(42)_{10}$ to its octal number equivalent is
(1) $(57)_8$ (2) $(42)_8$
(3) $(47)_8$ (4) $(52)_8$

32. Determine the octal equivalent of $(432267)_{10}$

(1) $(432267)_8$ (2) $(346731)_8$
(3) $(2164432)_8$ (4) None of these

33. Determine the decimal equivalent of $(456)_8$

(1) $(203)_{10}$ (2) $(302)_{10}$
(3) $(400)_{10}$ (4) $(402)_{10}$

34. Conversion of octal number $(3137)_8$ to its decimal equivalent is

(1) $(1631)_{10}$ (2) $(1632)_{10}$
(3) $(1531)_{10}$ (4) $(1931)_{10}$

35. Conversion of decimal number $(15)_{10}$ to hexadecimal number is

(1) $(14)_{16}$ (2) $(13)_{16}$ (3) $(F)_{16}$ (4) $(7F)_{16}$

36. Which of the following is a hexadecimal number equal to 3431 octal number?

(1) 197 (2) 917 (3) 791 (4) 971
(5) 719

37. The method used for the conversion of octal to decimal fraction is

(1) digit is divided by 8
(2) digit is multiplied by the corresponding power of 8
(3) digit is added with 8
(4) digit is subtracted with 8

38. MSD refers as

(1) Most Significant Digit
(2) Many Significant Digit
(3) Multiple Significant Digit
(4) Most Significant Decimal

39. LSD stands for

(1) Long Significant Digit
(2) Least Significant Digit
(3) Large Significant Digit
(4) Longer Significant Decimal

Directions (40 and 41) *Triangle represents Δ (1) and circle represents o (0). If triangle appears in unit's place then its value is 1. If it appears in 10's place its value is doubled to 2 like that it continues. Using the given terminology answer the following questions.*
For example,

$$\Delta = 1$$
$$\Delta o \Delta = 4, 0, 1 = 4 + 0 + 1$$
$$\Delta o = 2$$ **[IBPS PO Mains 2017]**

40. How will you represent '87' in this code language?

(1) oΔΔΔoΔΔ (2) ΔoΔoΔΔΔ
(3) ΔΔoΔΔΔΔ (4) ΔooΔooΔ
(5) ΔΔoΔΔΔo

41. What will be the code for ΔΔoooΔo ?

(1) 98 (2) 95 (3) 96 (4) 94
(5) 99

42. How many values can be represented by a single byte?

(1) 4 (2) 16
(3) 64 (4) 256

43. Which of the following is not a computer code?

(1) EBCDIC (2) ASCII
(3) CISC (4) UNICODE

44. ASCII stands for **[IBPS Clerk 2014, 2018]**

(1) American Special Computer for Information Interaction
(2) American Standard Computer for Information Interchange
(3) American Special Code for Information Interchange
(4) American Special Computer for Information Interchange
(5) American Standard Code for Information Interchange

45. The most widely used code that represents each character as a unique 8-bit code is **[UPSSSC 2017]**

(1) ASCII (2) UNICODE
(3) BCD (4) EBCDIC

46. Today's mostly used coding system is/are

(1) ASCII (2) EBCDIC
(3) BCD (4) Both (1) and (2)

47. In EBCDIC code, maximum possible characters set size is

(1) 356 (2) 756
(3) 556 (4) 256

48. Code 'EBCDIC' that is used in computing stands for

(1) Extension BCD Information Code
(2) Extended BCD Information Code
(3) Extension BCD Interchange Conduct
(4) Extended BCD Interchange Conduct

49. Most commonly used codes for representing bits are
(1) ASCII (2) BCD
(3) EBCDIC (4) All of these

50. The coding system allows non-english characters and special characters to be represented
(1) ASCII (2) UNICODE
(3) EBCDIC (4) All of these

51. Which of the following character set supports Japanese and Chinese fonts? **[IBPS Clerk Mains 2017]**
(1) EBCDIC (2) ASCII
(3) BC (4) ECBI
(5) UNICODE

52. Two inputs *A* and *B* of NAND gate have 0 output, if
(1) *A* is 0 (2) *B* is 0
(3) Both are zero (4) Both are 1

53. Gate having output 1 only when one of its input is 1 is called
(1) AND (2) NOT
(3) OR (4) NOR

54. ....gate is also known as inverter.
(1) OR (2) NOT
(3) XOR (4) NAND

55. The only function of NOT gate is to ....
(1) stop signal
(2) invert input signal
(3) act as a universal gate
(4) double input signal

56. Following diagram depicts which logic gate? **[IBPS PO Mains 2017]**

A $\bar{A}$

(1) NOR gate (2) NOT gate
(3) OR gate (4) NAND gate
(5) None of these

57. The NAND gate is AND gate followed by ......
(1) NOT gate (2) OR gate
(3) AND gate (4) NOR gate

58. The NOR gate is OR gate followed by ....
(1) AND gate (2) NAND gate
(3) NOT gate (4) OR gate

59. The NOR gate output will be high if the two inputs are
(1) 00 (2) 01 (3) 10 (4) 11

60. Which of following are known as universal gates?
(1) NAND and NOR (2) AND and OR
(3) XOR and OR (4) AND

61. Gate whose output is 0 only when inputs are different is called
(1) XOR (2) XNOR (3) NOR (4) NAND

62. If Δ represents '1' and o represents '0'. What will be the one's complement of oΔΔooΔ? **[IBPS PO Mains 2017]**
(1) 011001 (2) 100110
(3) 101010 (4) 000000
(5) 111111

ANSWERS

1. *(4)*	2. *(5)*	3. *(4)*	4. *(4)*	5. *(3)*	6. *(1)*	7. *(2)*	8. *(2)*	9. *(1)*	10. *(2)*
11. *(1)*	12. *(2)*	13. *(4)*	14. *(3)*	15. *(4)*	16. *(1)*	17. *(3)*	18. *(3)*	19. *(4)*	20. *(2)*
21. *(4)*	22. *(3)*	23. *(4)*	24. *(2)*	25. *(2)*	26. *(2)*	27. *(4)*	28. *(3)*	29. *(1)*	30. *(4)*
31. *(4)*	32. *(4)*	33. *(2)*	34. *(1)*	35. *(3)*	36. *(5)*	37. *(2)*	38. *(2)*	39. *(2)*	40. *(2)*
41. *(1)*	42. *(4)*	43. *(3)*	44. *(5)*	45. *(1)*	46. *(4)*	47. *(4)*	48. *(2)*	49. *(4)*	50. *(2)*
51. *(5)*	52. *(4)*	53. *(3)*	54. *(2)*	55. *(2)*	56. *(2)*	57. *(1)*	58. *(3)*	59. *(1)*	60. *(1)*
61. *(1)*	62. *(2)*								

CHAPTER

06

COMPUTER SOFTWARE

Software is a collection of computer programs and related data that provide the instructions for telling a computer what to do and how to do. A software is an interface between the user and the computer hardware. It is responsible for controlling, integrating and managing the hardware components of a computer system and for accomplishing specific tasks.

Types of Software

1. System software
2. Application software

System Software

It consists of several programs, which are directly responsible for controlling, integrating and managing the individual hardware components of a computer system. System software also provides the interface between the user and components of the computer.

Depending on the functionality, the system software can be further divided into following categories

1. **Operating System** It consists of programs which control, coordinate and supervise the activities of various components of a computer system. Its function is to provide link between the computer hardware and the user. It provides an environment to run the programs. *For example,* MS-DOS, Windows XP/2000/98, Unix, Linux, etc.

   Operating system performs the following functions

   (i) It recognises input from keyboard and sends output to the display screen.
   (ii) It makes sure that programs running at the same time do not interfere with each other.
   (iii) It is also responsible for security and ensures that unauthorised users do not access the system.

BIOS

The Basic Input/Output System (BIOS) is commonly known as **System BIOS.** BIOS controls various electronic components within the main computer system. The initial function of BIOS is to initialise system devices such as RAM, hard disk, CD/DVD drive, video display card and other hardwares.

2. **Device Driver** A software, which is written with the objective of making a device functional when it is connected to the computer is called device driver. It is a system software that acts like an interface between the device and the user.

   Every device, whether it is a printer, monitor, mouse or keyboard has a driver program associated with it for its proper functioning.

3. **Language Translator** It helps in converting programming language to machine language. The translated program is called object code. There are three different kinds of language translator : Assembler, Compiler and Interpreter.

Linker

It is a system program that links together several object modules and libraries to form a single and coherent program (executable). The main purpose of linker is to resolve references among files.

Loader

It is a kind of system software which is responsible for loading and relocation of the executable program in the main memory. It is a part of operating system that brings an executable file residing on disk into memory and starts its execution process.

Application Software

It is a computer software designed to help the user to perform single or multiple tasks. It is a set of instructions or programs designed for specific use or application, that enable the user to interact with a computer.

Application softwares are also called the end-user programs. These programs do the real work for users.

There are two types of application software

General Purpose Software

These types of software are used for any general purpose. They allow people to do simple computer tasks.

Some of the general purpose softwares are as follows

1. **Word Processing Software** A word processor is a software program capable of creating, storing and printing of documents. Word processors have the ability to create a document and make changes anywhere in the document.

   For example, Microsoft Word, WordPerfect (Windows only), AppleWorks (Mac only), OpenOffice.org Writer, etc.

2. **Electronic Spreadsheets** Spreadsheet applications are the computer programs that accept data in a tabular form and allow you to create and manipulate spreadsheets electronically.

   For example, Microsoft Excel, Corel Quattro Pro, Lotus 1-2-3, OpenOffice.org Calc, etc.

3. **Presentation Software** This software is used for creation of the slides and to display the information in the form of presentation of slides.

   For example, Microsoft PowerPoint, Corel Presentations, Lotus Freelance Graphics, OpenOffice.org Impress, etc.

4. **Database Management System** (DBMS) A DBMS refers to the software that is responsible for sorting, maintaining and utilising a database.

   For example, Microsoft Access, Corel Paradox, MySQL, OpenOffice.org Base, etc.

5. **Desktop Publishing (DTP) Software** It is a tool for graphic designers and non-designers to create visual communications for professional or desktop printing as well as for online or on screen electronic publishing.

   For example, Quark XPress, Adobe PageMaker, 3B2, CorelDraw, Corel Ventura, Illustrator, etc.

6. **Graphics Software** (Image Editing) It enables a person to manipulate visual images on a computer system. Most graphics softwares have the ability to import and export one or more graphics file formats.

   For example, DirectX, Adobe Photoshop, piZap, Microsoft Publisher, Picasa, etc.

7. **Multimedia Software** Multimedia includes a combination of text, audio, still images, animation, video or interactivity content forms.

   For example, Macro-Media Flash, Xilisoft Video Converter, VLC Media Player, Nimbuzz, etc.

Specific Purpose Software

These softwares are designed to perform specific tasks. This type of application software generally has one purpose to execute.

Some of the specific purpose application softwares are described below

1. **Inventory Management System and Purchasing System** Inventory is a list of goods and materials available in a stock. Inventory management system is generally used in departmental stores or in an organisation to keep the records of the stock of all the physical resources.

   For example, Fishbowl, AdvancePro, etc.
2. **Payroll Management System** It is used by all modern organisations to encompass every employee of the organisation who receives a regular wages or other compensation.
   For example, Namely, UltiPro, etc.
3. **Hotel Management System** It refers to the management techniques used in the hotel sector. These can include hotel administration, accounts, billing, marketing, housekeeping, front office or front desk.

   For example, Djubo, Aatithya HMS, Hotelogix PMS, etc.
4. **Reservation System** A reservation system or Central Reservation System (CRS) is a computerised system used to store and retrieve information and conduct transactions related to air travel, hotels, car rental or other activities. Today, number of websites like www.yatra.com, www.makemytrip.com provide online booking for tourists.
5. **Report Card Generator** It is an application software which is commonly used in schools by the examination department to prepare and generate the report cards of the students.
   For example, E-report card.
6. **Accounting Software** It is an application software that records and processes accounting transactions within functional modules such as accounts payable, accounts receivable, payroll and trial balance.

   For example, Tally. ERP9, HDPOS, MARG, Profit book etc.
7. **Billing System** It refers to the software that is used to perform the billing process. It handles the tracking of labled products and services delivered to a customer or set of customers.
   For example, Billing Manager, Billing Tracker, kBilling, etc.

System Utilities

These programs perform tasks related to the maintenance of the computer system. These are the packages which are loaded into computer during the time of installation of operating system.

They are used to support, enhance, expand and secure existing programs and data in the computer system.

System utility mainly consists of the following functions

1. **Disk Compression** It increases the amount of information that can be stored on a hard disk by compressing all information stored on it.
   For example, DiskDoubler, SuperStor Pro, DoubleDisk Gold , etc.
2. **Disk Fragmenter** It detects computer files whose contents are broken across several locations on the hard disk and moves the fragments to one location to increase efficiency.

   It can be used to rearrange files and unused space on your hard disk.

   For example, MyDefrag, Diskeeper, Defraggler, etc.
3. **Backup Utilities** It can make a copy of all information stored on a disk and restore either the entire disk or selected files.
4. **Disk Cleaners** It is used to find files that have not been used for a long time. This utility also serves to increase the speed of a slow computer.
   For example, Bleach Bit cleaner, etc.
5. **Anti-virus** It is the utility which is used to scan computer for viruses and prevent the computer system and files from being corrupt.
   For example, Kaspersky, AVG, McAfee, Avira, etc.

6. **Text Editor** It is a program that facilitates the creation and correction of text. A text editor supports special commands for text editing, i.e. you can write, delete, find and replace words, lines, paragraphs, etc.
   For example, MS-Word, WordPad, Notepad, etc., in which Notepad is the most popular text editor.

Open Source Software

Open source refers to something that can be modified and shared as its designed are publicly accessible.

Open Source Software (OSS) is any computer software that is distributed with its source code available for modification.

Examples of Open Source Software are Linux, Unix, MySQL, etc. To be considered as open source software by the software development industry, *certain criteria must be met are as follows*

- Software must be available free or at a low cost.
- Source code must be included.
- Anyone must be allowed to modify the source code.
- Modified versions can be redistributed.

Criteria for the Distribution of OSS

Open source software is normally distributed with the source code under an open source license. The distribution terms of open source software must comply with the following criteria

1. **Free Redistribution** The license shall not restrict any party from selling or giving away the software distribution containing programs from several different sources. The license shall not require a royalty or other fee for such sale.
2. **Source Code** The program must include source code and allows distribution with source code as well as a compiled form. The source code must be in the preferred form in which a programmer would modify the program.
3. **Integrity of the Author's Source Code** The license may restrict source code from being distributed in modified form only if the license allows the distribution of "patch files" with the source code for the purpose of modifying the program at build time.

Proprietary Software

It is a software that is owned by an individual or a company. There are always major restrictions on it to use and its source code is always kept secret. Proprietary software is copyrighted and bears limits against use, distribution and modification that are imposed by its publisher, vendor or developer.

Main Barriers for Using Proprietary Software

1. Licenses and maintenance of proprietary software is very expensive.
2. It is developed for a single purpose, applications are separately packaged.
3. Vendor support is conditional to maintenance subscription.
4. Users have to dependent on the developer of proprietary software for all updates, support and fixes.
5. Low level of customisation and adaptability.

Tit-Bits

- **Adobe Page Maker** is a typesetting tool which is used for desktop publishing.
- **Fully Backup** contains a copy of every program, data and system file on a computer.
- **Firmware** is a combination of software and hardware. e.g. ROMs, PROMs and EPROMs.
- **Freeware** is commonly used for copyrighted software that is given away for free by its owner.

QUESTION BANK

1. Which one of the following is defined as "a set of instructions, data or programs used to operate computers and execute specific tasks"? **[SSC CGL 2018]**
   (1) Processor (2) Hardware
   (3) Malware (4) Software

2. The term used to describe the intangible instructions that tell the computer what to do is **[IBPS Clerk 2015]**
   (1) hardware (2) software
   (3) storage (4) input/output
   (5) None of these

3. Software refers to
   (1) the physical components that a computer is made of
   (2) firmware
   (3) programs
   (4) people ware

4. Which of the following is software? **[IBPS Clerk 2014]**
   (1) Keyboard (2) Internet Explorer
   (3) Scanner (4) Mouse
   (5) Printer

5. The primary purpose of software is to turn data into **[RBI Grade B 2014]**
   (1) information (2) programs
   (3) objects (4) charts
   (5) websites

6. Computer software is **[SBI Clerk 2015]**
   (1) used only for output
   (2) a computer peripheral
   (3) used for input
   (4) a set of instructions
   (5) used only in operating systems

7. The steps and tasks needed to process data, such as responses to questions or clicking an icon, are called
   (1) instructions
   (2) the operating system
   (3) application software
   (4) the system unit

8. The two broad categories of software are
   (1) word processing and spreadsheet
   (2) transaction and application
   (3) Windows and Mac OS
   (4) system and application

9. System software
   (1) allows the user to diagnose and troubleshoot the device
   (2) is a programming language
   (3) is a part of productivity suite
   (4) helps the computer manage internal resources

10. A collection of various programs that helps to control your computer is called
    (1) system software **[SBI Clerk 2015]**
    (2) application software
    (3) Microsoft Excel
    (4) Microsoft Word
    (5) Microsoft Outlook

11. This type of software works with end-users, application software and computer hardware to handle the majority of technical details. **[RBI Grade B 2014, IBPS PO 2012]**
    (1) Communication software
    (2) Application software
    (3) Utility software
    (4) System software
    (5) None of the above

12. It is a set of programs that enables your computer's hardware device and application software to work together.
    (1) Management
    (2) Processing
    (3) Utility
    (4) System software

13. A(n) ...... is a software that helps a computer control to operate efficiently and keep track of data.
    (1) application system
    (2) hardware system
    (3) software system
    (4) operating system

14. A computer cannot 'boot' if it does not have the
(1) compiler (2) loader
(3) operating system (4) assembler

15. The .... tells the computer how to use its components.
(1) utility (2) application
(3) operating system (4) network

16. Operating system is a
(1) application software
(2) system software
(3) hardware
(4) language

17. The .... manual tells you how to use a software program. **[RBI Grade B 2012]**
(1) documentation (2) programming
(3) user (4) technical
(5) None of these

18. What does the acronym BIOS stand for? **[SBI Clerk 2014, RBI Grade B 2013]**
(1) Basic Input/Outer System
(2) Basic Internal Output System
(3) Basic Inner/Output System
(4) Basic Input/Output Systemisation
(5) Basic Input/Output System

19. ...... includes boot firmware and power management. **[SBI Clerk 2015]**
(1) CD-ROM (2) Internal buses
(3) BIOS (4) Chip Set
(5) RAM

20. Which category does best describe the BIOS? **[UPSSSC 2016]**
(1) Hardware (2) Malware
(3) Firmware (4) Utility

21. In computer terminology, which of the following best describes a device driver? **[UGC NET 2019]**
(1) Software that allows the user to control the operating system
(2) Hardware that allows the user to control the operating system
(3) Hardware that allows interaction between peripheral devices and the operating system
(4) Software that allows interaction between peripheral devices and the operating system

22. .... helps in converting programming language to machine language.
(1) Operating system (2) Device driver
(3) Language translator (4) Linker

23. A linker program
(1) places the program in the memory for the purpose of execution
(2) relocates the program to execute from the specific memory area allocated to it
(3) links the program with other programs needed for its execution
(4) interfaces the program with the entities generating its input data

24. The main purpose of .... is to resolve references among files.
(1) text editor (2) loader
(3) antivirus (4) linker

25. Which of the following system software resides in main memory always?
(1) Text editor (2) Assembler
(3) Linker (4) Loader

26. A kind of system software, which is responsible for loading and relocating of the executable program in the main memory
(1) loader
(2) linker
(3) translator
(4) presentation software

27. Specialised program that allows user to utilise in specific application is classified as **[IBPS RRB PO Mains 2017]**
(1) relative program
(2) application program
(3) appropriate program
(4) replicate program
(5) logical program

28. .... is a software which is used to do particular task. **[IBPS Clerk Mains 2017]**
(1) Operating system
(2) Program
(3) Data software
(4) Data
(5) Application software

29. Software designed for a specific purpose/ application such as pay calculations, processing of examination result, etc. are known as
(1) utility software
(2) system software
(3) application software
(4) customised software

30. Application software
(1) is used to control the operating system
(2) is designed to help programmers
(3) performs specific task for computer users
(4) is used for making design only

31. The software that is used to create text-based documents are referred to as .... **[SBI PO 2013]**
(1) DBMS
(2) suites
(3) spreadsheets
(4) presentation software
(5) Word processors

32. Which of the following general purpose softwares allow you to do mathematical or financial calculation?
(1) Word processing program
(2) Spreadsheet program
(3) Presentation program
(4) Database program

33. Spreadsheet software is used
(1) to keep simple company accounts
(2) calculate employee commission payments
(3) as simple stock control system
(4) All of the above

34. Which software is used to create presentations to show to customers or staff members?
(1) Report generation
(2) Graph generator
(3) Presentation software
(4) Picture generator

35. Database software is used to
(1) discard sales records
(2) store contacts list
(3) keep customer records
(4) generate report

36. DTP is a tool for graphic designers and non-designers to create visual communications for professional. DTP stands for
(1) Device Transfer Protocol
(2) Desktop Publishing
(3) Device Transfer Programs
(4) All of the above

37. Corel Ventura, Illustrator are examples of
(1) Word Processing (2) Graphic
(3) Multimedia (4) DTP

38. DirectX is a/an **[RBI Grade B 2013]**
(1) computer part
(2) user interface
(3) operating system
(4) software that drives graphic software
(5) None of the above

39. Which among the following is not an example of system software?
(1) Operating system
(2) Debugger
(3) Software Driver
(4) Adobe Photoshop

40. Which application software is used for a special purpose? **[IBPS RRB PO Mains 2018]**
(1) General purpose software
(2) Special purpose software
(3) Important software
(4) System software
(5) None of the above

41. Which types of software is used in organisations to keep track of products in stocks?
(1) Enterprise Resource Planning (ERP) software
(2) Payroll Software
(3) Human resource planning software
(4) Inventory management software

42. A software program that adds functionality to your computer or help your computer perform better is called as **[IBPS RRB PO Mains 2017]**
(1) utility program
(2) function program
(3) specialised program
(4) manufacturer program
(5) compiling program

43. Which of the following techniques can be used to store a large number of files in a small amount of storage space?
(1) File adjustment
(2) File copying
(3) File compatibility
(4) File compression

44. What type of software creates a smaller file that is faster to transfer over the Internet? **[IBPS Clerk Mains 2017]**
(1) Compression (2) Fragmentation
(3) Unzipped (4) Abstraction
(5) Encapsulation

45. .... is a Windows utility program that locates and eliminates unnecessary fragments and rearranges files and unused disk space to optimise operations. **[SBI PO 2013]**
(1) Backup (2) Disk cleanup
(3) Disk defragmenter (4) Restore
(5) Disk restorer

46. When files are broken up into small parts on a disk they are said to be
(1) fragmented (2) contiguous
(3) sectored (4) disbursed

47. It can make copies of all information stored on a disk or either restore the entire disk
(1) Restore utility
(2) Disk cleaner
(3) Backup software
(4) Defragmenter

48. What is backup?
(1) Connect the user's network to more component
(2) Copy to save a data from original source to other destination
(3) Filter on old data from new data
(4) Access data from tape

49. A(n) .... backup contains a copy of every program, data and system file on a computer. **[Allahabad Bank Clerk 2011]**
(1) restoration (2) bootstrap
(3) differential (4) full
(5) None of these

50. Disk cleaner helps to free
(1) data (2) recycle bin
(3) space (4) information

51. They can find files that are unnecessary to computer operation, or take up considerable amounts of space.
(1) Antivirus
(2) Sweep
(3) Disk cleaner
(4) Disk Formatting

52. Which of the following Windows utilities erase unneeded files?
(1) Backup or Restore Wizard
(2) Disk Cleanup
(3) Disk Defragmenter
(4) Antivirus

53. Text editor is a/an **[RBI Grade B 2013]**
(1) application software
(2) system software
(3) utility software
(4) all purpose software
(5) None of the above

54. Which of the following is not related to a utility software?
(1) Text editor
(2) Antivirus program
(3) Disk compression software
(4) Railway reservation system

55. Utility programs include
(1) virus scanning software
(2) backup software
(3) disk defragmenter
(4) All of the above

56. Which of the following is not related to an application software?
(1) Word processor
(2) DBMS
(3) Operating system
(4) Railway reservation system

57. .... disk encryption is a technology (hardware or software) where data is encrypted before storage. **[SCC CGL 2017]**
(1) Half (2) Whole
(3) Double (4) Triple

58. Which of the following software is any computer software that is distributed with its source code available for modification? **[SSC CGL 2018]**

(1) Application software
(2) System Software
(3) Open Source Software
(4) Proprietary Software

59. Example(s) of open source software is/are **[SSC CHSL 2019]**

(1) Linux (2) Unix
(3) MySQL (4) All of these

60. Which of the following is not an open source software? **[UPSSSC 2018]**

(1) Linux
(2) Microsoft Office
(3) Mozilla Firefox
(4) Android

61. This software is copyrighted and bears the limits against use. **[SSC CGL 2017]**

(1) Proprietary Software
(2) Open Source Software
(3) Application Software
(4) System Software

ANSWERS

1. *(4)*	2. *(2)*	3. *(3)*	4. *(2)*	5. *(1)*	6. *(4)*	7. *(1)*	8. *(4)*	9. *(4)*	10. *(1)*
11. *(4)*	12. *(4)*	13. *(4)*	14. *(3)*	15. *(3)*	16. *(2)*	17. *(3)*	18. *(5)*	19. *(3)*	20. *(3)*
21. *(4)*	22. *(3)*	23. *(3)*	24. *(4)*	25. *(4)*	26. *(1)*	27. *(2)*	28. *(5)*	29. *(3)*	30. *(3)*
31. *(5)*	32. *(2)*	33. *(4)*	34. *(3)*	35. *(3)*	36. *(2)*	37. *(5)*	38. *(4)*	39. *(4)*	40. *(2)*
41. *(5)*	42. *(1)*	43. *(4)*	44. *(1)*	45. *(3)*	46. *(1)*	47. *(3)*	48. *(2)*	49. *(4)*	50. *(3)*
51. *(3)*	52. *(2)*	53. *(3)*	54. *(4)*	55. *(4)*	56. *(3)*	57. *(2)*	58. *(3)*	59. *(4)*	60. *(4)*
61. *(1)*									

CHAPTER

07

OPERATING SYSTEM

An Operating System (OS) is a program which acts as an interface between the user and the computer hardware. The interface enables a user to utilise hardware resources very efficiently.

Operating system is an organised collection or integrated set of specialised programs that controls the overall operations of a computer. It is a program that must be on any computer for proper booting.

Functions of Operating System

Process Management A process is the basic unit of execution in the operating system. It is a process by which operating system can control the planning, monitoring and performance of a CPU.

Memory Management It is a process of controlling and coordinating computer memory. It ensures that all processes are able to access their memory or not.

File Management It is the main function of operating system. It manages all data files in a computer system. At the time of execution of a program, the operating system also performs the task of copying files from secondary memory to primary memory.

Device Management It is a process of managing the operation and maintenance of input/output devices. It also facilitates the interface between all the connected devices.

Types of Operating System

1. Batch Processing Operating System

In this operating system, a number of jobs are put together and executed as a group. This operating system is responsible for scheduling the jobs according to priority and the resource required. e.g. Unix.

2. Single User Operating System

It is a type of operating system which allows only one user at a time. Operating system for Personal Computer (PC) is a single user OS. They are designed to manage one task at a time.
e.g. MS-DOS, Windows 9X.

3. Multi User Operating System

This OS allows multiple users to access a computer system concurrently. It is used in computer networks that allow same data and applications to be accessed by multiple users at the same time. e.g. VMS.

4. Multi-Tasking Operating System

In this operating system, more than one process can be executed concurrently. It also allows the user to switch between the running applications. e.g. Linux, Unix, Windows 95.

Multi-tasking OS further classified into two types

(i) **Preemptive Multitasking OS** It is a type of multitasking OS that allows computer programs to share operating system and underlying hardware resources.

(ii) **Cooperative Multitasking OS** It is the simplest form of multitasking. In it, each program can control the CPU for as long as it need it.

5. Time Sharing Operating System

This operating system allows multiple programs to simultaneously share the computer resources. It provides to each process to be run on. e.g. Mac OS.

6. Real Time Operating Sytem (RTOS)

These operating systems are designed to respond to an event within a pre-determined time.

They are often used in applications such as flight reservation system, military applications, etc. This type of operating system increases the availability and reliability of the system. e.g. Linux.

There are two types of real time operating system

(i) **Hard Real Time OS** In this RTOS, all the tasks are required to be completed within the specified time limit.

(ii) **Soft Real Time OS** In this RTOS, all the tasks are not required to be completed within the specified time limit.

User Interface

The system which provides the facility to the user to interact with the computer is called user interface. It allows users to easily access and communicate with the applications and the hardware.

The user can interact with the computer by using mainly two kinds of interface

1. Graphical User Interface (GUI)

It is a computer program that enables a person to communicate with a computer through the use of symbols, visual metaphors and pointing devices. It is best known for its implementation in Apple products.

The first graphical user interface was designed by Xerox Corporation in 1970s. GUIs can be found in handheld devices such as MP3 players, portable media players, gaming devices, etc.

2. Character User Interface (CUI)

It is also known as Command Line Interface (CLI). CUI is a mechanism of interacting with a computer system or software by typing commands to perform specific tasks.

CUI only uses text types one after another just as commands used in MS-DOS.

Booting

Booting is starting up a computer or computer appliance until it can be used. It can be initiated by hardware such as a Start button or by Software command.

There are two types of booting

- **Cold Booting** When a computer is turned ON after it has been completely shutdown.
- **Warm Booting** When a computer is restarted by pressing the combination of Ctrl + Alt + Del keys or by Restart button.

Some Important Operating Systems

Some popular operating systems are as follows

1. **UNIX** The first version of Unix was developed in 1969 by Ken Thompson and Dennis Ritchie. It is primarily used to a server rather than a work station and should not be used by anyone who does not understand the system.

2. **Apple Macintosh** (Mac OS) It was introduced in January, 1984 by Steve Jobs and was initially named as system software, which was later renamed as Mac OS.

   Versions of Mac OSX are Yosemite, Mavericks, Mountain Lion, Tiger, Tiger Panther, Jaguar, etc.
3. **LINUX** The first Linux Kernel was released in September, 1991 by Linus Torvalds. It is an open source software.

   Linux is similar to Unix in operations. It is difficult to understand by anyone.

   Kernel is the core of the operating system that supports the process by providing a path to the peripheral devices.
4. **Microsoft Windows** It is an operating system, based on GUI, developed by Microsoft. Microsoft first introduced an operating environment named Windows in November 1985.

MS-DOS (Microsoft-Disk Operating System)

The DOS OS was developed by Microsoft in 1980 for micro computers. MS-DOS was the first operating system that run on PC developed by IBM Corporation in 1981.

DOS is a single user operating system. It is the only operating system which can be loaded in the main memory of the computer using a single disk.

Structure of DOS

There are four essential programs associated with the control of computer and the way it interacts with them

1. **Boot Record** It includes loading the operating system into main memory. It is the main program of MS-DOS.
2. **Basic Input/Output System** (BIOS. sys) It provides an interface between the hardware and programs.
3. **The MS-DOS. sys Program** It is a collection of program routines and data tables that provide high level programs such as application programs.
4. **The Command.com Program** It provides a standard set of commands that gives users access to file management, configuration and miscellaneous functions.

Configuration of DOS

Config. sys, Autoexec. bat and their files provide the environment to computer to set commands

(i) **Config. sys** It adjusts the system acoording to commands.

(ii) **Autoexec.bat** When the system is powered ON, this file executes in automatically command line.

Important Extensions and their Meanings

Extensions	Meanings
.exe	Executable files
.com	Command files
.bat	Batch files
.doc	Document files
.txt	Text files
.prg	Program files
.ovr	Over lays
.sys	System files

Types of MS-DOS Commands

There are two types of MS-DOS commands as follows

1. **Internal Commands** These commands are automatically loaded into main memory when the booting process gets completed.

   e.g. DATE, TIME, VER, VOL, DIR, COPY, CLS, etc.
2. **External Commands** These commands require external files to be loaded in the computer to run.

   e.g. Checking disk, comparing disk, formatting, etc.

Important Commands and their Uses

Commands	Uses
CALL	Call one batch program from another
CD	Change Directory-move to a specific folder
CLS	Clear the screen
COPY	Copy one or more files to another location
DATE	Display or set the date
DEL	Delete one or more files
DIR	Display a list of files and folders
ERASE	Delete one or more files
EDIT	View and edit files
EXIT	Quit the current script/routine and set an error level
FORMAT	To erase and prepare the disk drive
IF	Conditionally perform a command
MD	Create new folders
MOVE	Move files from one folder to another
PATH	Display or set a search path for executable files
PRINT	Prints data to a printer port
REN	Rename a file or directory
RD	Remove an empty directory
SORT	Sort input and displays the output to the screen
START	Start a program, command or batch file
TIME	Display or set the system time
TYPE	Display the content of a text file
VER	Display version information
XCOPY	Copy multiple files, directories or drives from one location to another

Mobile Operating System

This OS operates on Smartphones, Tablets and Digital Mobile devices. It controls mobile devices and its design supports wireless communication and different types of mobile applications. It has built-in support for mobile multimedia formats.

Some popular mobile operating systems are as follows

1. **Android** It is a mobile OS developed by Google, which is based on Linux (main part of operating system). It is basically designed for touch screen mobile devices like Tablets, Smartphones, etc. Now-a-days, it is most widely used in mobile phones. The latest version of Android is Android 11, which was released on 8th September, 2020.
2. **Symbian** It is the OS developed and sold by Symbian Ltd. It is an open source mobile OS designed for Smartphones.

   It has been used by many major handset manufacturers including Motorola, Nokia, Samsung, Sony, etc. The latest version of Symbian is Nokia Belle, which was released on 2 October, 2012.
3. **iOS** It is the popular mobile operating system developed by Apple Incorporation. This operating system is commonly used in Apple iPhone, iPod Touch, iPad, etc. The latest version of iOS is iOS 14.3, which was released on 14 December, 2020.
4. **Black Berry** It is the most secure operating system used in leading Smartphones developed by Black Berry company. It also supports WAP 1.2. The latest version of BlackBerry is Black Berry OS 7.1.0, which was released in 2013.
5. **Windows Phone** It is a mobile operating system developed by Microsoft in 2010, for smartphones. It is a commercial proprietary software. Its latest version is 8.1, which was released on 2 June, 2015.

QUESTION BANK

1. Which of the following is the type of software that controls the internal operations in the computer?
   (1) Shareware
   (2) Public domain software
   (3) Application software
   (4) Operating system software

2. .... controls the way in which the computer system does function and provides a means by which users can interact with the computer.
   (1) Operating system
   (2) Motherboard
   (3) Platform
   (4) Application software

3. A collection of programs that controls how your computer system runs and processes information is called **[IBPS Clerk 2014]**
   (1) operating system (2) computer
   (3) office (4) compiler
   (5) interpreter

4. It is the program that manages the hardware of the computer system including the CPU, memory storage devices and input/output devices.
   (1) Software (2) Operating system
   (3) Hardware (4) System software

5. An operating system is a/an **[UPPSC Computer Assistant 2019, SSC CGL 2013]**
   (1) accounting software
   (2) application software
   (3) system software
   (4) utility software

6. Which of the following is the correct reason to use an operating system?
   (1) To manage resources
   (2) To control the hardware
   (3) To provide an interface between the hardware and user
   (4) All of the above

7. The primary purpose of the Windows operating system is
   (1) to make the most efficient use of the computer hardware
   (2) to allow people to use the computer
   (3) to keep systems programmer's employed
   (4) to make computers easier to use

8. Every computer has a(n) ......, many also have ...... **[RBI Grade B 2014]**
   (1) operating system; a client system
   (2) operating system; instruction sets
   (3) application programs; an operating system
   (4) application programs; a client system
   (5) operating system; application programs

9. Which of the following is/are function(s) of operating system?
   (1) User interface
   (2) File system manipulation
   (3) Resource allocation
   (4) All of the above

10. A program in execution is called
    (1) process (2) instruction
    (3) procedure (4) function

11. Memory utilisation factor shall be computed as
    (1) memory in use/allocated memory
    (2) memory in use/total memory connected
    (3) memory allocated/free existing memory
    (4) memory committed/total memory available

12. Which one of the following is not the function of operating system?
    (1) Resource Management
    (2) File Management
    (3) Networking
    (4) Processor Management

13. When a file contains instruction that can be carried out by the computer, it is often called a(n) ...... file.
    (1) data (2) information
    (3) executable (4) application

14. Grouping and processing all of a firm's transactions at one time, is called
(1) a database management system
(2) batch processing
(3) a real time system
(4) on-time system

15. .... is used for very large files or where a fast response time is not critical. The files to be transmitted are gathered over a period and then send together as a batch.
(1) Batch processing (2) Online processing
(3) File processing (4) Data processing

16. Which of the following system is a function of dedicated PCs?
(1) Meant for a single user
(2) Meant for the single task
(3) Deal with single software
(4) Deal with only editing

17. Windows operating system is ...... and ....
(1) multitasking, multi user
(2) multi user, single tasking
(3) single user, multitasking
(4) single tasking, single user

18. Operating system that allows only one user to work on a computer at a time is known as **[IBPS Clerk 2015]**
(1) single user operating system
(2) multi user operating system
(3) single tasking operating system
(4) multitasking operating system
(5) real-time operating system

19. An operating system is said to be multi user, if
(1) more than one programs can run simultaneously
(2) more than one users can work simultaneously
(3) Either (1) or (2)
(4) None of the above

20. ...... provides process and memory management services that allow two or more tasks, jobs or programs to run simultaneously.
(1) Multitasking (2) Multithreading
(3) Multiprocessing (4) Multicomputing

21. Which of the following terms explains the execution of more than one file at the same on a single processor?
(1) Single tasking (2) Multitasking
(3) Scheduling (4) Multiprocessing

22. ...... is a feature for scheduling and multi-programming to provide an economical interactive system of two or more users. **[IBPS Clerk 2012]**
(1) Time sharing (2) Multisharing
(3) Time tracing (4) Multiprocessing
(5) None of these

23. The simultaneously processing of two or more programs by multiple processors, is
(1) multiprogramming (2) multitasking
(3) time sharing (4) multiprocessing

24. Real time systems must have
(1) pre-emptive kernels
(2) non-pre-emptive kernels
(3) Both (1) and (2)
(4) Either (1) or (2)

25. RTOS stands for
(1) Real Time Operating System
(2) Reliable Time Operating System
(3) Reboot Time Operating System
(4) None of the above

26. System running more than one processes concurrently are called **[SSC CGL 2016]**
(1) multiprocessing
(2) multiprogramming
(3) real time
(4) batch processing

27. Which of the following refers to the means by which an OS or any other program interacts with the user? **[SBI Clerk 2014]**
(1) Program front-end
(2) Programming interface
(3) User login
(4) User interface
(5) User compatibility

28. The first graphical user interface was designed by
(1) Apple Inc. (2) Microsoft
(3) Xerox Corporation (4) None of these

29. Which process refers to the starting up of a computer and the loading of the required parts of the operating system into the RAM? **[SSC CGL 2018]**

(1) Swipping (2) Booting
(3) Mapping (4) Tagging

30. Which process checks to ensure the components of the computer are operating and connected properly?

(1) Booting (2) Processing
(3) Saving (4) Editing

31. What happens when you boot up a PC? **[RBI Grade B 2012]**

(1) Portions of the operating system are copied from disk into memory
(2) Portions of the operating system are copied from memory onto disk
(3) Portions of the operating system are compiled
(4) Portions of the operating system are emulated
(5) The PC gets switched off

32. What do you understand by the term booting? **[RBI Grade B 2012]**

(1) The process of starting the computer from the power-off position
(2) Connecting computer of the electric switch
(3) Increasing the memory of the computer
(4) The process of shut down the computer
(5) None of the above

33. Restart of computer is called ...... when computer is already ON.

(1) cold booting (2) warm booting
(3) shut down (4) logging off

34. The first version of Unix was developed by

(1) Ken Thompson (2) Presper Eckert
(3) J W Mauchly (4) Herman Hollerith

35. UNIX operating system is generally known as **[SSC CGL 2014]**

(1) Multi user operating system
(2) General application
(3) Single user operating system
(4) Single user application program

36. Which is the programming tool in UNIX? **[UPPSC Computer Assistant 2019]**

(1) LINT (2) KERNEL
(3) C-Shell (4) None of these

37. In computers, what does Yosemite, Mavericks, Mountain Lion, Lion Snow Leopard, Leopard, Tiger, Tiger Panther, Jaguar, Puma and Cheetah stand for? **[RRB NTPC 2016]**

A. Versions of Mac OSX
B. Types of storage servers
C. Macintosh clones
D. None of the above

(1) D (2) A
(3) C (4) B

38. Which of the following is an operating system? **[SBI Clerk 2014]**

(1) Linux (2) Debugger
(3) Mozilla (4) Google Chrome
(5) Intel 8085

39. Linux is a type of ...... software.

(1) shareware (2) commercial
(3) proprietary (4) open source

40. Which one of the following is not an operating system? **[SSC CGL 2018]**

(1) Linux (2) Unix
(3) Intel (4) Windows

41. Who developed the operating system Linux started as a project by a student of Finland? **[SSC CGL 2018]**

(1) Barbara Liskov
(2) Linus Torvalds
(3) Leonard M. Adleman
(4) Leslie Lamport

42. Which of the following operating systems was first developed by Microsoft?

(1) Windows ME (2) Windows NT
(3) Windows 97 (4) MS-DOS

43. Which one of the following file names is invalid in DOS? **[RBI Grade B 2013]**

(1) RIT. bat (2) LISTEN.bin
(3) RLUA.btt (4) TALK.bas
(5) None of these

44. Which one of the following DIR commands lists a group of files? **[RBI Grade B 2013]**

(1) DIR INVOICE.bas (2) DIR RESCUE.bas
(3) DIR PAYROLL.bas (4) DIR TOOL?.bas
(5) None of these

45. 'DOS' floppy disk/operating system does not have **[SBI PO 2014]**
(1) a boot record (2) a file allocation table
(3) a root directory (4) a virtual memory
(5) All of these

46. Which file in MS-DOS contains internal commands that are loaded during booting process?
(1) CONFIG.sys (2) MSDOS.sys
(3) BIOS.sys (4) COMMAND.com

47. What is the name of the batch file that automatically run when MS-DOS is booted?
(1) Config.sys (2) Config. bat
(3) Autoexe.bat (4) Run.bat

48. MS-DOS is usually supplied on a
(1) hard disk (2) cartridge tape
(3) CD ROM (4) floppy disk

49. Which of the following is the main program of MS-DOS?
(1) Boot Record (2) ID.sys
(3) MSDOS.sys (4) Command.com

50. Which of the following operating systems is also known as single user operating system?
(1) Windows (2) Linux
(3) Unix (4) DOS

51. The main difference between Windows and DOS is the ability to
(1) multitasking (2) speed up
(3) run a program (4) run without power

52. '>' symbol in DOS commands is used to
(1) compare two values (2) redirect input
(3) redirect output (4) filter data

53. Usually, in MS-DOS, the primary hard disk drives has the drive letter .... **[RBI Grade B 2012]**
(1) A (2) B
(3) C (4) D
(5) None of these

54. Which of the following is not usual file extension in DOS? **[RBI Grade B 2012]**
(1) .exe (2) .bat
(3) .0 (4) .com
(5) None of these

55. Which commands are automatically loaded into main memory?
(1) Internal (2) External
(3) Viral (4) Situational

56. Which type of commands in MS-DOS needs external files to perform their action?
(1) Internal commands
(2) External commands
(3) Batch commands
(4) Redirectories

57. Which one of the following DOS commands sends contents of the screen to an output device? **[RBI Grade B 2013]**
(1) BREAK (2) DISK COPY
(3) MORE (4) ASSIGN
(5) None of these

58. Which of the following is not an external command of DOS?
(1) LABEL (2) FORMAT
(3) CHKDSK (4) CLS

59. CHKDSK can be used to find
(1) disk's bad portion (2) occupied space
(3) free space (4) All of these

60. While working with MS-DOS, which command transfers a specific file from one disk to another?
(1) Copy (2) Disk copy
(3) Time (4) Rename

61. DEL command is used to
(1) delete files (2) delete directory
(3) delete lables (4) Both (1) and (2)

62. This command is used to display a list of files and sub-directories that are in the directory you specify.
(1) DER (2) DIS
(3) DIR (4) DAR

63. The purpose of DISKCOPY command is to **[RBI Grade B 2014]**
(1) format the disk if it is not formatted before a write operation is initiated on it
(2) overwrite the existing contents of the destination disk as it copies the new information to it
(3) make an exact copy of a floppy disk
(4) All of the above
(5) None of the above

64. Which command is used to delete file from a directory in DOS?
(1) REN (2) DEL (3) CD (4) MD

65. In MS-DOS, which of the following commands is used to delete directory with all sub-directories and files?
(1) Delete (2) Del (3) Deltree (4) Move

66. Which one of the following DOS command sends contents of the screen to an output device?
(1) BREAK (2) DISK COPY
(3) MORE (4) ASSIGN

67. In DOS, the DIR command is used to **[SSC CGL 2013]**
(1) display content of a file
(2) delete file
(3) display list of files and sub-directories
(4) copy files

68. The DOS command, which cannot be executed with versions 1 and 2 is **[RBI Grade B 2014, RBI Grade B 2013]**
(1) GRAPHICS (2) FIND
(3) LABEL (4) MODE
(5) None of these

69. Which of the following is not an internal command of DOS?
(1) VER (2) COPY
(3) FORMAT (4) VOL

70. Which one of the following is an MS-DOS external command? **[SSC CHSL 2012]**
(1) DIR (2) COPY
(3) FORMAT (4) PROMPT

71. A command, in DOS, used to set a name to a disk, is
(1) VOL (2) REN
(3) LABEL (4) CLS

72. In DOS, the 'label' command is used to
(1) create the label of disk
(2) change the label of disk
(3) remove the label of disk
(4) Both (1) and (2)

73. Which among the following is not a mobile operating system? **[IBPS PO 2016]**
(1) Android (2) Safari
(3) Symbian (4) iOS
(5) BlackBerry

ANSWERS

1. *(4)*	2. *(1)*	3. *(1)*	4. *(2)*	5. *(3)*	6. *(5)*	7. *(4)*	8. *(5)*	9. *(4)*	10. *(1)*
11. *(2)*	12. *(3)*	13. *(3)*	14. *(2)*	15. *(1)*	16. *(1)*	17. *(3)*	18. *(1)*	19. *(2)*	20. *(1)*
21. *(2)*	22. *(1)*	23. *(4)*	24. *(1)*	25. *(1)*	26. *(2)*	27. *(4)*	28. *(3)*	29. *(2)*	30. *(1)*
31. *(1)*	32. *(1)*	33. *(2)*	34. *(1)*	35. *(1)*	36. *(2)*	37. *(2)*	38. *(1)*	39. *(4)*	40. *(3)*
41. *(2)*	42. *(4)*	43. *(3)*	44. *(4)*	45. *(5)*	46. *(3)*	47. *(3)*	48. *(1)*	49. *(1)*	50. *(4)*
51. *(1)*	52. *(3)*	53. *(3)*	54. *(3)*	55. *(1)*	56. *(2)*	57. *(5)*	58. *(4)*	59. *(4)*	60. *(1)*
61. *(4)*	62. *(3)*	63. *(4)*	64. *(2)*	65. *(3)*	66. *(2)*	67. *(3)*	68. *(3)*	69. *(3)*	70. *(3)*
71. *(3)*	72. *(4)*	73. *(2)*							

CHAPTER

08

PROGRAMMING CONCEPTS

Program can be defined as a set of instructions that need to be executed to accomplish a computing task. A person who writes or performs the program is known as **programmer**.

Programmer uses some specific languages to write program which is known as programming languages. e.g. C++, Java, etc.

Note *Ada Lovelace is regarded as the world's first programmer.*

Programming Language

It is a set of commands, instructions and other syntax use to create a software program. Programming language must be simple, easy to learn and use. It must be consistent in terms of syntax and semantics.

Programming languages are mainly categorised into three parts, which are as follows

Low Level Language (LLL)

These programming languages are more difficult to understand. It is designed to operate and handle the entire instruction set of a computer system directly which are generally used to write the system software.

There are two types of low level language, which are as follows

1. **Machine Language** It is the only language understood by the computers. Sometimes, it referred to as machine code or object code or binary language.

   It is a collection of binary digits (0 or 1) or bits that the computer reads and interprets.
2. **Assembly Language** It is a low level programming language which is used as an interface with computer hardwares.

   It uses structured commands as substitutions for numbers, allowing humans to read the code easier than looking at binary codes.

Medium Level Language (MLL)

It serves as the bridge between raw hardware and programming layer of a computer system. It is designed to improve the translated code before it is executed by the processor. e.g. C.

High Level Language (HLL)

It is an advanced computer programming language that is not limited to one computer, designed for a specific job and is easier to understand.

The main advantages of high level languages over low level languages is that they are easier to read, write and understand. e.g. BASIC, C, FORTRAN, Java, Python, etc.

Some High Level Languages and Their Application Areas

Language	Year	Developer	Application Area	Nature
FORTRAN (Formula Translation)	1957	A team of programmers at IBM	Calculation	Compiled
ALGOL (Algorithmic Language)	1958	A commitee of European and American computer scientists	Scientific purpose	Compiled
LISP (List Processing)	1958	John McCarthy at the Massachusetts Institute of Technology (MIT)	Artificial intelligence	Compiled and Interpreted
COBOL (Common Business Oriented Language)	1959	Grace Hopper	Business management, String oriented	Compiled
BASIC (Beginner's All purpose Symbolic Instruction Code)	1964	John G. Kemeny and Thomas E. Kurtz at Dartmouth College in New Hampshire	Programming for educational purpose	Interpreted
Pascal	1970	Niklaus Wirth	Education	Compiled
C	1972	Dennis Ritchie at Bell Labs	System programming	Compiled
C ++	1985	Bjarne Stroustrup at Bell Labs	System object programming	Compiled
Python	1991	Guido Van Rossum	Multimedia, Mobile app, Image processing	Interpreted
Java	1995	James Gosling at Sun Microsystems	Internet oriented programming	Compiled and Interpreted
Java Script	1995	Brendan Eich	Games, animated 2D and 3D graphics	Compiled and Interpreted

Terms Related to Programming

Program Documentation

It is a kind of documentation that gives a comprehensive procedural description of a program. It shows as to how software is written. The program documentation describes what exactly a program does by mentioning about the requirements of the input data and effect of performing a programming task.

OOPs

OOPs stands for Object Oriented Programmings in which programs are considered as a collection of objects. Each object is nothing but an instance of a class.

De-Bugging

It is the process of locating and fixing or bypassing bugs (errors) in computer program code.

Language Translator

It converts programming language into machine language.

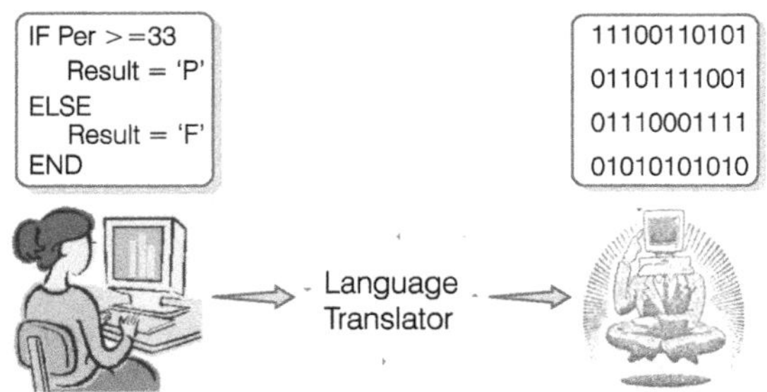

The translated program is called the **object code**. Depending upon used programming languages, *language translator is divided into three categories, which are as follows*

1. **Assembler** It converts a program written in assembly language into machine language. Assembly language consists of mnemonic code, which are difficult to learn and are machine dependent.
2. **Interpreter** It converts a HLL program into machine language by converting it line-by-line. If there is any error in any line, it stops the execution of the program immediately and reports to the user at the same time.

   Program execution cannot resume until the error is rectified by the user. Interpreter is very useful for de-bugging and suitable for novice programmer. This is a slow process and consumes less memory space.
3. **Compiler** It converts HLL program into machine language, which can be understood by the processor. For each high level language, the machine requires a separate compiler.

   A compiler creates a unique object program, i.e. if a source program is compiled, there is no need of that source program because output can be obtained by executing that object program.

   Compiler converts the entire HLL program in one go and reports all the errors of the program alongwith the line numbers.

Generation of Languages

The concept of language generations, sometimes called levels, is closely connected to the advances in technology that brought about computer generations. *The five generations of language are as follows*

(i) The **first generation languages** or **1 GLs** are low level languages like machine language.

(ii) The **second generation languages** or **2 GLs** are also low level languages that generally consist of assembly language.

(iii) The **third generation languages** or **3 GLs** are high level languages such as Java.

(iv) The **fourth generation languages** or **4 GLs** are the languages that consist of statements similar to the statements of human language. 4 GLs are commonly used in database programming and scripting programming.

(v) The **fifth generation languages** or **5 GLs** are programming languages that contain visual tools, which help to develop a program. A good example of 5 GLs is Visual Basic.

Algorithm

An algorithm is a step-by-step method of solving a problem. It is commonly used for data processing, calculation and other related computer and mathematical operations.

Flow Chart

A flow chart is a visual representation of the sequence of steps and decisions needed to perform a process. Each step in the sequence is noted within a diagram shape. Steps are linked by connecting lines and directional arrows.

Error

An error in a program is called bug. It is a term used to describe any issue that arises unexpectedly that cause a computers not function properly.

Types of Error

The types of error are classified into four categories, which are as follows

1. **Syntax Error** When the rules of the programming language are not followed, the compiler will show syntax error.

2. **Semantic Error** Semantic errors are reported by the compiler when the statements written in the program are not meaningful to the compiler.
3. **Logical Error** Logical errors are those errors that occur in the output of the program.The presence of logical errors leads to undesired or incorrect output.
4. **Runtime Error** Runtime errors are those errors that occur during the execution of a program. It generally occurs due to some illegal operation performed in the program.

Tit-Bits

- **Reserved words** are words that a programming language has set aside for its own use.
- **Pseudocode** is not a programming language, but simply an informal way of describing a program. It does not follow any syntax strictly.
- **Looping** is a control structure which is used in a program to execute a particular set of statements repeatedly.
- **Data Flow Diagram (DFD)** describes the processes that are involved in a system to transfer data from the input to the file storage and reports generation.

QUESTION BANK

1. The instructions that tell a computer how to carry out the processing tasks are referred to as computer **[IBPS PO 2015]**
(1) programs (2) processors
(3) input devices (4) memory modules
(5) None of these

2. A set of rules for telling the computer what operations to perform is called a **[IBPS PO 2012]**
(1) Procedural language
(2) Structures
(3) Natural language
(4) Command language
(5) Programming language

3. Which of the following contains specific rules and words that express the logical steps of an algorithm? **[IBPS Clerk 2014]**
(1) Programming language
(2) Syntax
(3) Programming structure
(4) Logical chart
(5) Flow chart

4. A(n) .... program is one that is ready to run and does not need to be altered in any way. **[IBPS Clerk 2013]**
(1) interpreter (2) high level
(3) compiler (4) COBOL
(5) executable

5. Who is regarded as the world's first programmer? **[RRB NTPC 2016]**
A. Alan Turing
B. Ada Lovelace
C. Tim Berners Lee
D. Steve Wozniak
(1) C (2) A
(3) B (4) D

6. A factor in the selection of source language is
(1) programmer's skill
(2) language availability
(3) program compatibility with other software
(4) All of the above

7. Languages which can easily interact with the hardware are called
(1) High level languages
(2) Low level languages
(3) Middle level languages
(4) All of the above

8. Machine language **[SBI PO 2013]**
(1) is the language in which programs were first written
(2) is the only language understood by the computer
(3) differs from one type of computer to another
(4) All of the above
(5) None of the above

9. The use of combination of 1's and 0's is feature of which of the following type of computer language? **[IBPS PO 2016]**
(1) High Level Language
(2) PASCAL
(3) Machine Language
(4) C
(5) COBOL

10. Each model of a computer has a unique
(1) assembly of a computer
(2) machine language
(3) high level language
(4) All of the above

11. All computers execute
(1) BASIC programs
(2) COBOL programs
(3) Machine language programs
(4) FORTRAN programs

12. The language which can be relocated easily is
(1) Machine language (2) Assembly language
(3) Low level language (4) Middle level language

13. Assembly language **[IBPS Clerk 2011]**
(1) uses alphabetic codes in place of binary numbers used in machine language
(2) is the easiest language to write programs
(3) need not be translated into machine language
(4) All of the above
(5) None of the above

14. Which language is CPU dependent ?
(1) C (2) Assembly
(3) Java (4) All except Java

15. .... serves as the bridge between raw hardware and programming layer of a computer system.
(1) Medium level language
(2) Low level language
(3) High level language
(4) Both (1) and (2)

16. Which of the following is a machine independent program?
(1) High level language
(2) Low level language
(3) Assembly language
(4) Machine language

17. Computer language used for calculation is
(1) LOGO (2) FORTRAN
(3) BASIC (4) C ++

18. Which of the following computer language is a mathematically oriented language used for scientific problems? **[UPSSSC 2015]**
(1) FORTRAN (2) COBOL
(3) LISP (4) PROLOG

19. FORTRAN stands for
(1) Formal Translation
(2) Formative Translation
(3) Formal Transaction
(4) Formula Translation

20. LISP is designed for
(1) artificial intelligence (2) GUI
(3) CUI (4) optical fibre

21. LISP is the second oldest high level programming language. Here, LISP stands for
(1) Level Program (2) Level Process
(3) List Processing (4) List Program

22. What does CO stand in COBOL? **[UPSSSC 2015, IBPS Clerk 2012]**
(1) Common Object (2) Common Oriented
(3) Common Operating (4) Computer Oriented
(5) None of these

23. Which of the following is not characteristic of COBOL?
(1) It is a very standardised language
(2) It is a very efficient in terms of coding and execution
(3) It had limited facilities for mathematical notation
(4) It is very readable language

24. A computer program used for business application is
(1) LOGO (2) COBOL
(3) BASIC (4) FORTRAN

25. Who among the following invented the computer language, COBOL? **[CHSL 2018]**
(1) Grace Murray Hopper
(2) John McCarthy
(3) Guido Van Rossum
(4) Brendan Eich

26. C programming language was developed by **[SSC CGL 2017]**
(1) Charles Babbage (2) Larry Wall
(3) James Gosling (4) Dennis Ritchie

27. C++ language developed by **[IBPS Clerk 2012]**
(1) Dennis Ritchie (2) Charles Babbage
(3) Niklaus Wirth (4) Bjarne Stroustrup
(5) John McCharthy

28. Python is a .... **[SSC CHSL 2019]**
(1) low level language (2) high level language
(3) machine language (4) assembly language

29. Java is referred to as a **[SBI PO 2014]**
(1) high level language
(2) complex language
(3) hardware device driver
(4) low level language
(5) programming mid level language

30. Computer language used on Internet is
(1) PASCAL (2) Java
(3) BASIC (4) LOGO

31. The language used for development of various games is
(1) C (2) C ++ (3) Java (4) SQL

32. Which of the following is a programming language for creating special programs like Applets? **[IBPS Clerk 2012]**
(1) Java (2) Cable
(3) Domain name (4) Net
(5) COBOL

33. Which is the official language for Android development? **[RRB NTPC 2016]**
A. Java B. COBOL
C. FORTRAN D. Ada
(1) C (2) A (3) B (4) D

34. Who invented Java Script programming language? **[SSC CGL 2016]**
(1) Brendan Eich (2) Willam Einthoven
(3) George Eastman (4) Emil Erlenmeyer

35. In which year did the Java Script programming language come into existence? **[SSC CHSL 2019]**
(1) 1995 (2) 1999
(3) 1990 (4) 2000

36. Which of the following is not a computer language ? **[UPSSSC 2016, SBI PO 2014]**
(1) BASIC (2) COBOL
(3) LOTUS (4) FORTRAN
(5) None of these

37. C, BASIC, COBOL and Java are examples of .... languages. **[IBPS Clerk 2015]**
(1) low level (2) computer
(3) system programming (4) high level
(5) None of these

38. .... is a written description of a computer program's functions. **[SBI PO 2014]**
(1) Explanatory instructions
(2) Graphical user interface
(3) Plug and play
(4) README files
(5) Documentation

39. De-bugging is the process of **[RRB NTPC 2016]**
A. rolling out a software program
B. modifying a software program
C. checking errors in a software program
D. changing the design structure of a program
(1) C (2) D (3) B (4) A

40. Translator program used in assembly language is called **[SBI Clerk 2012]**
(1) compiler (2) interpreter
(3) translation (4) translator
(5) assembler

41. The .... program is used to convert mnemonic code to machine code.
(1) Debug (2) C ++
(3) FORTRAN (4) Assembler

42. The function of an assembler is
(1) to convert basic language into machine language
(2) to convert high level language into machine language
(3) to convert assembly language into machine language
(4) to convert assembly language into low level language

43. An assembler is a
(1) programming language dependent
(2) syntax dependent
(3) machine dependent
(4) data dependent

44. Which of the following is not true about an assembler?
(1) Translates instructions of assembly language in machine language
(2) It translates the C program
(3) It is involved in program's execution
(4) It is a translating program

45. Compiler is a **[UPSSSC 2015]**
(1) computer program
(2) part of software
(3) program for converting from high level to machine language
(4) All of the above

46. Compiling creates a(n) **[RBI Grade B 2012]**
(1) error-free program (2) program specification
(3) subroutine (4) algorithm
(5) executable program

47. Computer programs are written in a high level programming language, however the human readable version of a program is called **[IBPS PO 2015]**
(1) word size (2) source code
(3) instruction set (4) application
(5) hard drive

48. Second generation languages are languages that consists of
(1) machine language (2) assembly language
(3) Java (4) visual basic

49. Which of the following generation languages consist of statements similar to the statements of human language?
(1) 1GL (2) 2GL (3) 3GL (4) 4GL

50. A set of step-by-step procedures for accomplishing a task is known as a(n) **[IBPS Clerk 2015]**
(1) Algorithm (2) Hardware program
(3) Software (4) Firmware program
(5) None of the above

51. Error in a program is called
(1) bug (2) debug
(3) virus (4) noise

52. Error which occurs when program tried to read from file without opening it is classified as
(1) execution error messages
(2) built in messages
(3) user defined messages
(4) half messages
(5) None of the above

53. .... are words that a programming language has set aside for its own use. **[IBPS PO 2011]**
(1) Control words (2) Control structures
(3) Reserved words (4) Reserved keys
(5) None of these

54. .... is a cross between human language and a programming language. **[IBPS PO 2012]**
(1) Pseudocode
(2) Java
(3) The Java virtual machine
(4) The compiler
(5) None of the above

55. In programming, repeating some statements is usually called **[SSC CGL 2013]**
(1) looping (2) control structure
(3) compiling (4) structure

56. What is the full name of DFD? **[UPPSC Computer Assistant 2019]**
(1) Data Flow Diagram (2) Data Full Document
(3) Data File Diagram (4) Data File Document

ANSWERS

1. *(1)*	2. *(5)*	3. *(3)*	4. *(5)*	5. *(3)*	6. *(3)*	7. *(2)*	8. *(4)*	9. *(3)*	10. *(2)*
11. *(3)*	12. *(2)*	13. *(1)*	14. *(2)*	15. *(1)*	16. *(1)*	17. *(2)*	18. *(1)*	19. *(4)*	20. *(1)*
21. *(3)*	22. *(2)*	23. *(2)*	24. *(2)*	25. *(1)*	26. *(4)*	27. *(4)*	28. *(2)*	29. *(1)*	30. *(2)*
31. *(3)*	32. *(1)*	33. *(2)*	34. *(1)*	35. *(1)*	36. *(3)*	37. *(4)*	38. *(5)*	39. *(1)*	40. *(5)*
41. *(4)*	42. *(3)*	43. *(3)*	44. *(2)*	45. *(4)*	46. *(5)*	47. *(2)*	48. *(2)*	49. *(4)*	50. *(1)*
51. *(1)*	52. *(1)*	53. *(3)*	54. *(1)*	55. *(1)*	56. *(1)*				

CHAPTER

09

MICROSOFT WINDOWS

Microsoft Windows (MS-Windows) stands for 'Microsoft-Wide Interactive Network Development for Office Work Solutions'. Microsoft Windows is a series of graphical interface operating system developed, marketed and sold by Microsoft.

A user can easily interact with the windows programs or applications by selecting relevant options, through the mouse or by entering characters through the keyboard.

Versions of MS-Windows

Some important versions of MS-Windows are as follows

Windows NT (New Technology)

A version of Windows NT was introduced in July, 1993 and made specifically for businesses. It offers better control over work station capabilities to help network administrators.

Features

(i) It is based on High Level Language.

(ii) It is able to run on DOS, Windows 3 and Win 32 applications.

(iii) It has a 32-bit Windows application.

(iv) It provides higher stability and security.

Windows 95

It is a graphical user interface based operating system. It was released on 24th August, 1995 by Microsoft.

Features

(i) It is a mixed of 16-bit/32-bit Windows operating system.

(ii) It is consumer-oriented.

(iii) It supports FAT32 File System, Multi-Display, Web TV and the Internet Explorer.

Windows 98

It was developed in 1998. This was produced in two main versions. The first Windows 98 version was plagued with programming errors but the Windows 98's second edition came out later was much better with many errors resolved.

Features

(i) It supports Internet Explorer 4.0.1.

(ii) Windows 98 was the first operating system to use the Windows Driver Model (WDM).

(iii) It includes a FAT32 converter utility for converting FAT16 drives to FAT32 without formatting the partition.

(iv) It also supports many peripheral devices (USB, DVD, etc.).

Windows ME

Windows ME (Millennium Edition) launched in June 2000, but it has been historically plagued with programming errors which may be frustrating for home users.

Features

(i) It is designed for single CPU.

(ii) The minimum internal storage is 64 MB and maximum 4 GB.

(iii) It introduced Multilingual User Interface (MUI).

Windows XP

It is an OS produced by Microsoft for use on personal computers. Microsoft released Windows XP on 25th October, 2001.

Some versions of Windows XP are as follows

(i) Windows XP Home edition is a version made for home users.

(ii) Windows XP Professional is made for business users.

Features

(i) It has various users with independent profiles.

(ii) It has 3.75 GB free space on the disk and that the total size of the disk is 19.5 GB.

(iii) Atleast 64 MB of RAM internal storage.

(iv) It provides 1.5 GB of available space on the hard disk.

(v) It includes video adapter and monitor with Super VGA (Video Graphics Array) or higher resolution.

(vi) It supports sound card, CD-ROM, DVD-ROM drive, speakers or headphones.

Windows Vista

It is an operating system developed by Microsoft for use on personal computers, including home and business desktops, laptops, tablets, PCs and media center PCs. It was released worldwide on 30th January, 2007.

Features

(i) It can be installed Pentium 4, higher, 512MB RAM, 32 MB video card and 40 GB hard disk.

(ii) It enhances the features of visual style.

Windows 7

It is an OS released by Microsoft on 22nd October, 2009. It is an upgrade of Windows XP and Vista. It does not include some standard applications like Windows Movie Maker, Windows Mail, etc.

Features

(i) It supports 64-bit processor.

(ii) It provides touch, speech, handwriting recognition.

(iii) It supports a playback of media in MP4.

(iv) It includes Windows Bio-Metric framework.

(v) It provides multiple firewall.

Windows 8

It is a personal computer operating system that was developed by Microsoft and released on 26th October, 2012.

Features

(i) It is a 64-bit logical CPU.

(ii) It provides 3D Graphic support and Internet Explorer-10.

(iii) It is based on Microsoft's Metro Design language.

(iv) It supports new emerging technology like USB 3.0, cloud computing.

Windows 10

It is a personal computer operating system developed and released by Microsoft on 29th July, 2015.

Features

(i) It is easy to use social media sites like Facebook and Twitter.

(ii) Windows 10 will also include a 'game DVR' mode to allow recordings of the last 30 seconds of play, all better for the social gaming.

(iii) Windows 10 interface is adapted by hardware it is running on.

Desktop

When we turn ON the computer then the first screen, which will be display on the computer is known as desktop. The background image of desktop is called wallpaper.

A small arrow or blinking symbol, moving on the desktop, is called cursor. Desktop contains Start menu, Task bar, icons, gadgets, etc.

STRUCTURE OF WINDOWS

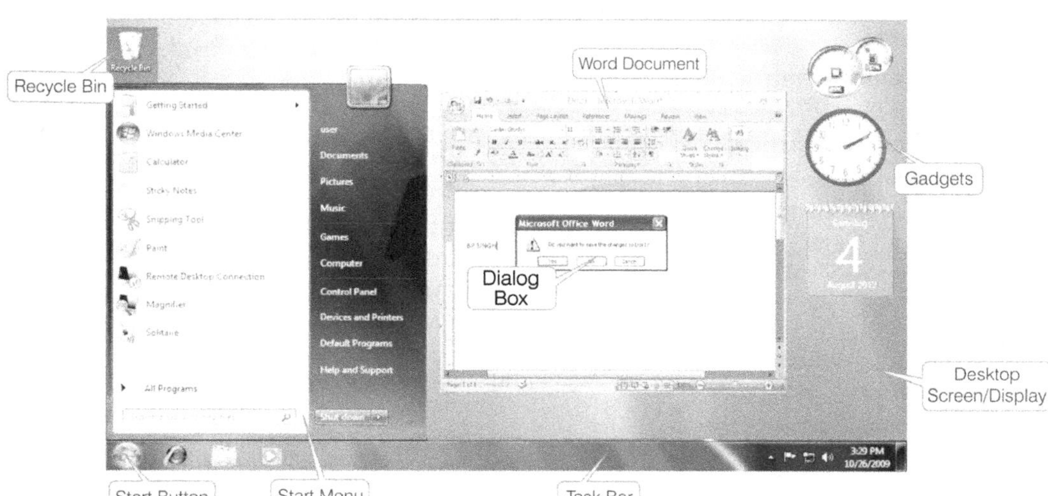

Some important components of desktop are organised as follows

Icon

A small image of a program, shown on the desktop with program name is known as icon. Icons are small pictures that represent files, folders, programs and other items.

Users can open these programs by double click on icons. If you move an icon on your desktop, this is called 'dragging' and after releasing it, it will be called 'dropping.'

Some of the icons displayed on the desktop are as follows

1. **Computer** It is the most important icon on the desktop, which contains icons of document folders, hard disk's partition, each removable disk drive. e.g. Floppy disk, CD, DVD, etc. It also allows the users to access drives, printers, removable disk or other system applications.
2. **Recycle Bin** It is also a form of icon on the desktop, which contains deleted files, folders or shortcuts. If we delete a file or folder then it goes to recycle bin. From recycle bin, we can restore the deleted files or folders on proper place.

   Once the recycle bin is empty then we won't be able to restore those files and folders again.

Task Bar

Initially, the long horizontal bar at the bottom of the desktop is known as Task Bar. When we open a program or any window, then the button of that program will be displayed on the task bar.

Generally, task bar consists of three parts

(i) Start button

(ii) Middle section

(iii) Notification area

Start Menu

This menu is the main gateway of our computer's program such as files, folders and settings. Start menu also contains most recently opened programs.

Start menu have following options

1. **All Programs** It contains a list of installed programs. When we install any software, it automatically shows in this menu.
2. **Favourites** It is a collection of book marked web pages.
3. **Documents** It shows a list of most recently opened documents.
4. **Setting** It includes Control Panel, Printers, Taskbar, etc.
5. **Find** It searches for specific files or folders.
6. **Log Off** It provides a password to protect from unauthorised access.
7. **Turn Off** (Shut down) To shut down or restart the system.

Window

Window is a rectangular area which provides an environment to run many programs.

Some parts of the window are as follows

Title Bar

It is located at the top of window or any dialog box, which displays the name of the window or software program. *Title bar contains atleast three small buttons, which are as follows*

1. **Close Button** At the right edge of the title bar, there is a square containing a [×] called the Close button. It helps to terminate the running program.
2. **Minimize Button** It reduces to window in the form of button which placed on the task bar. It helps to shrink the window.
3. **Maximize Button** It enlarges the window to occupy the whole desktop. It expands the size of window fit to the desktop.

Scroll Bar

It appears at the right (or left) side or at the bottom of the window. A window can display a document, i.e. larger than the window area, so with the help of scroll bar arrow, the user can scroll a document in the window area to bring the view of hidden portion of document.

There are two types of scroll bar; i.e. Horizontal scroll bar and Vertical scroll bar.

Menu Bar

Each window contains its own menu bar which performs specific actions when they have been selected.

The menu bar consists of several menus, which are as follows

1. **File menu** contains options like New, Open, Close, Save, Save As, Print, etc.
2. **Edit menu** contains options like Undo, Cut, Copy, Paste, Clear, etc.
3. **View menu** contains options like Normal, Toolbar, Print Layout, etc.
4. **Insert menu** contains options like Header, Footer, etc.
5. **Help menu** is used to provide information about window.

Dialog Box

When we perform certain operation on our document and click on the Close button without saving the document then dialog box will be appear on the screen.

Generally, dialog box contains message, Close button, Yes button, No button and Cancel button. It is mainly used to suggest that what to do next.

Main Programs Inside the Windows

Notepad

It is a text editor program. Notepad is most commonly used to edit or view text files. The file format of Notepad files is .txt (text document).

> ***To open*** Click on Start button → All Programs → Accessories → Notepad

WordPad

It is an another text editor program including some features such as complex formatting, pictures, etc. The extension of WordPad file is .rtf (rich text format).

> ***To open*** Click on Start button → All Programs → Accessories → WordPad

Paint

It is a drawing program, used to create drawing or edit digital pictures (images). The extension of paint file is .png or. jpg or. bmp.

> ***To open*** Click on Start button → All Programs → Accessories → Paint

Calculator

It performs addition, subtraction, multiplication, division, etc.

> ***To open*** Click on Start button → All Programs → Accessories → Calculator

Media Player

Windows media player is an easy-to-use interface to play digital media files, organise digital media collection, burn CDs, etc.

> ***To open*** Click on Start button → All Programs → Windows Media Player

Files

These are the collection of data stored on auxiliary storage media. In Windows, files are the basic unit to store data. The name given to a file or document by the user is called file name. Each file has a specific filename and has a file extension that identifies the file type.

Some common file name extensions are as follows

.docx	MS-Word document
.rtf	WordPad document
.txt	Notepad text file
.eml	E-mail file
.exe	Executable file
.xlsx	MS-Excel file
.htm / **.html**	HTML file (Web page)
.pptx	MS-PowerPoint presentation

ZIP File ZIP stands for Zone Information Protocol. This is an application that allows for the compression of application files.

Executable File When a file contains instructions that can be carried out by the computer, it is often called an executable file.

Folders

These are containers that you can use to store files. Folders can also store other folders, i.e. sub-folders. You can create any number of sub-folders and each can hold any number of files and additional sub-folders.

Windows Library

A windows library can contain files and folders stored on the local computer. Users interact with libraries in ways similar to how they would interact with other folders.

Different types of windows library are as follows

(i) **Documents Library** It is used to organise and arrange Word processing documents, Spreadsheets, Presentation and other text related files.

(ii) **Pictures Library** It is used to organise and arrange your digital pictures.

(iii) **Music Library** It is used to organise and arrange your digital music, such as songs, etc.

(iv) **Video Library** It is used to organise and arrange your videos, such as clips, recording, etc.

Tit-Bits

- To shut down the computer, we need to click Start button and then select Shut down key.
- **Windows Explorer** is a file manager application that is included with releases of the Microsoft Windows OS.
- **Clipboard** is a temporary storage in computer memory that stores the cutted or copied data.

MS-Windows Shortcut Keys

Keys	Description
Delete	Delete characters to the right of cursor
Backspace	Delete characters to the left of the cursor
Ctrl + A	Select all
F3	Search for a file or folder
Alt + Enter	View properties for the selected item
Alt + F4	Close the active item or quit the active program
Alt + Spacebar	Opens the shortcut menu for the active window
F2	Rename selected item
Ctrl + Right Arrow	Move the insertion point to the beginning of the next word
Ctrl + Left Arrow	Move the insertion point to the beginning of the previous word
Ctrl + Alt + Del	Restart the computer
Ctrl + Esc	Display the Start menu
F5	Refresh the active window
Esc	Cancel the current task
Window	To display or hide the Start menu
Window + D	To display the desktop
Window + L	To lock the keyboard

QUESTION BANK

1. In Windows NT, NT stands for
(1) New Terminology (2) New Technique
(3) New Technology (4) Normal Technique

2. If you are performing Windows 98 operating system to Windows XP you are performing a(n) **[IBPS Clerk 2014]**
(1) push up (2) China
(3) patch (4) pull down
(5) update

3. Which of the following is not a feature of Windows 98?
(1) It supports Internet Explorer 4.0.1
(2) It supports many peripheral devices
(3) It was the first operating system to use the WDM
(4) It provides multiple firewall

4. In Windows ME, what does ME stand for?
(1) Millennium Edition (2) Micro Expert
(3) Macro Expert (4) Multi Expert

5. Windows XP released in
(1) 2000 (2) 1998
(3) 1999 (4) 2001

6. Which of the following is an example of a system software?
(1) Windows 7 (2) MS Word 2010
(3) MS PowerPoint 2010 (4) OpenOffice Writer

7. Windows 95, Windows 98 and Windows NT are known as what?
(1) Processors (2) Domain names
(3) Modems (4) Operating systems

8. Which of the following is not a version of the Windows operating system software for the PC? **[IBPS PO 2015]**
(1) ME (2) 98 (3) XP (4) Linux
(5) 95

9. Which of the following is not an in-built software application found in MS Windows?
(1) Paint (2) CD Player
(3) Disk Defragmentor (4) Volume Control
(5) MS Word

10. What is Windows Explorer? **[SBI Clerk 2014]**
(1) Personal Computer (2) Network
(3) File Manager (4) Drive
(5) Web Browser

11. A screen in a software program that permits the user to view several programs at one time is called a **[SSC CGL 2018]**
(1) Spreadsheet (2) Word processor
(3) Window (4) Shareware

12. Background screen of computer is known as
(1) application (2) window
(3) desktop (4) frame

13. The background image of desktop is called as
(1) graphics (2) deskcover
(3) wallback (4) wallpaper

14. The desktop of a computer refers to
(1) the visible screen
(2) the area around the monitor
(3) the top of the mouse pad
(4) the inside of a folder

15. A blinking indicator that shows you where your next action will happen, is
(1) CPU (2) cursor
(3) toolbar (4) boot

16. Graphical pictures that represent an object like file, folder, etc., are **[RBI Grade B 2014]**
(1) task bar (2) windows
(3) desktop (4) icons
(5) None of these

17. A/An .... contains programs that can be selected.
(1) pointer (2) menu (3) icon (4) button

18. To open disk, mouse pointer is placed on disk icon and then
(1) mouse is dragged pushing the button
(2) mouse is double-clicked
(3) mouse is rotated around
(4) mouse is clicked after rotating it

19. When you want to move an icon on your desktop, this is called
(1) double clicking (2) highlighting
(3) dragging (4) pointing

20. To display the contents of a folder in Windows Explorer, you should....... **[SBI PO 2013]**
(1) click on it (2) collapse it
(3) name it (4) give it a password
(5) rename it

21. Factor making Windows popular is
(1) multitasking capacity
(2) desktop features
(3) user friendly
(4) being inexpensive

22. All the deleted files go to
(1) Recycle Bin (2) Task Bar
(3) Tool Bar (4) Computer

23. Generally, you access the recycle bin through an icon located
(1) on the desktop
(2) on the hard drive
(3) on the shortcut menu
(4) in the properties dialog box

24. Which of the following is used to access a file from the computer store? **[IBPS Clerk Mains 2017]**
(1) Insert (2) Retrieve
(3) File (4) Print
(5) Find

25. The taskbar is located
(1) on the start menu
(2) at the bottom of the screen
(3) on the quick launch toolbar
(4) at the top of the screen

26. In the split window mode, one title bar looks darker than the other, because **[RBI Grade B 2012]**
(1) darker title bar shows window not in use
(2) darker title bar shows active window
(3) darker title bar shows unavailable window
(4) Both (1) and (2)
(5) None of the above

27. Date and time are available on the desktop at
(1) Keyboard (2) Recycle Bin
(3) My Computer (4) Task Bar
(5) None of these

28. Which of the following is an appropriate method to shutdown computer?
(1) Click 'Start' then select 'Shut down'
(2) Click 'Start' then select 'Restart'
(3) Click 'Start' then switch user
(4) Switch off monitor

29. End menu is available at which button?
(1) End (2) Start
(3) Turn off (4) Restart

30. When you install a new program on your computer, it is typically added to the menu
(1) All Programs
(2) Select Programs
(3) Start Programs
(4) Desktop Programs

31. Why do you log-off from your computer when going out from your office? **[IBPS Clerk Mains 2017]**
(1) Someone might steal your files, passwords, etc.
(2) In order to save electricity
(3) Logging off is essential to increase performance
(4) Logging off is mandatory before you go out
(5) Logging off is a good exercise to perform regularly

32. Which of the following refers to the rectangular area for displaying information and running programs? **[SBI PO 2013]**
(1) Desktop (2) Dialog box
(3) Menu (4) Window
(5) Icon

33. Title bar, ribbon, status bar, views and document workspace are components of .... program.
(1) windows (2) browser
(3) explorer (4) Website

34. Active window means the
(1) active window is designated by a different color toolbar that other open window
(2) window that is currently open
(3) Both (1) and (2)
(4) window that is last used

35. To 'maximize' a window means to
(1) fill it to the capacity
(2) expand it to fit the desktop
(3) put only like files inside
(4) drag it to the recycle bin

36. To shrink a window to an icon,
(1) open a group window
(2) minimize a window
(3) maximize a window
(4) restore a window

37. Which of the following are lists of commands that appear on the screen? **[IBPS Clerk 2015]**
(1) GUIs (2) Icons
(3) Menus (4) Windows
(5) Stacks

38. Commands at the top of a screen such; FILE-EDIT-FONT-TOOLS to operate and change things within program comes under
(1) menu bar (2) tool bar
(3) user friendly (4) word processor

39. What is an on-screen display listing of available options of functions on a computer? **[SBI Clerk 2015]**
(1) Document (2) View
(3) Tool (4) Format
(5) Menu

40. Menus are the part of **[RBI Grade B 2014]**
(1) hardware (2) user interface
(3) status bar (4) monitor
(5) None of these

41. For creating a new document, you use which command at File menu?
(1) Open (2) Close (3) New (4) Save

42. What menu is selected to cut, copy and paste?
(1) File (2) Tools (3) Special (4) Edit

43. Help menu is available at which button?
(1) End (2) Start
(3) Turn off (4) Restart

44. It is easier to change the name of file using .... process.
(1) transforming (2) christening
(3) renaming (4) retagging

45. The steps involved to open a document are **[RBI Grade B 2013]**
(1) select the document to open from the File down menu
(2) click on the Open option in the Tools menu
(3) Both (1) and (2)
(4) can be different for different Word document
(5) None of the above

46. A computer message is "Do you really want to delete the selected file(s)"? The user clicks 'Yes' key. It is called
(1) program response
(2) user output
(3) user response
(4) program output

47. A symbol or question on the screen that prompts you to take action and tell the computer what to do next, is
(1) scanner (2) questionnaire
(3) information seeker (4) prompt and dialog box
(5) None of these

48. .... menu type is also known as a drop down menu.
(1) Fly-down (2) Pop-down
(3) Pop-up (4) Pull-up
(5) Pull-down

49. A .... is an additional set of commands that the computer displays after you make a selection.
(1) dialog box (2) sub menu
(3) menu selecting (4) All of these

50. Anything written on the screen is called
(1) cursor (2) text
(3) folder (4) boot
(5) None of these

51. ...... lets you leave a screen or program.
(1) Boot (2) Programs
(3) Exit (4) Text

52. A .... is an icon on the desktop that provides a user with immediate access to a program or file.
(1) kernel (2) buffer
(3) shortcut (4) spooler

53. What is the full form of RTF? **[IBPS Clerk Mains 2017]**
(1) Richer Text-Formatting
(2) Rich Text Format (3) Right Text Fishing
(4) Right Text Font (5) Rich Text Font

54. The extension(s) of paint file is/are
(1) .png (2) .jpg
(3) .bmp (4) All of these

55. Which of the following options is used to open calculator?
(1) Start button → All Programs → Accessories → Calculator
(2) Start button → All Programs → Calculator
(3) Start button → Accessories → Calculator
(4) All of the above

56. .... is an easy-to-use interface to play digital media files.
(1) WordPad (2) Notepad
(3) Media player (4) Games

57. When you cut or copy information it gets place in the .... **[IBPS Clerk 2013]**
(1) clipart (2) clipboard
(3) motherboard (4) Both (1) and (2)
(5) None of these

58. A clipboard **[RBI Grade B 2014]**
(1) is used to save data on disk in the event of a power failure
(2) is able to retain the contents even when computer is switched OFF
(3) is available only in Microsoft Word
(4) is a temporary storage in computer memory and temporarily stores the cutted or copied data
(5) None of the above

59. What is the command used to remove text or graphics from a document, the information is then stored on a clipboard so you can paste it?
(1) Chop (2) Cut
(3) Clip (4) Cart away

60. A saved document is referred to as a
(1) file (2) word
(3) folder (4) project
(5) None of these

61. The name given to a document by the user is called
(1) file name (2) program
(3) data (4) record

62. A .... is a collection of information saved as a unit.
(1) folder (2) file
(3) path (4) file extension

63. A file is often referred to as a **[RBI Grade B 2012]**
(1) wizard (2) document
(3) pane (4) device
(5) documentation

64. Which of the following statements is a false conceiving file names? **[IBPS Clerk 2014]**
(1) Every file in the same folder must have a unique name
(2) The file name comes before the dot (.)
(3) File extension is another name for the type
(4) The file extension comes before the dot (.) followed by the file name
(5) Files may share the same name or the same extension, but not both at the same time

65. File extensions are used in order to
(1) name the file
(2) ensure the file name is not lost
(3) identify the file
(4) identify the file type

66. Which of the following contained at the end of the file name and help to determine the type of file? **[SBI Clerk 2014]**
(1) File property (2) File type
(3) File name (4) File subname
(5) File extension

67. What are .bas, .doc, .htm examples of in computing? **[IBPS PO 2015]**
(1) Extensions (2) Protocols
(3) Database (4) Domains
(5) None of these

68. What is the default file extension for all Word documents? **[RBI Asstt. 2012]**
(1) WRD (2) TXT (3) DOC (4) FIL
(5) WD

69. You organise files by storing them in **[RBI Grade B 2012]**
(1) archives (2) lists
(3) indexes (4) folders
(5) None of these

70. .... may be included in other folder while making hierarchical structure folder.
(1) Mini-folder (2) Small folder
(3) Sub-folder (4) Object folder

71. Which of the following refers to containers used to store related documents located on the computer? **[SBI Clerk 2014]**
(1) Labels (2) Indexes
(3) Programs (4) Folders
(5) Sections

72. You can keep your personal files/folders in
(1) My Folder (2) Documents
(3) My Files (4) My Text

73. When embedding object into document, one of the following occurs. **[RBI Grade B 2014]**
(1) Embedded object becomes a part of the document
(2) Embedded object remains outside object to the document, but loaded with document
(3) Both becomes a zip file
(4) Both (1) and (2)
(5) None of the above

74. Which of the following shortcut keys represents the correct sequence for copy, paste and cut commands?
(1) Ctrl + V; Ctrl+C; Ctrl+V
(2) Ctrl + C; Ctrl+V; Ctrl+X
(3) Ctrl + X; Ctrl+C; Ctrl+V
(4) Ctrl + C; Ctrl+X; Ctrl+V

75. Which of the following keys is used to delete characters to the left of the cursor? **[SBI PO 2014]**
(1) Alt + Delete (2) Shift
(3) Esc (4) Delete
(5) Backspace

76. To restart the computer, following combination of keys is used.
(1) Del + Ctrl
(2) Backspace + Ctrl
(3) Esc + Ctrl
(4) Ctrl + Alt + Del

77. Which of the following shortcut keys is used to close current or active window? **[IBPS RRB PO Mains 2018]**
(1) Alt+F4 (2) Ctrl+F4
(3) Alt+F6 (4) Ctrl+F6
(5) Ctrl+Esc

ANSWERS

1. *(3)*	2. *(5)*	3. *(4)*	4. *(1)*	5. *(4)*	6. *(1)*	7. *(4)*	8. *(4)*	9. *(5)*	10. *(3)*
11. *(3)*	12. *(3)*	13. *(4)*	14. *(1)*	15. *(2)*	16. *(4)*	17. *(3)*	18. *(2)*	19. *(3)*	20. *(1)*
21. *(2)*	22. *(1)*	23. *(1)*	24. *(2)*	25. *(2)*	26. *(2)*	27. *(4)*	28. *(1)*	29. *(2)*	30. *(1)*
31. *(1)*	32. *(4)*	33. *(1)*	34. *(3)*	35. *(2)*	36. *(2)*	37. *(3)*	38. *(1)*	39. *(5)*	40. *(2)*
41. *(3)*	42. *(4)*	43. *(2)*	44. *(3)*	45. *(3)*	46. *(3)*	47. *(4)*	48. *(5)*	49. *(1)*	50. *(2)*
51. *(3)*	52. *(3)*	53. *(2)*	54. *(4)*	55. *(1)*	56. *(3)*	57. *(2)*	58. *(4)*	59. *(2)*	60. *(1)*
61. *(1)*	62. *(2)*	63. *(2)*	64. *(4)*	65. *(4)*	66. *(5)*	67. *(1)*	68. *(3)*	69. *(4)*	70. *(3)*
71. *(4)*	72. *(2)*	73. *(1)*	74. *(2)*	75. *(5)*	76. *(4)*	77. *(1)*			

CHAPTER

10

MICROSOFT OFFICE

Microsoft Office (MS-Office) was developed by Microsoft in 1988. It is a collection of softwares, based on specific purpose and mainly used in office work. You can start any software of MS-Office by using the Start button.

There are five packages of MS-Office listed below

1. MS-Word (Word Processing Software)
2. MS-Excel (Spreadsheet Software)
3. MS-PowerPoint (Presentation Software)
4. MS-Access (Database Management Software)
5. MS-Outlook (E-mail Client)

Microsoft Word

MS-Word is a Word processing application which is one of the most important and widely used applications found on computer. It provides tools for editing, formatting and printing of documents smaller than 45 KB.

The document can be a poster, report, letter, brochure, web page, news letter, etc.
e.g. WordStar, Notepad for Windows.

To start the MS-Word software, we can follow any one method out of them

(i) Click on Start button and then click on Run option. Run dialog box will be appear on the screen. Now, type winword on text box and press Enter key.

(ii) Click Start button → All Programs → Microsoft Office → Microsoft Word 2010.

It opens MS-Word with a blank document. By default, the name of the blank document is Document1.docx, where. docx are the extensions of a MS-Word file.

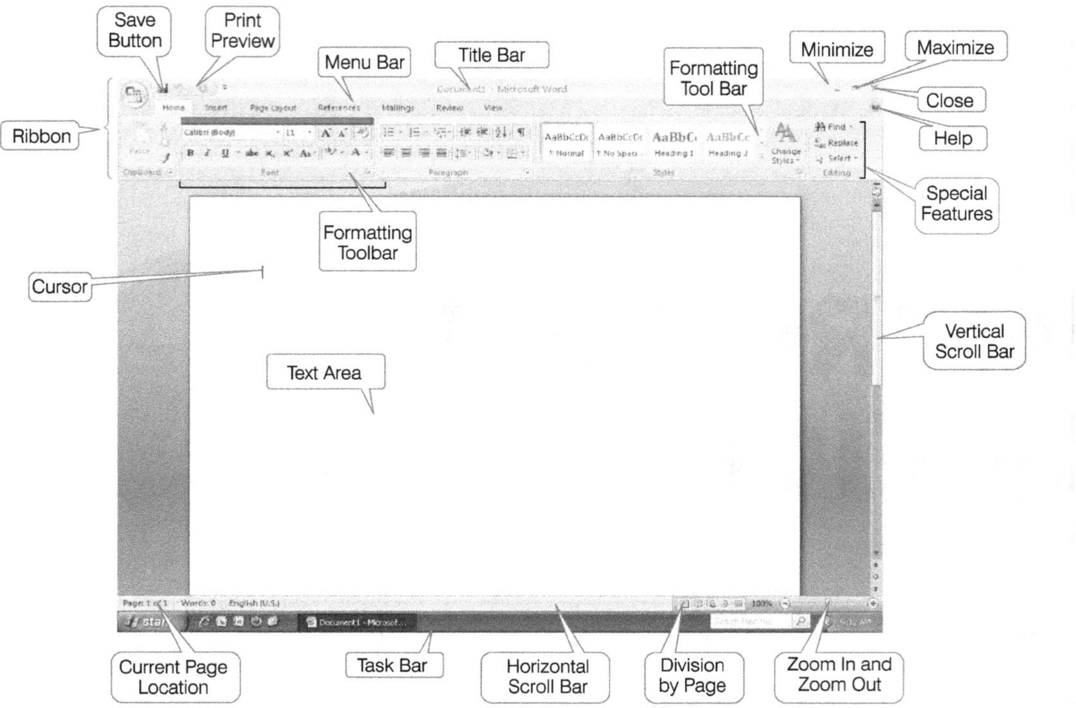

Components of Microsoft Word

The components of MS-Word are as follows

(i) **Title Bar** It shows the name of the application and name of the file. It consists of three control buttons, i.e.

(a) *Minimize* (reduces the window but application still active)

(b) *Restore* (brings Word window to the maximum original size)

(c) *Close* (close the Word window)

(ii) **Standard Tool Bar** It displays the symbol for the common operations like Open, Print, Save, etc.

(iii) **Ribbon** It is a set of tools and commands across the top of the screen. It consists of a panel of commands which are organised into a set of tabs.

(iv) **Tab** On the ribbon, it contains the buttons needed to edit characters, text and layout.

There are various tabs as follows

(a) **Home Tab** It consists of Clipboard, Font, Paragraph, Styles, Editing.

(b) **Insert Tab** It consists of Pages, Tables, Illustrations , Links, Header & Footer, Text, Symbols.

(c) **Page Layout Tab** It consists of Themes, Page Setup, Page Background, Paragraph, Arrange.

(d) **References Tab** It consists of Table of Contents, Footnotes, Citations & Bibliography, Captions, Index, Table of Authorities.

(e) **Mailings Tab** It consists of Create, Start Mail Merge, Write & Insert Fields, Preview Results, Finish.

(f) **Review Tab** It consists of Proofing, Language, Comments, Tracking, Changes, Compare, Protect.

(g) **View Tab** It consists of Document Views, Show, Zoom, Window, Macros.

(v) **Ruler** It appears on the top of the document window. It allows to format the horizontal or vertical alignment of text in a document.
There are two types of ruler
(a) **Horizontal Ruler** It indicates the width of the document and is used to set left and right margins.
(b) **Vertical Ruler** It indicates the height of the document and is used to set top and bottom margins.

(vi) **Status Bar** It displays the information such as page number, current page, current template, column number, line number, etc.

(vii) **Work Area** It is the rectangular area of the document window that can be use to type the text. It is also called as **workplace**.

(viii) **Cursor** It is also called **insertion pointer**. It denotes the place where text, graphics or any other item would be placed when you type, overwrite or insert them.

Features of Microsoft Word

The features of MS-Word are described below

(i) **Text Editing** It provides editing, adding and deleting text, modification of text content i.e. cut, copy and paste.

When we cut any text in our document, it will save in hard drive temporarily, till we paste it on any other place.

(ii) **Format Text** It offers to modify the text in any of the available hundreds of text designs. It formats text in various styles such as bold, italic, underline, etc.

(iii) **Indentation** It denotes the distance between text boundaries and page margins. It offers three types of indentation-positive, hanging and negative.

(iv) **Page Orientation** It facilitates selection of typed text printed or visible in horizontal view or vertical view on a specified size of the page. MS-Word offers Portrait–vertically oriented and Landscape–horizontally oriented.

(v) **Find & Replace** This feature allows flexibility and comfort to the user to replace a text with a substituted text at all places.

(vi) **Spell Check** This facilitates automatic and manual checking of spelling mistakes and also suggests a few possible alternate options for incorrect spelt words.

(vii) **Thesaurus** It contains a comprehensive dictionary and thesaurus feature that offers the synonym options for a word.

(viii) **Bullets and Numbering** A list of bullets and numbering features is used for tables, lists, pages and tables of content. Bullets are arranged in unordered lists and numbering is arranged in ordered lists.

(ix) **Graphics** It provides the facility of incorporating drawings in the documents which enhance their usefulness.

(x) **Object Linking and Embedding** (OLE) It is a program integration technology that is used to share information between programs through objects. Object save entities like charts, equations, video clips, audio clips, pictures, etc.

(xi) **Horizontal and Vertical Scroll Bars** They enable one to move up and down or left and right across the window. The horizontal scroll bar is located above the status bar. The vertical scroll bar is located along the right side of the screen to move up and down the document.

(xii) **Save a Document** When we create a new document, it will be saved into the hard drive.

To save a document, user has three common ways

(i) To click on Save option from File menu.
(ii) Select Save button from Standard toolbar.
(iii) Press Ctrl + S key.

Tit-Bits

- MS-Word was first released in 1983 under the name Multi-Tool Word for Xenix Systems.
- In MS-Word, a default alignment for the paragraph is left.
- MS-Word has a list of pre-defined typing, spelling, capitalisation and grammar errors that **Auto-correct** can detect and correct.

Shortcut Keys of MS-Word and their Descriptions

Standard Toolbar

Tool Name	Shortcut Keys	Description
New	Ctrl + N	Creates a new document.
Open	Ctrl + O or Ctrl + F12	Opens an existing document.
Save	Ctrl + S or Shift + F12	Saves the active document.
	F12	Opens a Save As dialog box.
Select	Ctrl + A	Selects all contents of the page.
Print	Ctrl + P or Ctrl + Shift + F12	Prints the active document.
Print Preview	Ctrl + F2	Displays full pages as they are printed.
Spelling	F7	Checks the spelling in the active document.
Cut	Ctrl + X	Cuts the selected text and puts it on the clipboard.
Copy	Ctrl + C	Copies the selected text and puts it on the clipboard.
Paste	Ctrl + V or Shift + Insert	Insert the clipboard contents at the insertion point.
Format Painter	Ctrl + Shift + C	Copies the formatting of the selected text to a specified location.
Undo	Ctrl + Z	Reverses certain commands.
Redo	Ctrl +Y	Reverses the action of the Undo button.
Help	F1	Provides the help for working on MS -Word.
Find	Ctrl + F	Opens Find & Replace dialog boxes with Find tab.
Insert	Ctrl + K	Insert link.
Delete	Ctrl + Del	Deletes word to the right of cursor.
	Ctrl + Backspace	Deletes word to the left of cursor.
Insert	Alt + Shift + D	Insert the current date.
	Alt + Shift + T	Insert the current time.

Formatting Toolbar

Tool Name	Shortcut Keys	Description
Style	Ctrl + Shift + S	Applies a style or records a style.
Font	Ctrl + Shift + F	Changes the font of the selected text.
Font Size	Ctrl + Shift + P	Changes the font size of the selected text.
Bold	Ctrl + B	Makes the selected text bold.
Italic	Ctrl + I	Makes the selected text italic.
Underline	Ctrl + U	Makes the selected text underline.
Aligned Left	Ctrl + L	Aligns the paragraph at left indent (By default).
Center	Ctrl + E	Centers the paragraph between the indents.
Aligned Right	Ctrl + R	Aligns the paragraph at right indent.
Justify	Ctrl + J	Aligns the paragraph at both right and left indents.
Line space	Ctrl + 5	To increase line spacing.

Microsoft Excel

A spreadsheet is a matrix of rows and columns similar to an accounting ledger.

An electronic spreadsheet is used for analysing, sharing and managing information for accounting purpose performing mathematical calculations, budgeting, billing etc.

The spreadsheet program also provides tools for creating graphs, inserting pictures and chart, analysing the data, etc.

e.g. Corel Quattro Pro, Visicalc, Lotus-1-2-3, Apple Numbers, etc.

To start MS-Excel software, we can follow any one method out of them

(i) Click on Start button and then click on Run option. Run dialog box will be appear on the screen. Now, type Excel on Text box and press Enter key.

(ii) Click Start button → All Programs → Microsoft Office → Microsoft Excel 2010.

It opens MS-Excel with a blank spreadsheet. By default, the name of the blank spreadsheet is Book1.xlsx, where .xls and .xlsx are the extensions of a MS-Excel spreadsheet.

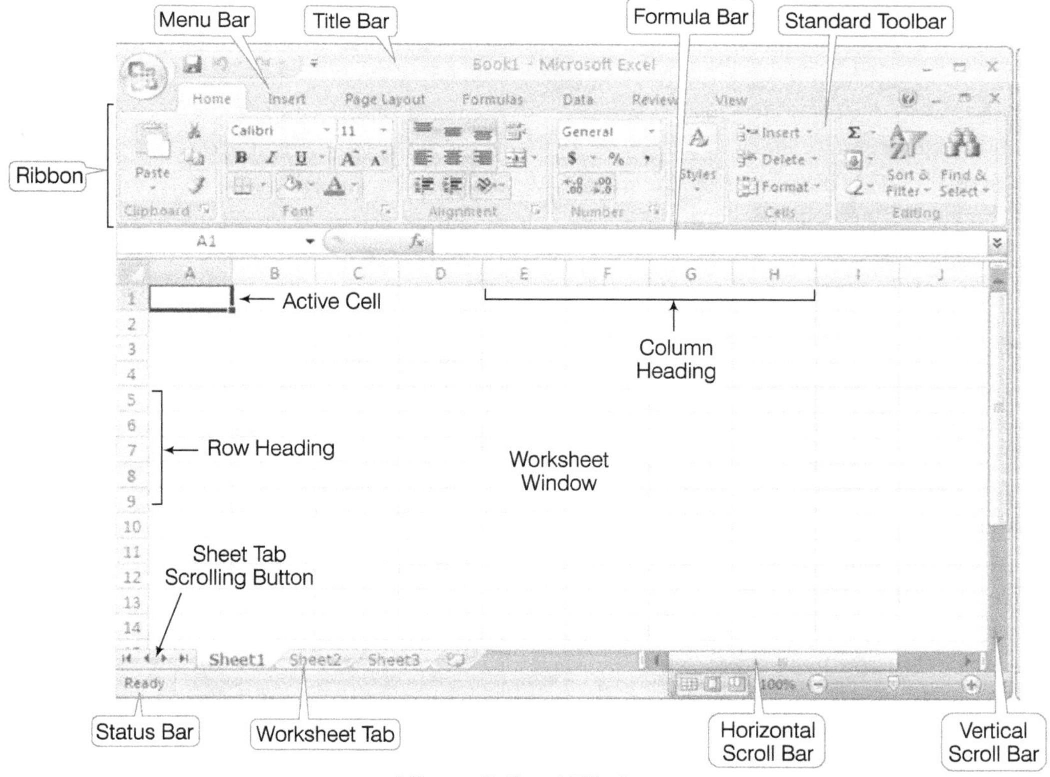

Microsoft Excel Window

Components of Microsoft Excel

The components of MS-Excel are as follows

1. **Title Bar** It shows the name of the application and name of the file. It consists of three control buttons, i.e. Minimize, Maximize and Close.
2. **Ribbon** It consists of a panel of commands which is organised into a set of tabs.
3. **Tab** On the ribbon, it contains the buttons needed to edit characters, text and layout.

   There are 7 tabs in MS-Excel as follows

   (i) **Home Tab** It consists of Clipboard, Font, Alignment, Number, Styles, Cells and Editing.

   (ii) **Insert Tab** It consists of Tables, Illustrations, Charts, Sparklines, Filter Links, Text and Symbols.

   (iii) **Page Layout Tab** It consists of Themes, Page Setup, Scale to Fit, Sheet Options and Arrange.

   (iv) **Formulas Tab** It consists of Function Library, Defined Names, Formula Auditing and Calculation.

   (v) **Data Tab** It consists of Get External Data, Connections, Sort & Filter, Data Tools and Outline.

   (vi) **Review Tab** It consists of Proofing, Language, Comments and Changes.

   (vii) **View Tab** It consists of Workbook Views, Show, Zoom, Window and Macros.
4. **Status Bar** It displays information about the currently active worksheet. It includes page number, view shortcuts, zoom slider, etc.
5. **Formula Bar** It is located below the ribbon. It is used to enter and edit worksheet data. *It includes*

   (i) **Name box** displays the all references or column and row location of the active cell.

   (ii) **Functions** are pre-defined formulas that perform calculations by using specific values, called arguments.

There are different types of functions

Functions	Descriptions	Examples
SUM	It is used to add all the values provided as argument.	= SUM (A1 : A5)
AVERAGE	This function calculates the average of all the values provided as argument.	= AVERAGE (A1 : A5)
COUNT	This function counts the number of cells that contain number.	=COUNT (A1 : A5)
MAX	This function is used to return maximum value from a list of arguments.	=MAX (A1 : A5)
MIN	This function is used to return minimum value from a list of arguments.	=MIN (A1 : A5)

where, A1 : A5 is a range between the cells of A1 and A5.

Basic Terms of Spreadsheet

The basic terms of spreadsheet are as follows

1. A **spreadsheet** is a software tool that lets one enter, calculate, manipulate and analyse set of numbers.
2. The intersection of each row and column is called **cell**. A cell is an individual container for data. *It may hold*

   (i) Numbers (Constants)

   (ii) Formulas (Mathematical equations)

   (iii) Text (Labels)
3. An array of cells is called a **sheet** or **worksheet**. A worksheet holds information presented in tabular format with text.
4. A **workbook** is a document that contains one or more worksheet. Each new workbook has created three worksheets by default.
5. A **row** is given a number that identifies it starts from 1, 2, 3, 4, 5, ... and so on.
6. A **column** is given a letter that identifies it starts from A ... Z, AA ... AZ, BA, BB ... BZ and so on.
7. **Active cell** is a cell in which you are currently working.

8. A **cell pointer** is a cell-boundary that specifies which cell is active at that moment.
9. A **formula** is an equation that calculates the value to be displayed. A formula must begin with Equal To (=) sign.
10. A **cell address** is used to specified the intersecting of row and column of the letter and number on the worksheet.

Charts

Charts are the graphical and pictorial representation of worksheet data.

Types of Chart

1. **Area Chart** It emphasises the magnitude of change over time.
2. **Column Chart** It shows data changes over a period of time or illustrates comparisons among items.
3. **Bar Chart** It illustrates comparisons among individual items. Categories are organised vertically and Values horizontally.
4. **Line Chart** It shows trends in data at equal intervals. It is useful for depicting the change in a value over a period of time.
5. **Pie Chart** It shows the proportional size of items that make up only one data series to the sum of the items.
6. **XY** (Scatter) **Chart** It shows the relationship among the numeric values in several data series or plots two groups of numbers as series of XY coordinates. Scatter compares pairs of values.

Components of Chart

1. **Chart Area** This is the total region surrounding the chart.
2. **Plot Area** The area where data is plotted. The plot area is bounded by axes in a 2D-Chart, whereas in 3D-Chart it is bounded by walls and floor.
3. **Chart Title** The descriptive text aimed at helping user identify the chart.
4. **Axis Title** This is the title given to three axis, i.e. X, Y and Z.
5. **Data Series** A row or column of numbers that are plotted in a chart is called a data series.
6. **Gridlines** These are horizontal and vertical lines, which inserted in the chart to enhance its readability.
7. **Legend** It helps to identify various plotted data series.
8. **Data Label** It provides additional information about the data marker.
9. **Data Table** It is defined as a range of cells that is used for testing and analysing outcomes on a large scale.

Tit-Bits

- **$ Sign** locks the cells location to a fixed position.
- **Stacked Bar Column** shows the relationship of individual items to the whole.
- **Chart Wizard** is used to create charts in MS-Excel.
- **Embedded Chart** is a chart that is drawn on an existing sheet.

Shortcut Keys of MS-Excel and their Descriptions

Shortcut Keys	Descriptions
F2	Edit the selected cell.
F5	Go to a specific cell. e.g. C6.
F7	Checks the spellings.
F11	Create chart.
Ctrl + Shift + ;	Enter the current time.
Ctrl + ;	Enter the current date.
Alt + Shift + F1	Insert new worksheet.
Shift + F3	Opens the Insert Function window.
Shift + F5	Opens Find & Replace dialog boxes with Find tab.
Ctrl + A	Select all contents of the worksheet.
Ctrl + B	Bold highlighted selection.
Ctrl + I	Italic highlighted selection.
Ctrl + K	Insert link.
Ctrl + U	Underline highlighted selection.
Ctrl + P	Bring up the Print dialog box to begin printing.
Ctrl + Z	Undo the last action.
Ctrl + F9	Minimise current workbook.
Ctrl + F10	Maximise currently selected workbook.
Ctrl + F6	Switch between open workbooks/ windows.
Ctrl + Page Up	Move to the previous sheet between Excel worksheets in the same Excel document.
Ctrl + Page Down	Move to the next sheet between Excel worksheets in the same Excel document.
Ctrl + Tab	Move between two or more open Excel files.
Alt + =	Create a formula to sum all of the above cells.
Shift + Home	Go to the first cell in the current row.
Ctrl + Shift + !	Format number in comma format.
Ctrl + Shift + $	Format number in currency format.
Ctrl + Shift + #	Format number in date format.
Ctrl + Shift + %	Format number in percentage format.
Ctrl + Shift + @	Format number in time format.
Ctrl + Space	Select entire column.
Shift + Space	Select entire row.

Microsoft PowerPoint

Presentation is the practice of showing and explaining the contents of a topic to an audience or a learner visually.

The application software that can create professional looking visual aids is called presentation graphics software.

The presentation software is used for creation of the slides and to display the information in the form of presentation of slides.

A presentation software provides tools like editor that allows insertion and formatting of text and methods for inserting and manipulating graphics images along with sound and visual effects.

To start the MS-PowerPoint software, we need to

Click Start button → All Programs → Microsoft Office → Microsoft PowerPoint 2010.

By default, the name of the blank document is Presentation1. ppt, where .ppt or .pptx is the extension of a PowerPoint file.

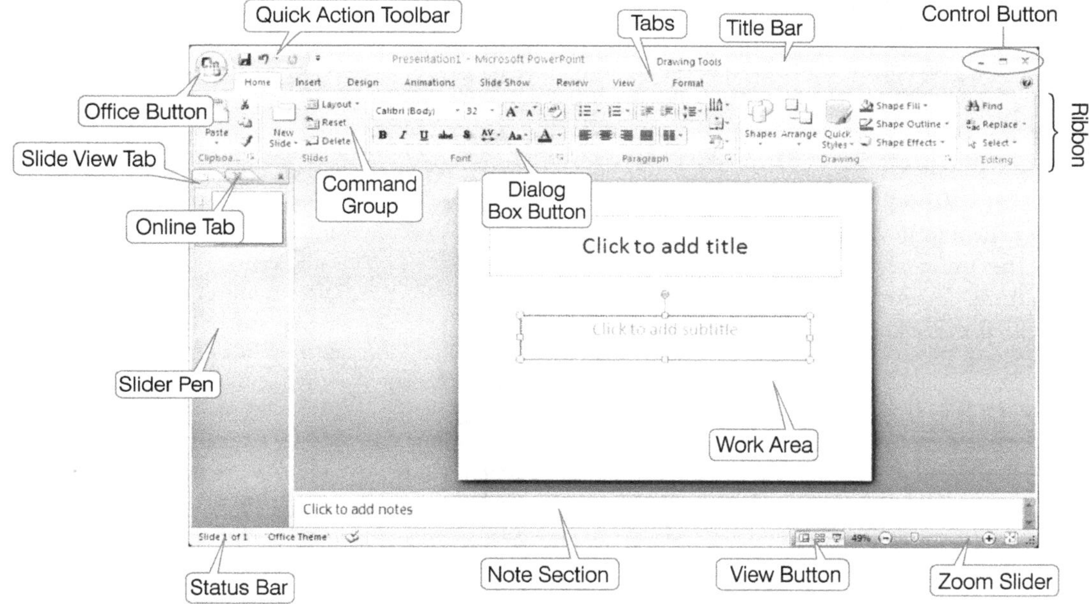

Microsoft PowerPoint Window

Components of Microsoft PowerPoint

Various components of MS-PowerPoint 2010 window are described below

1. **Title Bar** It contains the name of currently opened file followed by software name.
2. **Ribbon** It is same as Word and Excel, just few tabs are different like Animations, Slide Show, etc.
3. **Slide** It appears in the centre of the window. You can create your presentation by adding content to the slides.
4. **Slide Pane** This area of PowerPoint window displays all the slides that are added in the presentation.
5. **Slide View Tab** This tab displays a thumbnail view of all the slides.
6. **Outline View Tab** This tab displays the text contained in the presentation in an outline format.
7. **Notes Section** This section can be used for creating notes.
8. **Status Bar** It displays the number of the slide that is currently being displayed.

PowerPoint Views

Different types of views available in PowerPoint 2010 are explained below

1. **Normal View** This view is the main editing view, where you write and design your presentations, i.e. actual screen which is displayed.
2. **Slide Sorter View** It provides a view of slides in thumbnail form. This view makes it easy to sort and organise the sequence of the slides at the time of creating presentation.

3. **Notes Page View** In this view, the notes page is located just below the slide page. Here, notes that apply to the current slide can be typed. Later, these notes can be printed and referred while giving actual presentation.
4. **Slide Show View** This view is used to deliver a presentation to the audience. Slide Show View takes up the full computer screen, like an actual presentation. To exit Slide Show View, press **Esc** key from the keyboard.
5. **Master View** This view includes Slide View, Handout View and Notes View. They are the main slides that store information about the presentation, including background color, fonts effects, placeholder sizes and positions.

Tit-Bits

- **Trigger** is defined as an object or item that performs on the slide when we click the mouse.
- The MS-PowerPoint can maximum zoom to 400% only.
- In MS-PowerPoint, we can add many types of **image and sound** format such as .gif, .bmp, .png, .jpg, .giv, .wav, .mid, etc.

Shortcut Keys of Microsoft PowerPoint and their Descriptions

Shortcut Keys	Descriptions
F5	View the Slide Show.
Shift + Ctrl + Home	Selects all text from the cursor to the start of the active text box.
Shift + Ctrl + End	Selects all text from the cursor to the end of the active text box.
S	Stops the slide show press S again to restart the slide show.
Esc	Ends the slide show.
Ctrl + A	Selects all items on the page or the active text box.
Ctrl + B	Applies bold to the selected text.
Ctrl + F	Opens the Find and replace Dialog box with Find tab.
Shift + click each slide	Selects more than one slide.
Ctrl + H	Opens the Find and replace Dialog box with Replace tab.
Ctrl + I	Applies italic to the selected text.
Ctrl + M	Inserts a new slide.
Ctrl + N	Opens a new blank presentation.
Ctrl + O	Opens the Open dialog box.
Ctrl + T	Opens the Font dialog box.
Ctrl + U	Applies underlining to the selected text.
Ctrl + V	Paste the cutted or copied text.
Ctrl + W	Closes the presentation.
Ctrl + Y	Repeats or undo the last command entered.
Home	Moves cursor to the beginning of the current line of the text.
End	Moves cursor to the end of the current line of text.
Ctrl + Home	Moves cursor in beginning of presentation.
Ctrl + End	Moves cursor to end of presentation.
Shift + Click each side	Selects more than one slide in a presentation.
F1	Opens the help dialog box.

Microsoft Access

A database is a collection of logically related and similar data. Database stores similar kind of data for a specific purpose that is organised in such a manner that any information can be retrieved from it, when needed. Microsoft Access is an application which allows the creating of database. Microsoft Access is a Relational Database Management System (RDBMS).

Microsoft Outlook

It is an E-mail client and personal information manager that is available as a part of Microsoft Office suite.

Windows mobile devices are the version of MS-Outlook, enables users to synchronise their E-mails data to their smartphones.

MS-Outlook can work with Microsoft exchange server and Microsoft sharepoint server for multiple users in an organisation such as shared mail boxes, calendars, exchange public folders, sharepoint lists and meeting schedules.

QUESTION BANK

1. Microsoft Office was developed by........ in ...
(1) Microsoft Inc, 1970s
(2) Microsoft Inc, 1980s
(3) Sun Microsoft, 1980s
(4) Sun Microsoft Inc, 1970s

2. Which of the following is a basic software of MS-Office?
(1) MS-Word (2) MS-Excel
(3) MS-PowerPoint (4) All of these

3. MS-Word is a
(1) tabular data formatting software
(2) Word processing software
(3) presentation software
(4) E-mail client

4. What is MS-Word? **[SBI Clerk 2015]**
(1) It is a calculating tool.
(2) It is a planning tool.
(3) It is a chart.
(4) It is a networking tool.
(5) It is a document typing tool.

5. Microsoft Office Word is a(n)
(1) area in the computer's main memory in which Microsoft Office text files are stored temporarily
(2) program included with Windows 2000 that can be used only to create or edit text files, smaller than 64k, that do not require formatting
(3) classified password that prevents unauthorised users from accessing a protected Microsoft Office item or document
(4) full featured Word processing program that can be used to create and revise professional looking documents easily

6. A program which helps to create written documents and lets you go back and make corrections as necessary.
(1) Spreadsheet
(2) Personal writer
(3) Word printer
(4) Word processor

7. A Word processor would be used best to
(1) paint a picture
(2) draw a diagram
(3) type a story
(4) work out income and expenses

8. This program is made by Microsoft and embedded with Windows and used to view Web document. **[RBI Grade B 2013]**
(1) Netscape (2) Outlook Express
(3) Internet Explorer (4) MS-Word
(5) None of these

9. You can start Microsoft Word by using which button?
(1) New (2) Start
(3) Program (4) All of these

10. When you start MS-Word, the opening document has the name as
(1) DOC1 (2) Document1
(3) Document (4) Workbook

11. What is the default file extension for all Word documents?
[RBI Grade B 2012, IBPS Clerk 2014]
(1) WRD (2) TXT
(3) DOC (4) FIL
(5) WD

12. The first bar of MS-Word is
(1) menu bar (2) status bar
(3) title bar (4) formatting toolbar

13. Editing a document that has been created means **[IBPS Clerk 2015]**
(1) saving it (2) printing it
(3) scanning it (4) correcting it
(5) None of these

14. A ...... is an additional set of commands that the computer displays after you make a selection from main menu.
(1) Dialog box (2) Sub menu
(3) Menu selection (4) All of these

15. Microsoft Word is a word processor developed by Microsoft. In MS-Word, Spelling Check is a feature available in which tab?
(1) File (2) Home
(3) Insert (4) Review

16. MS-Word is a text or document editing application program that comes in the package of MS-Office Suite. Which among the given options is not related with MS-Word? **[IBPS PO 2016]**
(1) Page Layout (2) Anti-virus
(3) Mailings (4) Format Painter
(5) SmartArt

17. In order to choose the font for a sentence in a Word document **[IBPS Clerk 2011]**
(1) select Font in the Format menu
(2) select Font in the Edit menu
(3) select Font in the Tools menu
(4) select Font in the View menu
(5) None of the above

18. When computer users ...... a document, they change its appearance.
(1) Edit (2) Create
(3) Save (4) Format

19. In MS-Word, the Replace option is available on
(1) File menu (2) Edit menu
(3) Insert menu (4) View menu

20. Which of the following is not an option of Edit menu?
(1) Cut (2) Copy
(3) Paste (4) Page Setup

21. Which bar is usually located below the title bar that provides categorised options?
(1) Menu bar (2) Status bar
(3) Tool bar (4) Scroll bar

22. The process of making changes to an existing document is referred to as **[SBI Clerk 2014]**
(1) editing (2) changing
(3) modifying (4) creating
(5) adjusting

23. Most of the editing tools are available under which menu?
(1) File (2) Format
(3) Edit (4) All of these

24. To move to the beginning of a line of text, press the ... key.
(1) Page Up (2) A
(3) Home (4) Enter

25. In which menu, we will find the command document? **[RBI Grade B 2013]**
(1) File (2) Insert
(3) Tools (4) Data
(5) None of these

26. Which of the following is not a font style?
(1) Bold (2) Italic
(3) Regular (4) Superscript

27. Portrait and landscape are
(1) page orientation (2) paper size
(3) page layout (4) page margin

28. Which of the following should be used to move a paragraph from one place to another in a Word document?
(1) Copy and paste (2) Cut and paste
(3) Delete and retype (4) Find and replace

29. To move the text from its original position to another position without deleting it is called
(1) scrolling (2) searching
(3) moving (4) copying

30. Which of the following displays the buttons for changing text style, alignment and size?
(1) Standard toolbar
(2) Status bar
(3) Drawing toolbar
(4) Formatting toolbar

31. Which of the following commands is used in MS-Word to underline the statement? **[UPPSC Computer Assistant 2019]**
(1) Underline (2) U
(3) I (4) P

32. Where we can insert a page number in document? **[UPPSC Computer Assistant 2019]**
(1) Header (2) Footer
(3) Both (1) and (2) (4) None of these

33. After selecting the 'Replace' option from the Edit menu, the following dialog box will be appear.
(1) Replace (2) Find
(3) Find & Replace (4) Edit

34. Which of the following justifications align the text on both the sides, left and right of the margin? **[IBPS Clerk 2012]**
(1) Right (2) Justify
(3) Both sides (4) Balanced
(5) None of these

35. Auto-text can be used to insert ..... in document. **[RBI Grade B 2014]**
(1) Text (2) Graphics
(3) Either (1) or (2) (4) Both (1) and (2)
(5) None of these

36. About margins **[RBI Grade B 2014]**
(1) all sections in a document need to have same margin
(2) different sections can have different margins
(3) Word have pre-defined margins settings for all documents
(4) can't say, depend on the version of Word
(5) None of the above

37. When entering text within a document, the Enter key is normally pressed at the end of every **[IBPS PO 2011, IBPS Clerk 2013]**
(1) line (2) sentence
(3) paragraph (4) word
(5) file

38. In order to delete a sentence from a document, you would use **[IBPS Clerk 2015]**
(1) highlight and copy
(2) cut and paste
(3) copy and paste
(4) highlight and delete
(5) select and paste

39. Soft page breaks **[RBI Grade B 2013]**
(1) are induced by the user
(2) are inserted by word automatically at the end of the page
(3) can be deleted
(4) are the one to show end of paragraph
(5) None of the above

40. In Word, you can force a page break **[IBPS PO 2011]**
(1) by positioning your cursor at the appropriate place and pressing the F1 key
(2) by positioning your cursor at the appropriate place and pressing the Ctrl+Enter
(3) by using the insert/section break
(4) by changing the font size of your document
(5) None of the above

41. Where you can find the horizontal split bar on MS-Word screen?
(1) On the left of horizontal scroll bar
(2) On the right of horizontal scroll bar
(3) On the top of vertical scroll bar
(4) On the bottom of vertical scroll bar

42. In MS-Word, the default alignment for paragraph is
(1) left aligned (2) centered
(3) right aligned (4) justified

43. Which of the following is not available on the ruler of MS-Word screen?
(1) Left indent (2) Right indent
(3) Centre indent (4) All of these

44. You specify the save details of your file in the **[RBI Grade B 2013]**
(1) "Save as a file" dialog box
(2) "Save the file as" dialog
(3) "File save" dialog box
(4) Any of (1) and (2)
(5) None of the above

45. To save an existing document with a different file name, click
(1) Save button on the Standard toolbar
(2) Save on the File menu
(3) Save As button on the Standard toolbar
(4) Save As on the File menu

46. In how many ways, you can save a document? **[SBI PO 2012]**
(1) 3 (2) 4
(3) 5 (4) 6
(5) 8

47. Word has a list of pre-defined typing, spelling, capitalisation and grammar errors that .... can defect and correct.
(1) autoentry (2) autocorrect
(3) autoadd (4) autospell

48. Where header appears?
(1) Top (2) Bottom
(3) Centre (4) All of these

49. Keyboard shortcut for Cut command is **[SBI Clerk 2015]**
(1) Ctrl + W (2) Ctrl + Y
(3) Ctrl + Z (4) Ctrl + X
(5) Ctrl + V

50. To increase the line spacing, use the .... shortcut keys.
(1) Ctrl + L (2) Ctrl + E
(3) Ctrl + I (4) Ctrl + 5

51. Shortcut for displaying the full page as they are printed.
(1) Ctrl + F1 (2) Ctrl + F2
(3) Shift + F1 (4) Shift + F2

52. The shortcut key to print document is **[IBPS PO 2012]**
(1) Ctrl + D (2) Ctrl + A
(3) Ctrl + B (4) Ctrl + C
(5) Ctrl + P

53. Which of the following keys should be pressed simiultaneously for highlighting the text to the default font? **[RRB NTPC 2016]**
A. Ctrl + Home B. Ctrl + Space bar
C. Ctrl + Shift + Z D. Ctrl + Alt + F2
Codes
(1) B (2) C (3) D (4) A

54. To move to the bottom of a document while working on MS-Word, which command is used? **[IBPS Clerk 2014]**
(1) Home key
(2) End key
(3) Ctrl + Page Down Key
(4) Insert key
(5) Ctrl + End key

55. To undo the last work, we have to use which of the following Windows shortcut key? **[SBI PO 2014]**
(1) Ctrl + P (2) Ctrl + U
(3) Ctrl + A (4) Ctrl + Z
(5) Ctrl + W

56. Shortcut key to go to last line in the document. **[SBI PO 2014]**
(1) Ctrl + Last (2) Ctrl + L
(3) Ctrl + End (4) Alt + End
(5) Alt + L

57. Which of the following can be used to select the entire document? **[IBPS Clerk 2013]**
(1) Ctrl + A (2) Alt + F5
(3) Shift + A (4) Ctrl + K
(5) Ctrl + H

58. What is the shortcut key for centering the text selected by the user in Word?
(1) Ctrl + A (2) Ctrl + B
(3) Ctrl + C (4) Ctrl + E

59. Which of the following is a computer software program that is used for storing, organising and manipulating data? **[UPSSSC 2018]**
(1) Firefox (2) Excel
(3) Outlook (4) PowerPoint

60. What kind of software would you most likely use to keep track of a billing account? **[IBPS PO 2015]**
(1) Web Authoring (2) Electronic Publishing
(3) Spreadsheet (4) Word Processing
(5) PowerPoint

61. Excel worksheet data can be shared with Word document by **[RBI Grade B 2014]**
(1) inserting an Excel file into Word
(2) copy and paste Excel worksheet into Word document
(3) link Excel data in a Word document
(4) All of the above
(5) None of the above

62. A worksheet is made of columns and rows, wherein **[RBI Grade 2013]**
(1) columns run horizontally and rows run vertically
(2) columns run vertically and rows run horizontally
(3) the run is dependent on the application being used
(4) Both (2) and (3)
(5) None of the above

63. Which of the following software applications would be the most appropriate for performing numerical and statistical calculations? **[RBI Grade B 2012]**
(1) Database (2) Document processor
(3) Graphics package (4) Spreadsheet
(5) PowerPoint

64. The file responsible for starting MS-Excel is **[RBI Grade B 2013]**
(1) MS.Excel (2) MS.exe
(3) Excel.exe (4) Excel.com
(5) None of these

65. Anything that is typed in a worksheet appears **[RBI Grade B 2013]**
(1) in the formula bar only
(2) in the active cell only
(3) in both active cell and formula bar
(4) All of the above
(5) None of the above

66. Which one is the example of spreadsheet package?
(1) VisiCalc (2) Unity
(3) Ada (4) Snowball

67. Which option will we use to give heading in the form ?
(1) Label (2) Text box
(3) Option group (4) Insert

68. The extension of saved file in MS-Excel is
(1) .xis (2) .xas
(3) .xlsx (4) .xll

69. Alignment buttons are available on which toolbar?
(1) Status (2) Standard
(3) Formatting (4) All of these

70. In Excel, the intersection of a column and a row is called **[RBI Grade B 2014]**
(1) cell (2) grid
(3) table (4) box
(5) None of these

71. What does an electronic spreadsheet consist of?
(1) Rows (2) Columns
(3) Cells (4) All of these

72. A collection of worksheets is called **[RBI Grade B 2014, UPPSC Computer Assistant 2019]**
(1) Excel book (2) Worksheets
(3) Excel sheets (4) Workbook
(5) None of these

73. All of the following terms are related to spreadsheet software except
(1) worksheet (2) cell
(3) formula (4) virus detection

74. Which of the following is an active cell in Excel?
(1) Current cell (2) Formula
(3) Range (4) Cell address

75. How is the data organised in a spreadsheet?
(1) Lines and spaces
(2) Layers and planes
(3) Height and width
(4) Rows and columns

76. The basic unit of a worksheet into which you enter data in Excel is called a
(1) tab (2) cell
(3) box (4) range

77. The advantage of using a spreadsheet is
(1) calculations can be done automatically
(2) changing data automatically updates calculations
(3) more flexibility
(4) All of the above

78. A .... is rectangular grid of rows and columns used to enter data.
(1) cell
(2) worksheet
(3) spreadsheet
(4) Both (2) and (3)

79. The default view in Excel is ...... view.
(1) Work (2) Auto
(3) Normal (4) Roman

80. It is a software tool that lets one enter, calculate, manipulate set of numbers.
(1) Speedsheet (2) Spreadsheet
(3) Slide sheet (4) All of these

81. Borders can be applied to
(1) cells (2) paragraph
(3) text (4) All of these

82. The cell having bold boundary is called
(1) relative (2) active
(3) absolute (4) mixed

83. You can create hyperlinks from the Excel workbook to
(1) a Web page on company Internet
(2) a Web page on the Internet
(3) other Office 97 application documents
(4) All of the above

84. To select a column, the easiest method is to
(1) double click any cell in the column
(2) drag from the top cell in the column to the last cell in the column
(3) click the column heading
(4) click the row heading

85. Which of the following groups is not present in the Insert tab of MS-Excel? **[UPSSSC Gram Panchayat Officer 2019]**
(1) Illustrations (2) Paragraph
(3) Links (4) Symbols

86. Which of the following will you use as an option for saving a file?
(1) Save button on Standard toolbar
(2) Save option from File menu
(3) Pressing Ctrl + S
(4) All of the above

87. What function displays row data in a column or column data in a row?
(1) Hyperlink (2) Index
(3) Transpose (4) Rows

88. In Excel, ... allows users to bring together copies of workbooks that other users gave worked on independently. **[SBI Clerk 2011]**
(1) copying (2) merging
(3) pasting (4) compiling
(5) None of these

89. Insert date, format page number and insert auto text are buttons on the .... toolbar.
(1) formatting (2) header and footer
(3) standard (4) edit

90. On saving a worksheet, the 'Save As' dialog box **[RBI Grade B 2013, 14]**
(1) is used to open the saved Excel files
(2) is used for saving the file for the first time
(3) is used for saving the file by some alternative name
(4) Both (2) and (3)
(5) None of the above

91. The letter and number of the intersecting column and row is the **[IBPS PO 2012]**
(1) cell location (2) cell position
(3) cell address (4) cell coordinates
(5) cell contents

92. Which of the following is not a valid formula in Microsoft Excel? **[IBPS Clerk 2014]**
(1) = A2 + A1 (2) = A2 + 1
(3) = 1 + A2 (4) = 1A + 2
(5) = A1 + A2

93. The function TODAY ( ) in Excel, enters the current **[RBI Grade B 2014]**
(1) system time in a cell
(2) system date and time in a cell
(3) system date only
(4) time at which the current file was opened
(5) None of the above

94. Which of the following characteristics is used to compute dynamically the results from Excel data? **[IBPS Clerk 2012]**
(1) Goto (2) Table
(3) Chart (4) Diagram
(5) Formula and function

95. Which area in an Excel window allows entering values and formulas? **[RBI Grade B 2013]**
(1) Standard Toolbar (2) Menu Bar
(3) Title Bar (4) Formula Bar
(5) None of these

96. = Sum (B1 : B10) is an example of a
(1) function (2) formula
(3) cell address (4) value

97. You can copy data or formulas
(1) with the copy, paste and cut commands on the Edit menu
(2) with commands on a shortcut menu
(3) with buttons on the standard toolbars
(4) All of the above

98. A cell entry can be edited in the cell or in the
(1) menu bar (2) edit menu
(3) function bar (4) formula bar

99. In Excel, this is a pre-recorded formula that provides a shortcut for complex calculations.
(1) Value (2) Data series
(3) Function (4) Field

100. In Excel, an active cell can be represented by
(1) 4A (2) A4
(3) A$4 (4) A4

101. Three types of data can be entered in a worksheet, as number/characters, text and
(1) formulas (2) functions
(3) logic (4) All of these

102. The physical arrangement of elements on a page is referred to as a document's
(1) Features (2) Format
(3) Pagination (4) Grid

103. Cell address $A4 in a formula means it is a
(1) mixed cell reference
(2) absolute cell reference
(3) relative cell reference
(4) All of the above

104. In this chart, only one data series can be plotted.
(1) Pie (2) Line
(3) Bar (4) Column

105. This chart shows the relationship of parts to a whole.
(1) Pie (2) Line
(3) Stacked bar (4) Embedded

106. A chart placed in a worksheet is called
(1) formatting chart (2) embedded chart
(3) aligning chart (4) hanging chart

107. Scatter chart is also known as
(1) XX chart (2) YX chart
(3) XY chart (4) YY chart

108. In Excel, charts are created using which option?
(1) Chart wizard (2) Pivot table
(3) Pie chart (4) Bar chart

109. Pie charts are typically created by using which of the following?
(1) Browser software
(2) Database software
(3) Desktop publishing software
(4) Spreadsheet software

110. To select the current column, press
(1) Ctrl + Spacebar (2) Ctrl + B
(3) Shift + Enter (4) Ctrl + Enter

111. The cell accepts your typing as its contents, if you press
(1) Enter (2) Ctrl + Enter
(3) Tab (4) Insert

112. Which key is used in combination with another key to perform a specific task?
(1) Function (2) Space bar
(3) Arrow (4) Control

113. Which of the following commands in Office 2010, can be used to go to the first cell in the current row? **[IBPS Clerk 2014]**
(1) Tab (2) Shift + Tab
(3) Esc + Home (4) Shift + Home
(5) Home

114. In a worksheet in MS-Excel, what is short-cut key to hide entire row? **[SBI PO 2014]**
(1) Ctrl + 2 (2) Ctrl + 9
(3) Ctrl + N (4) Ctrl + –
(5) Ctrl + N

115. To select entire row, which shortcut is used? **[SBI PO 2014]**
(1) Shift + space (2) Ctrl + space
(3) Alt + space (4) None of these
(5) None of these

116. Which software is used to create presentation?
(1) Microsoft Word
(2) Microsoft Excel
(3) Microsoft PowerPoint
(4) Microsoft Access

117. What is the extension of PowerPoint in Microsoft Office 2007?
(1) .ptp (2) .pptx (3) .ppx (4) .ptx

118. You can add any picture in your document from which menu?
(1) File (2) Edit
(3) Insert (4) Format

119. Which of the following should you use if you want all the slides in the presentation to have the same 'look'?
(1) The slide layout option
(2) Add a slide option
(3) Outline view
(4) A presentation design template

120. The .... defines the appearance and shape of letters, numbers and special characters.
(1) Font (2) Font size
(3) Point (4) Paragraph formatting

121. .... shows how the contents on printed page will appear with margin, header and footer.
(1) Draft
(2) Full screen reading
(3) Outline
(4) Page layout

122. By default, on which page the header or footer is printed? **[IBPS Clerk 2011]**
(1) On first page (2) On alternative page
(3) On every page (4) All of these
(5) None of these

123. To find the paste special option, or use the Clipboard group on the ...... tab of Power Point. **[IBPS Clerk 2013]**
(1) Design (2) Slide Show
(3) Page Layout (4) Insert
(5) None of these

124. This is to insert an object, which is not missprint to its originating document into a destination document? **[RBI Grade B 2014]**
(1) Cell (2) Embed
(3) Defaults (4) Any of these
(5) None of these

125. Selecting Portrait changes our page from **[RBI Grade B 2014]**
(1) a wide to tall orientation
(2) a tall to wide orientation
(3) a normal font size to a condensed one
(4) a condensed font size to a normal one
(5) None of the above

126. Which of the following controls the format and placement of the titles and text you on slides, as well as, background items and graphics you want to appear on every slide? **[IBPS Clerk 2015]**
(1) Slide (2) Copyright
(3) Layout (4) Design
(5) None of these

127. Which of the following views is the best view to use when setting transition effects for all slides in presentation?
(1) Slide sorter view (2) Notes page view
(3) Slide view (4) Outline view

128. Which PowerPoint view displays each slide of the presentation as a thumbnail and is useful for re-arranging slides? **[IBPS Clerk 2013]**
(1) Slide sorter (2) Slide show
(3) Slide master (4) Notes page
(5) Slide design

129. Which is a feature included in Microsoft PowerPoint software that allows the user to see all the slides in a presentation at one time? **[IBPS PO 2016]**
(1) Slide Sorter (2) Slide Master
(3) Handout Master (4) Slide Header
(5) Reading View

130. To add a header or footer to your handout, you can use the
(1) Title master (2) Slide master
(3) Handout master (4) All of these

131. The maximum zoom percentage in MS-PowerPoint is **[IBPS Clerk 2009]**
(1) 100% (2) 200%
(3) 400% (4) 500%
(5) None of these

132. In Microsoft PowerPoint, two kinds of sound effect files can be added to the presentation are
(1) .wav files and .mid files
(2) .wav files and .gif files
(3) .wav files and .jpg files
(4) .jpg files and .gif files

133. Which file format can be added to a PowerPoint show?
(1) .jpg (2) .giv
(3) .wav (4) All of these

134. PowerPoint provides .... number of layouts for use with blank presentation.
(1) 20 (2) 22
(3) 24 (4) 26

135. In PowerPoint, the Header and Footer buttons can be found on the Insert tab in which group? **[IBPS PO 2012, Clerk 2013]**
(1) Illustrations group (2) Object group
(3) Insert group (4) Tables group
(5) None of these

136. Which command brings you to the first slide in your presentation?
(1) Next slide button (2) Page up
(3) Ctrl + Home (4) Ctrl + End

137. Which of the following allows you to select more than one slide in a presentation?
(1) Alt + click each slide
(2) Shift + drag each slide
(3) Shift + click each slide
(4) Ctrl + click each slide

138. Which of the following will not advance the slides in a slide show view?
(1) Esc key
(2) Spacebar
(3) Enter key
(4) Mouse button

139. Which of the following bypasses the Print dialog box when printing individual slides or an entire presentation?
(1) File, Print preview
(2) Print button
(3) File, Print
(4) Ctrl + P

140. Which key on the keyboard can be used to view slide show?
(1) F1 (2) F2 (3) F5 (4) F10

ANSWERS

1. (2)	2. (4)	3. (2)	4. (5)	5. (2)	6. (4)	7. (3)	8. (4)	9. (2)	10. (2)
11. (3)	12. (3)	13. (4)	14. (2)	15. (4)	16. (2)	17. (1)	18. (1)	19. (2)	20. (4)
21. (1)	22. (1)	23. (3)	24. (3)	25. (4)	26. (3)	27. (1)	28. (2)	29. (4)	30. (4)
31. (2)	32. (3)	33. (3)	34. (2)	35. (4)	36. (2)	37. (1)	38. (4)	39. (2)	40. (3)
41. (3)	42. (1)	43. (3)	44. (1)	45. (4)	46. (1)	47. (2)	48. (1)	49. (4)	50. (4)
51. (2)	52. (5)	53. (2)	54. (3)	55. (4)	56. (3)	57. (1)	58. (4)	59. (2)	60. (3)
61. (4)	62. (2)	63. (4)	64. (3)	65. (3)	66. (1)	67. (1)	68. (3)	69. (3)	70. (1)
71. (4)	72. (4)	73. (4)	74. (1)	75. (4)	76. (2)	77. (3)	78. (4)	79. (3)	80. (2)
81. (4)	82. (2)	83. (4)	84. (2)	85. (2)	86. (4)	87. (3)	88. (2)	89. (1)	90. (3)
91. (3)	92. (4)	93. (4)	94. (5)	95. (4)	96. (2)	97. (4)	98. (4)	99. (3)	100. (2)
101. (4)	102. (2)	103. (1)	104. (1)	105. (3)	106. (2)	107. (3)	108. (1)	109. (4)	110. (1)
111. (1)	112. (4)	113. (3)	114. (2)	115. (1)	116. (3)	117. (2)	118. (3)	119. (4)	120. (1)
121. (4)	122. (4)	123. (5)	124. (2)	125. (1)	126. (3)	127. (1)	128. (1)	129. (1)	130. (3)
131. (3)	132. (1)	133. (4)	134. (3)	135. (5)	136. (3)	137. (3)	138. (1)	139. (4)	140. (3)

CHAPTER

11

DATABASE CONCEPTS

A database is a collection of logically related information in an organised way so that it can be easily accessed, managed and updated.

Some other operations can also be performed on database such as adding, updating and deleting data.

Fundamentals of Database

1. **Data** These are raw and unorganised facts that need to be processed such as digital representation of text, numbers, graphical images or sound.

   e.g. A student's test score is one piece of data.
2. **Information** When data is processed, organised, structured or presented in a given context to make it useful or meaningful, it is called information.

   e.g. The class's average score is the information that can be concluded from the given data.

Types of Database

1. **Network Database** In this type of database, data is represented as a collection of records and relationships among data that are represented as links.
2. **Hierarchical Database** In this type of database, data is organised in the form of tree with nodes. Nodes are connected *via* links.
3. **Relational Database** This database is also known as **structured database** in which data is stored in the form of tables. Where, columns define the type of data stored in the table and rows define the information about the data.

Components of Database

A database consists of several different components. Each component listed, is called an **object**.

Database components are described below

1. **Tables** These are the building blocks or relation of any relational database model where all the actual data is defined and entered.

   Different types of operation are done on the tables such as storing, filtering, retrieving and editing of data. Tables consist of cells at the intersection of records (rows) and fields (columns), *which are described below*

   (i) **Field** It is an area (within the record) reserved for a specific piece of data.

   e.g. Customer number, Customer name, Street address, City, State, Phone number, Current address, etc. Field of a table is also known as **column**.

(ii) **Record** It is the collection of data items of all the fields pertaining to one entity, i.e. a person, company, transition, etc. Record of a table is also known as **row** or a **tuple** and the number of records in a relation is called the **cardinality** of that relation.

2. **Queries** These are basically questions based on the data available in a database. A query consists of specifications indicating which fields, records and summaries a user wants to fetch from the database.

   Queries allow you to extract data based on the criteria that you define.

3. **Forms** Although you can enter and modify data in datasheet view of tables but you neither control the user's action very well nor you can do much to facilitate the data-entry process. To overcome this problem, forms are introduced. Like tables, forms can be used to view and edit your data. However, forms are typically used to view the data in an underlying table, one record at a time.

   e.g. A user can create a data entry form that looks exactly like a paper form. People generally prefer to enter data into a well-designed form, rather than a table.

4. **Reports** When you want to print those records which are fetched from your database, design a report. Access even has a **wizard** to help produce mailing labels.

Database Management System (DBMS)

A DBMS is a collection of inter-related data and a set of programs to retrieve data from the database.

It is an organised collection of data viewed as a whole, instead of a group of separate unrelated files.

The primary goal of DBMS is to provide an environment that is both convenient and efficient for user to store and retrieve database information.

e.g. MySQL, Oracle, FoxPro, dBASE, SyBase, MS-Access. The purpose of database management system is to bridge the gap between information and data.

The basic processes that are supported by DBMS are as follows

(i) Specification of data types, structures and constraints to be considered in an application.

(ii) Storing the data.

(iii) Manipulation of the database.

(iv) Querying the database to retrieve desired information.

(v) Updating the content of the database.

Architecture of DBMS

The architecture of DBMS is divided into three levels are as follows

1. **Internal Level** It is the lowest level of data abstraction that deals with the physical representation of the database on the computer. It is also known as **physical level**.

   It defines how the data is actually stored and organised in the storage medium.

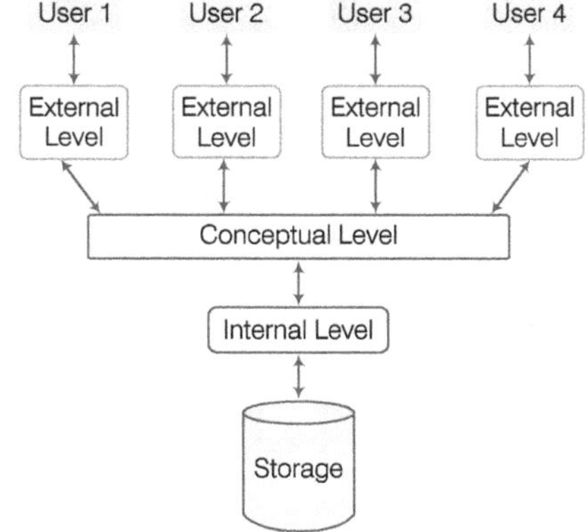

Architecture of DBMS

2. **Conceptual Level** It is the overall view of the database and includes all the information that is going to be represented in the database.

   It describes what type of data is stored in the database, the relationship among the data without effecting to the physical level. It is also known as **logical level**.

3. **External Level** This is the highest level of data abstraction which describes the interaction between the user and the system.

   It permits the users to access data in a way that is customised according to their needs, so that the same data can be seen by different users in different ways, at the same time. It is also known as **view level**.

Advantages of DBMS

1. **Reduction in Data Redundancy** The duplication of data refers to data redundancy. DBMS cannot make separate copies of the same data. All the data is kept at a place and different applications refer to data from centrally controlled system.
2. **Better Interaction with Users** In DBMS, the availability of uptodate information improves the data to be access or respond as per user requests.
3. **Improvement in Data Security** DBMS can allow the means of access to the database through the authorised channels.

   To ensure security, DBMS provides security tools, i.e. username and password.
4. **Maintenance of Data Integrity** Data integrity ensures that the data of database is accurate. In DBMS, data is centralised and used by many users at a time, it is essential to enforce integrity controls.
5. **Backup and Recovery** The DBMS provides backup and recovery sub-system that is responsible to recover data from hardware and software failures.

Disadvantages of DBMS

1. **Cost of Hardware and Software** A processor with high speed of data processing and memory of large size is required to run the DBMS software. It means that you have to upgrade the hardware used for file based system. Similarly, database software is also very costly.
2. **Complexity** The provision of the functionality that is expected from a good DBMS makes the DBMS an extremely complex piece of software. Failure to understand the system can lead to bad design decisions, which can have serious consequences for an organisation.
3. **Cost of Staff Training** Mostly DBMSs are often complex systems, so the training for user to use the database is required. The organisation has to pay a lot of amount for the training of staff to run the DBMS.
4. **Appointing Technical Staff** The trained technical persons such as database administrator, application programmers, etc., are required to handle the database. You have to pay a lot of amount to these persons. Therefore, the system cost increases.
5. **Database Failure** In most of the organisations, all data is integrated into a single database. If database is corrupted due to power failure or it is corrupted on the storage media, then our valuable data may be lost or whole system stop.

Applications of DBMS

1. **Banking** For customer information, accounts, loans and other banking transactions.
2. **Reservation** For reservation and schedule information.
3. **Universities** For student information, course registration, grades, etc.
4. **Credit Card Transaction** For purchase of credit cards and generation of monthly statements.
5. **Tele-communication** For keeping records of calls made, generating monthly bill, etc.
6. **Finance** For storing information about holdings, sales and purchase of financial statements.
7. **Sales** For customer, product and purchase information.

Relational Database

In a relational database, data is stored in different tables with relationships to each other. In the case of relational database, a Relational Database Management System (RDBMS) performs this task.

An important feature of this database system is that a single database can be spread across several tables.

e.g. Base, Oracle, DB2, SyBase, Informix, etc.

Terms Related to Relational Database

1. **Relation** It is a table with columns and rows which represent the data items and relationships among them. It has three important properties, a name, cardinality and a degree.

   These properties help us to further define and describe relations

   (i) **Name** The first property of a relation is its name, which is represented by the tide or the entity identifier.

   (ii) **Cardinality** The second property of a relation is its cardinality, which refers to the number of tuples (rows) in a relation.

   (iii) **Degree** The third property of a relation is its degree, which refers to the number of attributes (columns) in each tuple.

2. **Domain** It is a collection of all possible values from which the values for a given column or an attribute is drawn. A domain is said to be atomic, if elements are considered to be indivisible units.

3. **Attributes** The heading columns of a table are known as **attributes**. Each attribute of a table has a distinct name.

4. **Tuples** The rows in a relation are also known as **tuples**. Each row or tuple has a set of permitted values for each attribute.

Key

A key is defined as the column or set of columns in a table that is used to identify either row of data in a table or establish relationship with another table.

If a table has Id, name and address as the column names, then each one is known as the **key** for that table. The keys are also used to uniquely identify each record in the database table.

Types of Key

1. **Primary Key** It is a set of one or more attributes that can uniquely identify tuples (rows) within the relation. The primary key should be chosen in such a way, i.e. its value must not be changed.

   There should not be duplicacy in the record of primary key. Primary key can be atomic or composite. The field chosen as primary key, cannot accept null value.

2. **Candidate Key** The set of all attributes which can uniquely identify each tuple (row) of a relation, is known as **candidate key**. Each table may have one or more candidate keys and one of them will become the primary key. The candidate key of a relation is always a minimal key.

3. **Alternate Key** From the set of candidate keys after selecting one of the keys as primary key, all other remaining keys are known as alternate keys.

4. **Foreign Key** It is a non-key attribute whose value is derived from the primary key of the same or some another table. The relationship between two tables is established with the help of foreign key.

   A table may have multiple foreign keys and each foreign key can have a different referenced table.

Database Languages

1. **Data Definition Language** (DDL) It is used to define structure of your tables and other objects in database. In DBMS, it is used to specify a database schema as a set of definitions.

2. **Data Manipulation Language** (DML) It provides various commands used to access and manipulate data in existing database. This manipulation involves inserting data into database tables, retrieving existing data,

deleting data from existing tables and modifying existing data.

3. **Data Control Language** (DCL) These commands are used to assign security levels in database which involves multiple user setups. They are used to grant defined role and access privileges to the users.

Entity-Relationship Model (E-R Model)

It represents the entities contained in the database. It is a diagrammatically representation of entities and relationship between them. It is also known as **E-R Diagram**.

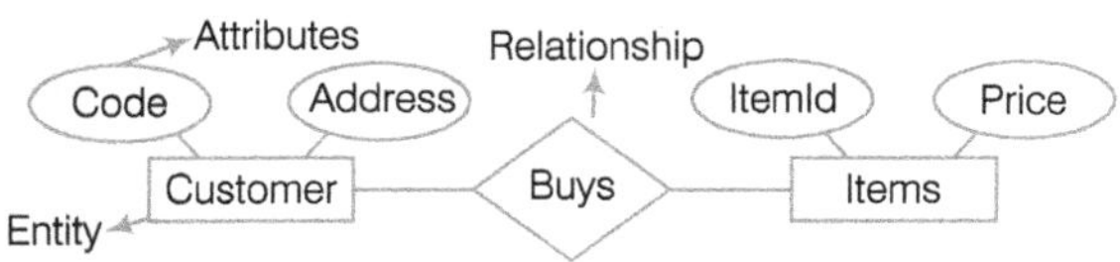

E-R Diagram

Some terms related to E-R Model are described below

Entity

It is an object that has its existence in the real world. It includes all those things about which the data are collected. "Entities are represented in rectangles". e.g. Customer buys items, it means Customer and Items are entities.

Attributes

It describes the characteristics or properties of entity. In tables, attributes are represented by columns. Attributes are drawn in elliptical shapes. e.g. Items entity may contain ItemId and Price.

Entity Set

It is a set of entities of the same type that shares same properties or attributes. e.g. Students are an entity set of all student entities in the database.

Entity set is of two types which are as follows

1. **Strong Entity Set** It has a primary key or can be easily distinguishable each attribute.
2. **Weak Entity Set** It does not posses sufficient attributes to form a primary key.

Relationship

It is an association among several entities. A relationship describes how two or more entities are related to each other. It is represented by diamond shape.

Relationship can be divided into three parts

(i) **One-to-One** This relationship tells us that a single record in Table A is related to a single record in Table B and *vice-versa.*

(ii) **One-to-Many** This entails one data in Table A to have links to multiple data in Table B. However, a single data in Table B, will have link to a single data in Table A.

(iii) **Many-to-Many** Each data in Table A is linked to all the data in Table B and *vice-versa.*

Tit-Bits

- Dr. EF Codd represented 12 rules for Relational Database Management System (RDBMS) in 1970.
- **Schema** is a logical structure of the database.
- **Instances** are the actual data contained in the database at a particular point of time.
- **Data Duplication** wastes the space, but also promotes a more serious problem called data inconsistency.
- **Data Mining** is the process of sorting through large data sets to identify patterns and establish relationships to solve problems through data analysis.

QUESTION BANK

1. A .... is a collection of data that is stored electronically as a series of records in a table.
   (1) Spreadsheet (2) Presentation
   (3) Database (4) Web page

2. A collection of interrelated records is called a **[RBI Grade B 2012]**
   (1) utility file
   (2) management information system
   (3) database
   (4) spreadsheet
   (5) datasheet

3. Which of the following is the organised collection of large amount of interrelated data stored in a meaningful way used for manipulation and updation? **[IBPS Clerk Mains 2017]**
   (1) Database (2) File
   (3) Folder (4) Data-mining
   (5) None of these

4. Items such as names and addresses are considered as
   (1) input (2) data
   (3) output (4) records

5. Which type of database, organised the data in the form of tree with nodes?
   (1) Network Database
   (2) Hierarchical Database
   (3) Relational Database
   (4) Multiple Database

6. The database stores information in
   (1) rows and columns
   (2) blocks
   (3) tracks and sectors
   (4) All of the above

7. To locate a data item for storage is
   (1) field (2) feed
   (3) database (4) fetch

8. Devices that could be used to input data into a database are
   (1) keyboard, fax roller ball
   (2) mouse, keyboard, monitor
   (3) mouse, keyboard, touch screen
   (4) All of the above

9. In a relational database, a data structure that organises the information about a single topic into rows and columns, is
   (1) block (2) record (3) tuple (4) table

10. The smallest unit of information about a record in a database is called a
    (1) cell (2) field (3) record (4) query

11. .... are distinct items that do not have much meaning to you in a given context. **[SBI PO 2012]**
    (1) Fields (2) Data
    (3) Queries (4) Properties
    (5) None of these

12. A collection of related files is called a **[SBI PO 2011, IBPS Clerk 2013]**
    (1) character (2) field
    (3) database (4) record
    (5) None of these

13. Which of the following contains information about a single 'entity' in the database like a person, place, event or thing?
    (1) Query (2) Form
    (3) Record (4) Table

14. DBMS is comprised of tables that made up of rows called .... and columns called ....
    (1) fields, records (2) records, fields
    (3) address, fields (4) ranges, sheet

15. What is a stored question about information in a database? **[SBI Clerk 2015]**
    (1) Query (2) Sort
    (3) Report (4) Record
    (5) Field

16. A program that generally has more user-friendly interface than a DBMS is called a
(1) front end (2) repository
(3) back end (4) form

17. Which of the following object(s) is/are contained in database?
(1) Table (2) Query
(3) Form (4) All of these

18. Which of the following places the common data elements in order from smallest to largest?
(1) Character, File, Record, Field, Database
(2) Character, Record, Field, File, Database
(3) Character, Field, Record, File, Database
(4) Bit, Byte, Character, Record, Field, File, Database

19. What is the overall term for creating, editing, formatting, storing, retrieving a text document? **[IBPS PO 2012]**
(1) Word processing (2) Spreadsheet design
(3) Web design (4) Database management
(5) Presentation generation

20. The database administrator's function in an organisation is
(1) to be responsible for the technical aspects of managing the information contained in organisational databases
(2) to be responsible for the executive level aspects of decision regarding the information management
(3) to show the relationship among entity classes in a data warehouse
(4) to define which data mining tools must be used to extract data

21. The code that relational database management systems use to perform their database task is referred to as
(1) QBE (2) SQL
(3) OLAP (4) Sequel Server

22. DBMS helps to achieve
(1) data independency
(2) centralised control of data
(3) selection of data
(4) Both (1) and (2)

23. Which out of the following is not a DBMS software?
(1) dBASE (2) FoxPro
(3) Oracle (4) Database 2000

24. In which, the database can be restored up to the last consistent state after the system failure?
(1) Backup (2) Recovery
(3) Redundancy (4) Security

25. .... provides total solutions to reduce data redundancy, inconsistency, dependency and unauthorised access of data.
(1) DBMS **[IBPS Clerk 2012]**
(2) Tables
(3) Database
(4) Protection password
(5) Centralisation of data

26. Periodically adding, changing and deleting file records is called .... file.
(1) updating (2) upgrading
(3) restructuring (4) renewing

27. Architecture of database management can be viewed as
(1) two levels (2) four levels
(3) three levels (4) one level

28. A collection of conceptual tools for describing data, relationships, semantics and constraints is referred to as **[IBPS Clerk 2012]**
(1) E-R model (2) database
(3) data model (4) DBMS
(5) None of these

29. .... is one reason for problems of data integrity. **[IBPS Clerk 2012]**
(1) Data availability constraints
(2) Data inconsistency
(3) Security constraints
(4) Unauthorised access of data
(5) Data redundancy

30. .... means that the data contained in a database is accurate and reliable.
(1) Data redundancy
(2) Data integrity
(3) Data reliability
(4) Data consistency

31. Which of the following contains data descriptions and defines the name, data type and length of each field in the database?
(1) Data dictionary (2) Data table
(3) Data record (4) Data filed

32. An advantage of the database management approach is
(1) data is dependent on programs
(2) data redundancy increases
(3) data is integrated and can be accessed by multiple programs
(4) All of the above

33. Which of the following is the drawback of DBMS?
(1) Improvement in data
(2) Backup and recovery
(3) Complexity
(4) Maintenance of data integrity

34. In which of the following, database is used?
(1) Banking (2) Finance
(3) Sales (4) All of these

35. A database that contains tables linked by common fields is called a
(1) centralised database
(2) flat file database
(3) relational database
(4) All of the above

36. Oracle is a(n) **[IBPS Clerk Mains 2017]**
(1) hardware (2) high level language
(3) operating system (4) system software
(5) RDBMS

37. The cardinality property of a relation, refers to the
(1) number of database
(2) number of columns
(3) number of rows
(4) number of tables

38. Rows of a relation are called
(1) relation (2) tuples
(3) data structure (4) entities

39. A set of possible data values is called
(1) attribute (2) degree
(3) tuple (4) domain

40. The purpose of the primary key in a database is to **[IBPS Clerk 2015]**
(1) unlock the database
(2) provide a map of the data
(3) uniquely identify a record
(4) establish constraints on database operations
(5) None of the above

41. In case of entity integrity, the primary key may be
(1) not null (2) null
(3) Both (1) and (2) (4) any value

42. In files, there is a key associated with each record which is used to differentiate among different records. For every file, there is atleast one set of keys that is unique. Such a key is called
(1) unique key (2) prime attribute
(3) index key (4) primary key

43. Which of the following types of table constraints will prevent the entry of duplicate rows?
(1) Primary key (2) Unique
(3) Null (4) Foreign key

44. The particular field of a record that uniquely identifies each record is called the **[SBI PO 2012]**
(1) key field (2) primary field
(3) master field (4) order field
(5) None of these

45. .... is a primary key of one file that also appears in another file. **[IBPS Clerk 2013]**
(1) Physical key (2) Primary key
(3) Foreign key (4) Logical key
(5) None of these

46. .... is an invalid type of database key.
(1) Structured primary key **[IBPS Clerk 2013]**
(2) Atomic primary key
(3) Primary key
(4) Composite primary key
(5) None of the above

47. Key to represent relationship between tables is called **[SBI Clerk 2010]**
(1) primary key (2) secondary key
(3) foreign key (4) composite key
(5) None of these

48. Which database language is used to access data in existing database?
(1) DDL (2) DML
(3) DCL (4) None of these

49. An E-R diagram is a graphic method of presenting **[IBPS Clerk 2011]**
(1) primary keys and their relationships
(2) primary keys and their relationships to instances
(3) entity classes and their relationships
(4) entity classes and their relationships to primary keys
(5) None of the above

50. In an E-R diagram, an entity set is represented by
(1) rectangle (2) square
(3) ellipse (4) triangle

51. In an E-R diagram, attributes are represented by
(1) rectangle (2) square
(3) ellipse (4) circle

52. In E-R diagram, relationship type is represented by **[IBPS Clerk 2012]**
(1) ellipse (2) dashed ellipse
(3) rectangle (4) diamond
(5) None of these

53. An entity set that does not have sufficient attributes to form a primary key, is a **[IBPS Clerk 2011]**
(1) strong entity set (2) weak entity set
(3) simple entity set (4) primary entity set
(5) None of these

54. Relationship can be divided into
(1) One-to-one
(2) Many-to-one
(3) One-to-many
(4) All of the above

55. Dr. E F Codd represented .... rules that a database must obey if it has to be considered truly relational. **[IBPS Clerk 2012]**
(1) 10 (2) 8
(3) 12 (4) 6
(5) 5

56. A logical schema
(1) is the entire database
(2) is a standard way of organising information into accessable part
(3) describes how data is actually stored on disk
(4) All of the above

57. Data duplication wastes the space, but also promotes a more serious problem called
(1) isolated **[IBPS PO 2015]**
(2) data inconsistency
(3) other than those given as options
(4) program dependency
(5) separated data

58. When data changes in multiple lists and all lists are not updated. This causes **[RBI Grade B 2012]**
(1) Data redundancy
(2) Information overload
(3) Duplicate data
(4) Data consistency
(5) Data inconsistency

ANSWERS

1. (3)	2. (3)	3. (1)	4. (2)	5. (2)	6. (1)	7. (4)	8. (3)	9. (4)	10. (2)
11. (1)	12. (4)	13. (3)	14. (2)	15. (1)	16. (4)	17. (4)	18. (3)	19. (4)	20. (1)
21. (2)	22. (4)	23. (4)	24. (2)	25. (4)	26. (1)	27. (3)	28. (3)	29. (1)	30. (2)
31. (1)	32. (3)	33. (3)	34. (4)	35. (3)	36. (5)	37. (3)	38. (2)	39. (4)	40. (3)
41. (1)	42. (4)	43. (1)	44. (2)	45. (3)	46. (1)	47. (3)	48. (2)	49. (3)	50. (1)
51. (3)	52. (4)	53. (2)	54. (4)	55. (3)	56. (2)	57. (2)	58. (5)		

CHAPTER

12

DATA COMMUNICATION AND NETWORKING

The term 'communication' means sending or receiving information. When we communicate, we share information or data.

A communication system can be defined as the collection of hardware and software that facilitates inter-system exchange of information between different devices.

Data Communication

It is the exchange of data between two devices using some form of transmission media.

It includes the transfer of data or information and the method of preservation of data during the transfer process. Data is transferred from one place to another in the form of signals.

There are three types of signal

1. **Digital Signal** In this signal, data is transmitted in electronic form, i.e. binary digits (0 or 1).
2. **Analog Signal** In this signal, data is transmitted in the form of radiowaves like in telephone line.
3. **Hybrid Signal** These signals have properties of both analog signal and digital signal.

Components of Data Communication

Whenever we talk about communication between two computing devices using a network, five most important aspects come to our mind. These are sender, receiver, communication medium, the message to be communicated and certain rules called protocols to be followed during communication. The communication media is also called transmission media.

Five components of data communication are

(i) **Sender** It is a computer or any such device which is capable of sending data over a network. It can be a computer, mobile phone, smartwatch, walkie-talkie, video-recording device, etc.

(ii) **Receiver** It is a computer or any such device which is capable or receiving data from the network. It can be any computer, printer, laptop, mobile phone, television, etc. The sender and receiver are known as nodes in a network.

(iii) **Message** It is the data or information that needs to be exchanged between the sender and the receiver. Messages can be in the form of text, number, image, audio, video, multimedia, etc.

(iv) **Communication Media** It is the path through which the message travels between source and destination. It is also called medium or link which is either wired or wireless.

(v) **Protocol** It is a set of rules that need to be followed by the communicating parties in order to have successful and reliable data communication.

Characteristics of Data Communication

1. **Delivery** The data must be delivered from the source device to the correct destination in the right order.
2. **Accuracy** The data must be delivered error-free. If there exists any inaccuracy during transmission, the data should be re-transmitted.
3. **Timeliness** The data must be delivered during the specified time period. The late delivered data becomes useless.

Communication Channel

The communication channel refers to the direction of signal flow between two linked devices.

There are mainly three types of communication channels which are as follows

1. **Simplex Channel** In this channel, the flow of data is always in one direction with no capability to support response in other direction.

   This communication is uni-directional. Only one of the communicating devices transmits information and the other can only receive it.

   E.g. Radio, Television, Keyboard, etc.
2. **Half Duplex Channel** In this channel, the data can flow in both directions, but not at the same time. When one device transmits information, the other can only receive at that point of time. E.g. Walkie –Talkie.
3. **Full Duplex Channel** In this channel, the flow of data is in both directions at a time i.e., both stations can transmit and receive information simultaneously.

   E.g. Wireless handset (mobile phone).

Communication Media

Communication media of a network refers to the transmission media or the connecting media used in the network. It can be broadly defined as anything that can carry information from a source to the destination.

It refers to the physical media through which communication signals can be transmitted from one point to another.

Transmission media can be divided into two broad categories

Guided Media or Wired Technologies

The data signal in guided media is bound by the cabling system that guides the data signal along a specific path.

It consists of a cable composed of metals like copper, tin or silver.

Basically, they are divided into three categories

1. **Ethernet Cable or Twisted Pair Cable** In this cable, wires are twisted together which are surrounded by an insulating material and an outer layer called jacket. One of the wires is used to carry signals to the receiver and the other is used only as a ground reference.

   E.g. Local area networks use twisted pair cable.
2. **Co-axial Cable** It carries the signal of higher frequency data through the network. It has a single inner conductor that transmits electric signals and the outer conductor acts as a ground and is wrapped in a sheet of teflon or PVC. Co-axial cable is commonly used in transporting multi-channel television signals in cities.

   E.g. Cable TV network.

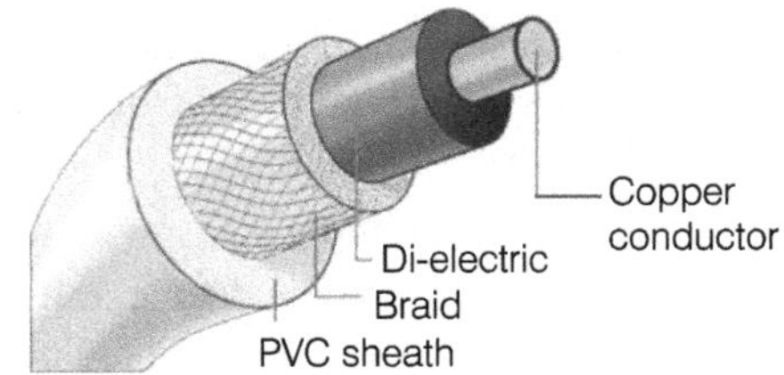

Co-axial Cable

3. **Fibre Optic Cable** It is made up of glass or plastic and transmits signals in the form of light from a source at one end to another.

   Optical fibres allow transmission over longer distance at higher bandwidth which is not affected by electromagnetic field. The speed of optical fibre is hundred times faster than co-axial cables.

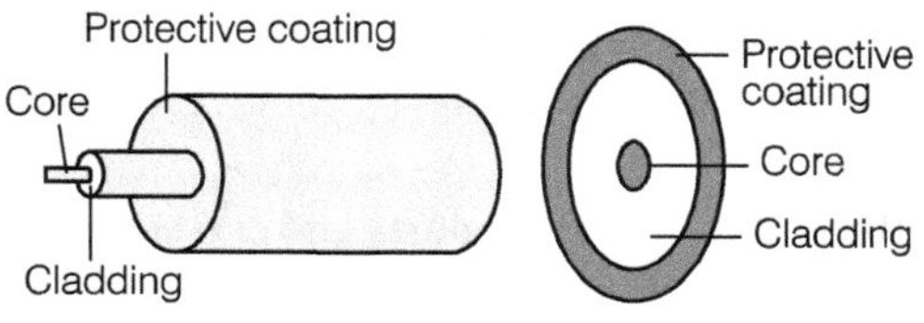

Fibre Optic Cable

Note *Tamil Nadu, the Indian state decided to implement Bharat Net Service which will connect all the village panchayats through optical fibre.*

Unguided Media or Wireless Technologies

It is the transfer of information over a distance without the use of enhanced electrical conductors or wires. When the computers in a network are interconnected and data is transmitted through waves, then they are said to be connected through unguided media.

Some commonly used unguided media of transmission are as follows

1. **Radiowave Transmission** When two terminals communicate by using radio frequencies than such type of communication is known as radiowave transmission. This transmission is also known as Radio Frequency (RF) transmission. The frequencies range from 3Hz to 1GHz. These are omni-directional. Radio waves, particularly those waves that propagate in the sky mode, can travel long distances.
2. **Microwave Transmission** Microwaves are electromagnetic waves having frequencies range from 0.3 to 300 GHz. Microwaves are uni-directional. It have higher frequency than that of radiowaves. It is used in cellular network and television broadcasting.
3. **Infrared Wave Transmission** Infrared waves are the high frequency waves used for short-range communication. The frequencies range from 300 GHz to 400 THz. These waves can not pass through the solid-objects. They are mainly used in TV remote and wireless speakers, etc.
4. **Satellite Communication** The communication across longer distances can be provided by combining radio frequency transmission with satellites.

   It works over long distances and allows fast communication. It is used for communication to ships, vehicles, planes and handheld terminals.

Note ***Bluetooth*** *It is a short range wireless communication technology that allows devices such as mobile phones, computers and peripherals to transmit data or voice wirelessly over a short distance.*

Computer Network

It is a collection of two or more computers, which are connected together to share information and resources.

Computer network is a combination of hardware and software that allows communication between computers over a network.

Note *ARPANET stands for Advanced Research Projects Agency Network. It was the first network developed by Vint Cerf in 1969.*

Benefits of Computer Network

Some of the benefits of computer network are discussed below

1. **File Sharing** Networking of computer helps the users to share data/files.
2. **Hardware Sharing** Users can share devices such as printers, scanners, CD-ROM drives, hard drives, etc., in a computer network.
3. **Application Sharing** Applications can be shared over the network and this allows implementation of client/server applications.
4. **User Communication** This allows users to communicate using E-mail, news groups, video-conferencing, etc. within the network.

Types of Computer Network

Computer network is broadly classified into various types which are as follows

Local Area Network (LAN)

LAN is a small and single-site network. It connects network devices over a relatively short distance.

It is a system in which computers are inter-connected in the geographical area such as home, office, building, school, etc. which are within a range of 1 km. Its speed is upto 1000 Mbps. On most LANs, cables are used to connect the computers.

LANs are typically owned, controlled and managed by a single person or organisation. They also use certain specific connectivity technologies, primarily Ethernet and Token Ring. LAN provides a sharing of peripherals in an efficient or effective way.

Wide Area Network (WAN)

WAN is a geographically dispersed collection of LANs. A WAN like the Internet spans most of the world. A network device called a router connects LANs to a WAN. Its speed is upto 150 Mbps.

Like the Internet, most WANs are not owned by any one organisation, but rather exist under collective or distributed ownership and management. WANs use technology like ATM, Frame Relay and X.25 for connectivity.

Metropolitan Area Network (MAN)

It is a data network designed for a town or city. It connects an area larger than a LAN, but smaller than a WAN. Its speed is upto 100 Mbps.

Its main purpose is to share hardware and software resources by various users. Cable TV network is an example of metropolitan area network. The computers in a MAN are connected using co-axial cables or fibre optic cables.

Personal Area Network (PAN)

PAN refers to a small network of communication. These are used in a few limited range, which is in reachability of individual person. Its speed is upto 3 Mbps. Few examples of PAN are Bluetooth, Wireless USB, Z-wave and Zig Bee.

- **Server** is a system that responds to requests across a computer network to provide a network service. It can be run on a dedicated computer. It is one of the most powerful and typical computer.
- **File Server** is a type of computer used on network that provides access to files. It allows users to share programs and data over LAN network.

Computer Network Devices

These devices are required to amplify the signal to restore the original strength of signal and to provide an interface to connect multiple computers in a network.

There are many types of computer network devices used in networking. Some of them are described below

1. **Repeater** It has two ports and can connect two segments of a LAN. It amplifies the signals when they are transported over a long distance so that the signal can be as strong as the original signal. A repeater boosts the signal back to its original level.
2. **Hub** It is like a repeater with multiple ports used to connect the network channels. It acts as a centralised connection to several computers with the central node or server. When a hub receives a packet of data at one of its ports from a network channel, it transmits the packet to all of its ports to all other network channel.
3. **Gateway** It is an inter-connecting device, which joins two different network protocols together. They are also known as protocol converters. It accepts packet formatted for one protocol and converts the formatted packet into another protocol.

   The gateway is a node in a network which serves as a proxy server and a firewall system and prevents the unauthorised access.
4. **Switch** It is a small hardware device that joins multiple computers together within one LAN. It helps to reduce overall network traffic.

   Switch forwards a data packet to a specific route by establishing a temporary connection between the source and the destination. There is a vast difference between a switch and a hub. A hub forwards each incoming packet (data) to all the hub ports, while a switch forwards each incoming packet to the specified recipient.
5. **Router** It is a hardware device which is designed to take incoming packets, analyse packets, moving and converting packets to the another network interface, dropping the packets, directing packets to the appropriate locations, etc.
6. **Bridge** It serves a similar function as switches. A bridge filters data traffic at a network boundary. Bridges reduce the amount of traffic on a LAN by dividing it into two segments.

Traditional bridges support one network boundary, whereas switches usually offer four or more hardware ports. Switches are sometimes called multiport bridges.

7. **Modem** It is a device that converts digital signal to analog signal (modulator) at the sender's end and converts back analog signal to digital signal (demodulator) at the receiver's end, in order to make communication possible via telephone lines. Modem is always placed between a telephone line and a computer.

Network Topology

The term 'topology' refers to the way a network is laid out, either physically or logically. Topology can be referred as the geometric arrangement of a computer system. Each computer system in a topology is known as node.

The most commonly used topologies are described below

1. **Bus Topology** It is such that there is a single line to which all nodes are connected. It is usually used when a network installation is small, simple or temporary.

   In bus topology, all the network components are connected with a same (single) line.

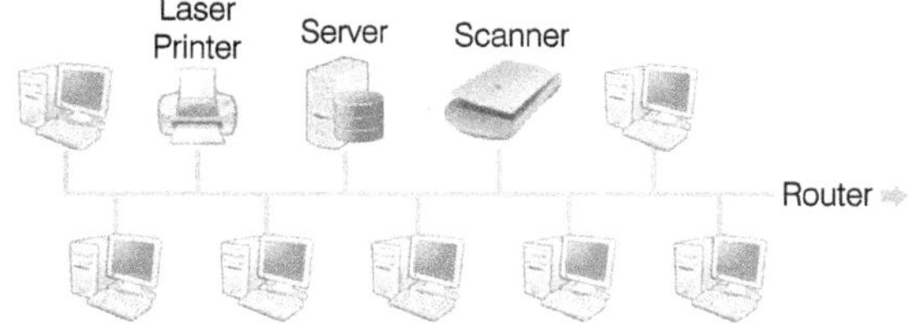

Bus Topology

2. **Star Topology** In this network topology, the peripheral nodes are connected to a central node, which re-broadcasts all transmissions received from any peripheral node to all peripheral nodes across the network. A star network can be expanded by placing another star hub.

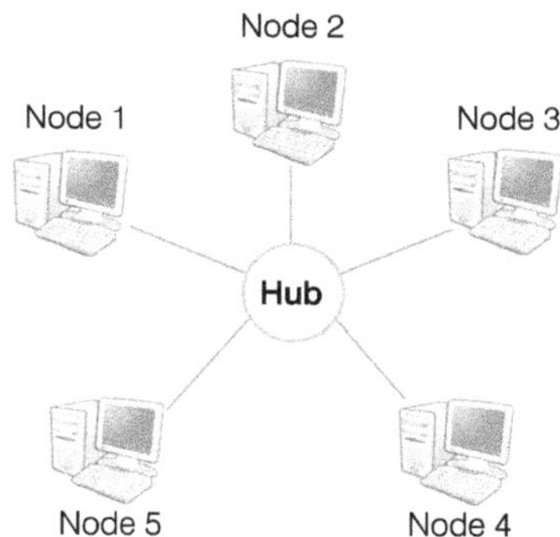

Star Topology

3. **Ring or Circular Topology** This topology is used in high-performance networks where large bandwidth is necessary. The protocols used to implement ring topology are Token Ring and Fiber Distributed Data Interface (FDDI). In ring topology, data is transmitted in the form of token over a network.

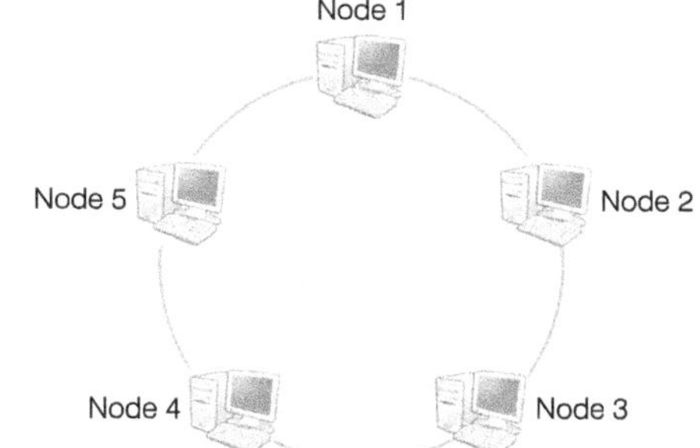

Ring or Circular Topology

4. **Mesh Topology** It is also known as completely inter-connected topology. In mesh topology, every node has a dedicated point-to-point link to every other node.

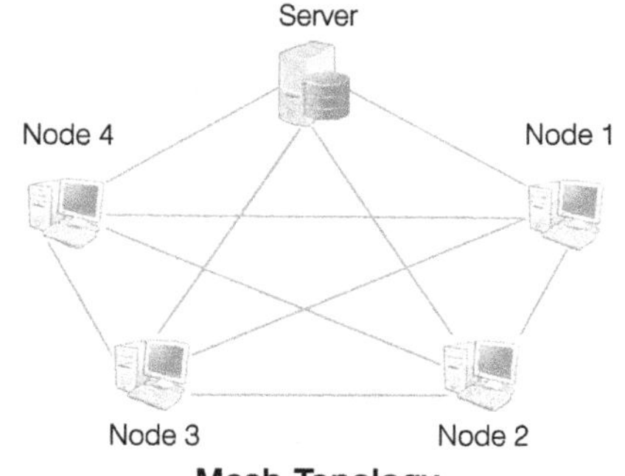

Mesh Topology

5. **Tree Topology** This is a network topology in which nodes are arranged as a tree. The function of the central node in this topology may be distributed.

   Its basic structure is like an inverted tree, where the root acts as a server. It allows more devices to be attached to a single hub.

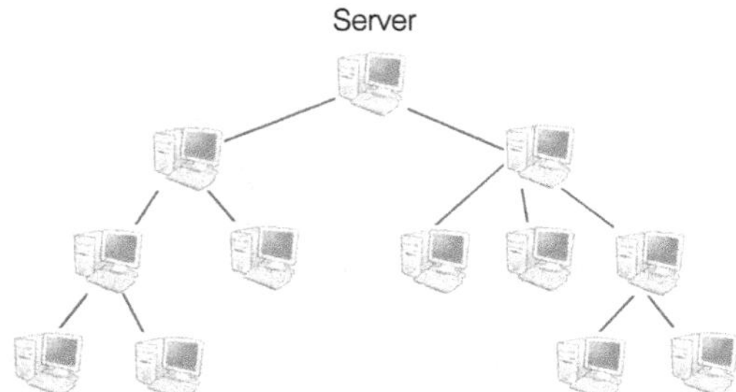

Tree topology

Models of Computer Networking

There are mainly two models of computer networking which are as follows

1. Peer-to-Peer Network

It is also known as P2P network. It relies on computing power at the edges of a connection rather than in the network itself.

P2P network is used for sharing content like audio, video, data or anything in the digital format.

In P2P connection, a couple of computers are connected via a Universal Serial Bus (USB) to transfer files. In peer-to-peer networking, each or every computer can work as server or client.

2. Client-Server Network

The model of interaction between two application programs in which a program at one end (client) requests a service from a program at the other end (server).

It is a network architecture which separates the client from the server. It is scalable architecture, where one computer works as server and others as client. Here, client acts as the active device and server behaves passively.

OSI Model

Open System Inter-connection (OSI) is a standard reference model for communication between two end users in a network. In 1983, the International Standards Organisation (ISO) published a document called Basic Reference Model for Open System Inter-connection, which visualises network protocols as a Seven Layered Model.

OSI is a layered framework for the design of network system that allows communication between all types of computer systems. It mainly consists of seven layers across a network.

Seven Layers of OSI Model and their Functions

Name of the Layer	Functions
Application Layer [User-Interface]	Re-transferring files of information, login, password checking, packet filtering, etc.
Presentation Layer [Data formatting]	It works as a translating layer, i.e. encryption or decryption.
Session Layer [Establish and maintain connection]	To manage and synchronise conversation between two systems. It controls logging ON and OFF, user identification, billing and session management.
Transport Layer [Transmission Control Protocol (TCP) accurate data]	It decides whether transmission should be parallel or single path, multi-plexing, splitting or segmenting the data, to break data into smaller units for efficient handling, packet filtering.
Network Layer [Internet Protocol (IP) routers]	Routing of the signals, divide the outgoing message into packets, to act as network controller for routing data.
Data Link Layer [Media Access Control (MAC) switches]	Synchronisation, error detection and correction. To assemble outgoing messages into frames.
Physical Layer [Signals-cables or operated by repeater]	Make and break connections, define voltages and data rates, convert data bits into electrical signal. Decide whether transmission is simplex, half duplex or full duplex.

In OSI model, physical layer is the lowest layer which is implemented on both hardware and software and application layer is the highest layer.

Computer Network Addressing

Network addresses are always logical, i.e. these are software based addresses which can be changed by appropriate configurations.

A network address always points to host/node/server or it can represent a whole network.

Network address is always configured on network interface card and is generally mapped by system with the MAC address of the machine for layer-2 communication.

There are different kinds of network addresses as

- IP
- IPX
- AppleTalk

Terms Related to Computer Network

1. **Multi-plexing** It is a technique used for transmitting signals simultaneously over a common medium. It involves single path and multiple channels for data communication.
2. **Code Division Multiple Access** (CDMA) It is a channel access method used by various radio communication technologies.

   CDMA employs spread spectrum technology and a special coding scheme, where each transmitter is assigned a code to allow multiple users to be multi-plexed over the same physical channel.
3. **Packet Switching** It refers to the method of digital networking communication that combined all transmitted data regardless of content, type or structure into suitable sized blocks known as packets.
4. **Public Switched Telephone Network** (PSTN) It is designed for telephone, which requires modem for data communication. It is used for FAX machine also.
5. **Integrated Services Digital Network** (ISDN) It is used for voice, video and data services. It uses digital transmission and combines both circuit and packet switching.
6. **Ethernet** It is a widely used technology employing a bus technology. An ethernet LAN consists of a single co-axial cable called Ether. It operates at 10 Mbps and provides a 48-bits address. Fast ethernet operates at 100 Mbps.
7. **Token** It is a small message used to pass between one station to another.

Tit-Bits

- **Bandwidth** determines the data transfer rate which is measured in Cycle Per Second (CPS) or Hertz (Hz).
- **Throughput** is the amount of data that is actually transmitted between two computers. It is specified in bits per second (bps). Giga bits per second (Gbps) is the fastest speed unit per data transmission.
- **GPS** (Global Positioning System) is a global navigation satellite system that provides location, velocity and time synchronisation. GPS is everywhere. You can find GPS system in your car, your smartphone and your watch.

QUESTION BANK

1. .... is the transmission of data between two or more computers over communication links.
(1) Communication (2) Networking
(3) Data communication (4) Data networking

2. Communication channel having.........type(s).
(1) 1 (2) 2 (3) 3 (4) 4

3. In simplex channel, flow of data is
(1) always in one direction
(2) always in both direction
(3) in both direction, but one at a time
(4) All of the above

4. Communication between a computer and a keyboard involves .... transmission. **[IBPS Clerk Mains 2017]**
(1) Automatic (2) Half duplex
(3) Full-duplex (4) Simplex
(5) None of these

5. Mobile phone is an example of which type of communication channel?
(1) Simplex (2) Half duplex
(3) Full duplex (4) None of these

6. Which of the following is not a property of twisted pair cabling?
(1) Twisted pair cabling is a relatively low speed transmission
(2) The wires can be shielded
(3) The wires can be unshielded
(4) Twisted pair cable carries signals as light waves

7. In twisted pair, wires are twisted together, which are surrounded by an insulating material and an outer layer called
(1) frame (2) cover
(3) disk (4) block
(5) jacket

8. Which of the following is the greatest advantage of co-axial cabling?
(1) High security (2) Physical dimensions
(3) Long distances (4) Easily tapped

9. Which of the following cables can transmit data at high speed? **[IBPS Clerk 2014]**
(1) Flat cable (2) Co-axial cable
(3) Optic fibre cable (4) Twisted pair cable
(5) UTP cable

10. Which Indian state decided to implement Bharat Net Service which will connect all the village panchayats through optical fibre? **[RRB NTPC 2016]**
A. Maharashtra B. Punjab
C. Tamil Nadu D. Uttar Pradesh
1. D 2. B 3. A 4. C

11. Networking using fibre optic cable is done as **[RBI Grade B 2012]**
(1) it has high bandwidth
(2) it is thin and light
(3) it is not affected by electro magnetic interference/power surges, etc
(4) All of the above
(5) None of the above

12. Which of the following is not a property of fibre optic cabling? **[IBPS Clerk Mains 2017]**
(1) Transmits at faster speed than copper cabling
(2) Easier to capture a signal from the copper cabling
(3) Very resistant to interference
(4) Carries signals as light waves
(5) Less attenuation

13. A device that connects to a network without the use of cables is said to be **[IBPS Clerk 2012, RBI Grade B 2012]**
(1) distributed (2) cabled
(3) centralised (4) open source
(5) wireless

14. Which of the following is the fastest communication channel?
(1) Radiowave
(2) Microwave
(3) Optical fibre
(4) All are operating at nearly the same propagation speed

15. Bandwidth refers to **[RBI Grade B 2013]**
(1) the cost of the cable required to implement a WAN
(2) the cost of the cable required to implement a LAN
(3) the amount of information a peer-to-peer network can store
(4) the amount of information a communication medium can transfer in a given amount of time
(5) None of the above

16. Which of the following represents the fastest data transmission speed? **[SBI Clerk 2012]**
(1) Bandwidth (2) bps
(3) gbps (4) kbps
(5) mbps

17. A(n) .... is composed of several computers connected together to share resources and data. **[RBI Grade B 2014]**
(1) Internet (2) Network
(3) Backbone (4) Hyperlink
(5) Protocol

18. What do we call for the arrangement when two or more computers physically connected by cables to share information or hardware? **[SBI Clerk 2015]**
(1) URL (2) Network
(3) Server (4) Internet
(5) Modem

19. A combination of hardware and software that allows communication and electronic transfer of information between computers is a **[SBI Clerk 2012]**
(1) network (2) backup system
(3) server (4) peripheral
(5) modem

20. Which of the following terms is associated with networks? **[SBI Clerk 2014]**
(1) MS-Excel
(2) Mouse
(3) Word
(4) Connectivity
(5) Plotter

21. What type of resource is most likely to be a shared common resource in a computer network? **[Allahabad Bank Clerk 2010]**
(1) Printers
(2) Speakers
(3) Floppy disk drives
(4) Keyboards
(5) None of the above

22. The first network that has planted the seeds of Internet was
(1) ARPANET (2) NSFnet
(3) V-net (4) I-net

23. Pathways that support communication among the various electronic components on the system board are called **[SBI PO 2014]**
(1) network lines (2) processors
(3) logic paths (4) bus lines
(5) gateway

24. What do we call a network whose elements may be separated by some distance? It usually involves two or more network and dedicated high speed telephone lines. **[SBI Clerk 2015]**
(1) LAN (2) WAN
(3) URL (4) Server
(5) World Wide Web

25. LAN can use .... architecture.
(1) peer-to-peer
(2) client and server
(3) Both (1) and (2)
(4) Neither (1) nor (2)

26. Ethernet, token ring and token bus are types of **[SBI Associates 2012, RBI Grade B 2014]**
(1) WAN
(2) LAN
(3) communication channels
(4) physical media
(5) None of the above

27. The advantage of LAN is **[SBI Clerk 2012]**
(1) sharing peripherals
(2) backing up your data
(3) saving all your data
(4) accessing the web
(5) automatic printing of data

28. Computer connected to a LAN can .... **[IBPS Clerk 2013]**
(1) run faster
(2) share information and/or share peripheral equipment
(3) go online
(4) E-mail
(5) None of the above

29. .... allows LAN users to share computer programs and data.
(1) Communication server
(2) Print server
(3) File server
(4) All of the above

30. What is the use of bridge in network?
(1) To connect LANs
(2) To separate LANs
(3) To control network speed
(4) All of the above

31. Which of the following items is not used in Local Area Network (LAN)? **[SSC CGL 2012]**
(1) Interface card (2) Cable
(3) Computer (4) Modem

32. Which type of network would use phone lines? **[IBPS Clerk 2015]**
(1) WAN (2) LAN
(3) WWAN (4) Wireless
(5) None of these

33. Which of the following refers to a small, single-site network?
(1) PAN (2) DSL
(3) RAM (4) USB
(5) CPU

34. These servers store and manage files for network users.
(1) Authentication (2) Main
(3) Web (4) File

35. .... is the most important/powerful computer in a typical network. **[SBI PO 2013]**
(1) Desktop (2) Network client
(3) Network server (4) Network station
(5) Network switch

36. A protocol is a set of rules governing a time sequence of events that must take place
(1) between peers (2) between an interface
(3) between modems (4) across an interface

37. A .... is an agreement between the communication parties on how communication is to proceed. **[SSC CGL 2016]**
(1) Path (2) SLA
(3) Bond (4) Protocol

38. A device operating at the physical layer is called a
(1) bridge (2) router
(3) repeater (4) All of these

39. Which of the following devices that joins multiple computers together within one LAN?
(1) Repeater (2) Hub
(3) Gateway (4) Switch
(5) Router

40. Which of the following is used for modulation and demodulation?
(1) Modem (2) Protocols
(3) Gateway (4) Multi-plexer
(5) None of these

41. What is the name of the derive that links your computer with other computers and information services through telephone lines? **[SBI Clerk 2015]**
(1) Modem (2) LAN
(3) URL (4) WAN
(5) Server

42. What is the function of a modem? **[RBI Grade B 2012]**
(1) Encryption and decryption
(2) Converts data to voice and vice- versa
(3) Converts analog signals to digital signals and vice-versa
(4) Serves as a hardware anti-virus
(5) None of the above

43. The hardware device or software program that sends messages between network is known as a **[IBPS Clerk 2014]**
(1) bridge (2) backbone
(3) router (4) gateway
(5) Other than those given as options

44. Which of the following is not a network device?
(1) Router (2) Switch
(3) Bus (4) Bridge

45. Geometric arrangement of devices on the network is called
(1) topology (2) protocol
(3) media (4) LAN

46. Which of the following topologies is not of broadcast type?
(1) Star (2) Bus
(3) Ring (4) All of these

47. Network components are connected to the same cable in the .... topology.
(1) star (2) ring
(3) bus (4) mesh
(5) tree

48. Hub is associated with .... network. **[SBI Clerk 2011]**
(1) bus (2) ring
(3) star (4) mesh
(5) All of these

49. In a ring topology, the computer in possession of the .... can transmit data.
(1) packet (2) data
(3) access method (4) token

50. In which topology, every node is connected to two other nodes? **[IBPS RRB PO Mains 2018]**
(1) Bus topology (2) Ring topology
(3) Star topology (4) Mesh topology
(5) None of these

51. Which is the name of the network topology in which there are bi-directional links between each possible node? **[SSC CGL 2012]**
(1) Ring (2) Star
(3) Tree (4) Mesh

52. An alternate name for the completely inter-connected network topology is **[SSC CGL 2012]**
(1) mesh (2) star
(3) tree (4) ring

53. Which is the highest reliability topology? **[IBPS RRB PO Mains 2018]**
(1) Mesh topology (2) Tree topology
(3) Bus topology (4) Star topology
(5) None of these

54. P2P is a .... application architecture. **[IBPS Clerk 2012]**
(1) client/server (2) distributed
(3) centralised (4) 1-tier
(5) None of these

55. A packet filtering firewall operates at which of the following OSI layers?
(1) At the application layer
(2) At the transport layer
(3) At the network layer
(4) At the gateway layer

56. Encryption and decryption are the functions of
(1) transport layer (2) session layer
(3) presentation layer (4) All of these

57. Name the fourth layer of OSI model. **[SBI PO 2014]**
(1) Application layer (2) Data link layer
(3) Transport layer (4) Session layer
(5) None of these

58. In OSI network architecture, the routing is performed by **[IBPS Clerk 2012]**
(1) Network layer (2) Data link layer
(3) Transport layer (4) Session layer
(5) None of these

59. In the following list of devices which device is used in network layer? **[SSC CGL 2016]**
(1) Repeaters
(2) Router
(3) Application Gateway
(4) Switch

60. Switches work on which OSI layer?
(1) Data link layer
(2) Physical layer
(3) Transport layer
(4) Network layer
(5) Application layer

61. In IT networking, which of the following device is used in physical layer? **[SSC CGL 2016]**
(1) Repeater
(2) Router
(3) Transport Gateway
(4) Bridge

62. Multi-plexing involves .... path(s) and .... channel(s). **[SBI Clerk 2011]**
(1) one, one
(2) one, multiple
(3) multiple, one
(4) multiple, multiple
(5) None of the above

63. A processor that collects the transmissions from several communication media and send them over a single line that operates at a higher capacity is called **[RBI Grade B 2013]**
(1) multi-plexer (2) bridge
(3) hub (4) router
(5) None of these

64. To send data/message to and from computers, the network software puts the message information in a
(1) NIC (2) packet
(3) trailer (4) header
(5) None of these

65. How many bits are there in the ethernet address? **[SBI Clerk 2011]**
(1) 64 bits (2) 48 bits
(3) 32 bits (4) 16 bits
(5) None of these

66. Ethernet uses
(1) bus topology
(2) ring topology
(3) mesh topology
(4) All of the above

67. In networks, a small message used to pass between one station to another is known as **[SSC CGL 2016]**
(1) Token (2) Byte
(3) Word (4) Ring

68. ISDN is a tele-communication technology, where **[UPSSSC 2016]**
(a) Voice, video and data all are transmitted simultaneously
(b) Only sound is transmitted
(c) Only video is transmitted
(d) Only data is transmitted

69. What is the frequency range of data transmission under computer system? **[UPSSSC Village Panchayat Officer]**
(a) Band (b) Bandwidth
(c) Byte (d) Bit

ANSWERS

1. (3)	2. (3)	3. (1)	4. (4)	5. (3)	6. (4)	7. (5)	8. (2)	9. (3)	10. (4)
11. (4)	12. (3)	13. (5)	14. (2)	15. (4)	16. (3)	17. (2)	18. (2)	19. (1)	20. (4)
21. (1)	22. (1)	23. (2)	24. (1)	25. (3)	26. (2)	27. (1)	28. (2)	29. (3)	30. (1)
31. (4)	32. (1)	33. (1)	34. (4)	35. (3)	36. (4)	37. (4)	38. (3)	39. (4)	40. (1)
41. (1)	42. (3)	43. (5)	44. (3)	45. (1)	46. (2)	47. (3)	48. (3)	49. (4)	50. (2)
51. (4)	52. (1)	53. (1)	54. (1)	55. (1)	56. (3)	57. (3)	58. (1)	59. (2)	60. (1)
61. (1)	62. (2)	63. (1)	64. (2)	65. (2)	66. (1)	67. (1)	68. (1)	69. (2)	

CHAPTER

13

INTERNET AND ITS SERVICES

The Internet is a worldwide network of computers that are able to exchange information with each other. Internet stands for International Network, which began in 1950's by Vint Cerf known as the Father of Internet.

Internet is a 'network of networks' that consists millions of private and public networks of local to global scope. Basically, network is a group of two or more computer systems linked together.

History of Internet

In 1969, the University of California at Los Angeles, and the University of Utah were connected for the beginning of the ARPANET (Advanced Research Projects Agency Network) using 50 kbits circuits. It was the world's first operational packet switching network. The goal of this project was to connect computers at different universities and U.S. defence.

In mid 80's another federal agency, the National Science Foundation, created a new high capacity network called NSFnet, which was more capable than ARPANET.

The only drawback of NSFnet was that it allowed only the academic research on its network and not any kind of private business on it. So, private organisations and people started working to build their own networks, which were later inter-connected with ARPANET and NSFnet to form the Internet.

Advantages of Internet

The advantages of Internet are as follows

- Allows you to easily communicate with other people.
- Global reach enables one to connect anyone on the Internet.
- Publishing documents on the Internet saves paper.
- A valuable resource for companies to advertise and conduct business.
- Greater access to information reduces research time.

Disadvantages of Internet

The disadvantages of the Internet are as follows

- It is a major source of computer viruses.
- Messages sent across the Internet can be easily intercepted and are open to abuse by others.
- Much of the information is not checked and may be incorrect or irrelevant.

- Unsuitable and undesirable material available that sometimes is used by notorious people such as terrorists.
- Cyber frauds may take place involving Credit/ Debit card numbers and details.

Internet Connections

Bandwidth and cost are the two factors that help you in deciding which Internet connection is to use. The speed of Internet access depends on the bandwidth.

Some of the Internet connections available for Internet access are as follows

Dial-Up Connection

Dial-up is a method of connecting to the Internet using an existing telephone. When a user initiates a dial-up connection, the modem dials a phone number of an Internet Service Provider (ISP) that is designated to receive dial-up calls.

The ISP then establishes the connection, which usually takes about ten seconds and is accompanied by several beeping and buzzing sounds. Its transfer speed is 56 kbit/s.

Broadband Connection

The term 'broadband' commonly refers to high speed Internet access that is always on and faster than the traditional dial-up access. It uses a telephone line to connect to the Internet. The transfer speed of broadband connection is 256 Kbit/s.

Broadband includes several high speed transmission technologies such as

1. **Digital Subscriber Line** (DSL) It is a popular broadband connection. It provides Internet access by transmitting digital data over the wires of a local telephone network. DSL is the most common type of broadband service. It uses the existing copper telephone lines. Its transfer speed is 256 kbits.
2. **Cable Modem** This service enables cable operators to provide broadband using the same co-axial cables that deliver pictures and sound to your TV set.

   Most cable modems are external devices that have two connections, one to the cable wall outlet and the other to a computer. They provide transmission speed of 1.5 Mbps or more.
3. **Broadband over Power Line** (BPL) BPL is the delivery of broadband over the existing low and medium voltage electric power distribution network. Its transfer speed is upto 3 Mbps.

   BPL is good for areas, where there are no other broadband connections, but power infrastructure exists. *For example,* rural areas.

Wireless Connection

Wireless broadband connects a home or business to the Internet using a radio link between the customer's location and the service provider's facility. Wireless broadband can be mobile or fixed. Unlike DSL and cable, wireless broadband requires neither modem nor cables. It can be easily established in areas where it is not feasible to deploy DSL or cable.

Some ways to connect the Internet wirelessly are as follows

1. **Wireless Fidelity** (Wi-Fi) It is a universal wireless networking technology that utilises radio frequencies to transfer data. Wi-Fi allows high speed Internet connections without the use of cables or wires. Wi-Fi networks can be use for public Internet access at 'hotspot' such as restaurants, coffee shops, hotels, airports, convention centers and city parks.
2. **Worldwide Interoperability for Microwave Access** (WiMAX) WiMAX systems are expected to deliver broadband access services to residential and enterprise customers in an economical way.

   It has the ability to provide service even in areas that are difficult for wired infrastructure to reach and the ability to overcome the physical limitations of traditional wired infrastructure.
3. **Mobile Wireless Broadband Services** These services are also becoming available from mobile telephone service providers and others. These services are generally appropriate for mobile customers and require a special PC card with a

built-in antenna that plugs into a user's computer. Generally, they provide lower speeds in the range of several hundred kbps.

Intranet is a private network for Internet tools, but available within an organisation. In large organisation, Intranet allows an easy access to corporate information for employees.

Extranet is a private network that uses the Internet protocol and the public tele-communication system to securely share part of a business information.

Podcast is a form of audio broadcasting on the web. It can be listened to on the go, while commuting to office or even while working.

Interconnecting Protocols

A protocol is a set of rules that govern data communications. It defines what is communicated, how it is communicated and when it is communicated.

Some of the protocols generally used to communicate via Internet are as follows

1. **Transmission Control Protocol/Internet Protocol** (TCP/IP)
   (a) **Transmission Control Protocol** (TCP) It provides reliable transport service, i.e. it ensures that message sent (from sender to receiver) is properly routed. TCP converts messages into a set of packets at the source which are then reassembled back into messages at the destination.
   (b) **Internet Protocol** (IP) It allows different computers to communicate by creating a network of networks. IP handles the dispatch of packets over the network. It maintains the addressing of packets with multiple standards. Each IP packet must contain the source and the destination addresses.

   Note *An IP address is a 32 bit number.*
2. **File Transfer Protocol** (FTP) It can transfer files between any computers that have an Internet connection and also works between computers using totally different operating systems. Some examples of FTP software are FileZilla, Kasablanca, gFTP, Konqueror, etc.
3. **HyperText Transfer Protocol** (HTTP) HTTP defines how messages are formatted and transmitted and what actions should be taken by the Web servers and browsers in response to various commands.

HyperText Markup Language (HTML)
It is used for designing Web pages. A markup language is a set of markup (angular bracket, <>) tags which tells the Web browser how to display the Web page's words and images for the user. Each individual markup code is referred to as an element or tag.

4. **Telnet Protocol** Telnet is a program that runs on the computer and connects PC to a server on the network. Telnet session starts by entering valid **username** and **password**.
5. **Usenet Protocol** The usenet service allows a group of Internet users to exchange their views/ideas and information on some common topic that is of interest to all the members belonging to that group.

   Several such groups exist on the Internet are called newsgroups. Usenet has no central server or administration.
6. **Point-to-Point Protocol** (PPP) It is a dial account which puts your computer directly on the Internet. A modem is required for such connection which transmits the data at 9600 bits per second.
7. **Simple Mail Transfer Protocol** (SMTP) It is the standard protocol for E-mail services on a TCP/IP network. It provides the ability to send and receive E-mail messages.
8. **Wireless Application Protocol** (WAP) A WAP browser is a commonly used Web browser for small mobile devices such as cell phones.
9. **Voice over Internet Protocol** (VoIP) It allows delivery of voice communication over 'IP' networks. *For example,* IP calls.
10. **Post Office Protocol version 3** (POP3) It is an Internet standard protocol used by local email software clients to retrieve emails from a remote mail server over a TCP/IP connection.

Terms Related to Internet

World Wide Web (WWW)

The world wide web is a system of Internet servers that supports hypertext and multimedia to access several Internet protocols on a single interface. WWW was introduced on 13th March, 1989.

The world wide web is often abbreviated as the Web or WWW. The world wide web is a way of exchanging information between computers on the Internet.

Web Page

The backbone of the world wide web is made of files, called **pages** or **Web pages**, containing information and links to resources - both text and multimedia - throughout the Internet. It is created using HTML.

There are basically two main types of web page i.e., static and dynamic. The main or first page of a Website is known as home page.

Note *Bookmarks are links to web pages that make it easy to get back to your favourite page.*

Hyperlink is a piece of text which connects different documents on a web page. It is a reference data that the user can follow by simply clicking on it.

Website

A group of Web pages that follow the same theme and are connected together with hyperlinks is called Website.

In other words, "A Website is a collection of digital documents, primarily HTML files, that are linked together and that exist on the Web under the same domain."

For example, http://www.carwale.com is a Website while http://www.carwale.com/new/ is a Web page.

Web Browser

It is a software application that is used to locate, retrieve and display content on the world wide web, including Web pages. Web browsers are programs used to explore the Internet.

We can install more than one Web browser on a single computer. The user can navigate through files, folders and websites with the help of a browser.

Note *F11 key on a windows keyboard sets to full screen mode in most browsers.*

The two types of Web browser are as follow

1. **Text Web Browser** A Web browser that displays only text-based information is known as text web browser. *For example,* Lynx, which provides access to the Internet in the text mode only.
2. **Graphical Web Browser** A Web browser that supports both text and graphic information is known as graphical web browser. *For example,* Internet Explorer, Firefox, Netscape, Safari, Google Chrome and Opera.

Note *The first graphical web browser was NCSA Mosaic.*

Web Server

A web server is a computer that runs websites. The server computer will deliver those Web pages to the computers that request them and may also do other processing with the Web pages. The web browser is a client that requests HTML files from Web servers.

Every Web server that is connected to the Internet is given a unique address, i.e. IP address, made up of a series of four numbers between 0 to 255 separated by periods (.). *For example,* Apache HTTP Server, Internet Information Services (IIS), Lighttpd, etc.

Note *Cookie is a small message given to a web browser by a web server. It stores information about the user's web activity.*

Web Address and URL

A Web address identifies the location of a specific Web page on the Internet, such as http://www.learnyoga.com.

On the Web, Web addresses are called URLs. It stands for Uniform Resource Locator. Tim Berners Lee created the first URL in 1991 to allow the publishing of hyperlinks on the world wide web. *For example,* "http://www. google.com/services/index.htm"

http://	–	Protocol identifier
www	–	World Wide Web
google.com	–	Domain name
/services/	–	Directory
index.htm	–	Web page

Domain Name

Domain is a group of network resources assigned to a group of users. A domain name is a way to identify and locate computers connected to the Internet. A domain name must be unique. It always have two or more parts, separated by period/dot (·). *For example,* google.com, yahoo.com, etc.

Domain Abbreviation

Domains are organised by the type of organisations and the country. A three-letter abbreviation indicating the organisation and usually two-letter abbreviation indicates the country name.

Most common domain abbreviations for organisation are as follow

.info	Informational organisation
.com	Commercial
.gov	Government
.edu	Educational
.mil	Military
.net	Network resources
.org	Non-profit organisation

Some domain abbreviations for country are as follow

.in	India
.au	Australia
.fr	France
.nz	New Zealand
.uk	United Kingdom

Domain Name System (DNS)

DNS stores and associates many types of information with domain names, but most importantly, it translates domain names (computers host names) to IP addresses. It also lists mail exchange servers accepting E-mail for each domain. DNS is an essential component of contemporary Internet use.

Blog

A blog is a Website or Web page in which an individual records opinions and links to other site on regular basis. A typical blog combines text, images, and links to other blogs, web pages and media related to its topic.

Most blogs are primarily textual, although some focus on art, photographs, videos, music and audio. These blogs are referred to as edublogs. The entries of a blog is also known as posts.

Newsgroup

A newsgroup is an online discussion forum accessible through usenet, devoted to discussion on a specified topic.

Online discussion group allows interaction through electronic bulletin board system and chat sessions.

Search Engine

It is a Website that provides the required data on specific topics. Search engines turn the Web into a powerful tool for finding information on any topic.

When a search engine returns the links to web pages corresponding to the keywords entered is called a hit, otherwise called a miss.

Many search engines also have directories or lists of topics that are organised into categories. Browsing these directories, is also a very efficient way to find information on a given topic.

Here are some of the most popular search engines

Google	http://www.google.com
AltaVista	http://www.altavista.com
Yahoo	http://www.yahoo.com
Hotbot	http://www.hotbot.com
Lycos	http://www.lycos.com
Excite	http://www.excite.com
WebCrawler	http://www.webcrawler.com

Note *Project loan is a search engine project by Google for providing internet access to rural and remote areas using high altitude helium filled balloons.*

Services of Internet

An Internet user can access to a wide variety of services such as electronic mail, file transfer, interest group membership, multimedia displays, real-time broadcasting, shopping, etc.

Some of the important services provided by the Internet are described below

Chatting

It is the online textual or multimedia conversation. It is a widely interactive communication process that takes place over the Internet.

Chatting, i.e. a virtual means of communication that involves the sending and receiving of messages, sharing audio and video between users located in any part of the world.

For example, Skype, Yahoo, Messenger, etc.

E-Mail (Electronic Mail)

E-mail is an electronic version of sending and receiving letter. Electronic mail lets you send and receive messages in electronic form.

E-mail address consists of two parts separated by @ symbol – the first part is user name and the second part is host name (domain name). However, spaces are not allowed within the E-mail address.
For example, arihantbooks@gmail.com

Here, *arihantbooks* is a username and *gmail.com* is a host name.

E-mail is transmitted between computer systems, which exchange messages or pass them onto other sites according to certain Internet protocols or rules for exchanging E-mail.

To use E-mail, a user must have an E-mail address. Emoticons or smileys are used in an E-mail to express emotions or feelings clearly. Storage area for E-mail messages is called mail box.

Video-Conferencing

It is a communication technology that integrates video and audio to connect users anywhere in the world as if they were in the same room.

This term usually refers to communication between three or more users who are in atleast two locations. Each user or group of users who are participating in a video-conference typically must have a computer, a camera, a microphone, a video screen and a sound system.

E-Learning

E-Learning (Electronic Learning) refers to the electronic mode of delivering learning, training or educational programs to users. It is the mode of acquiring knowledge by means of the Internet and computer based training programs.

E-Banking

E-Banking (Electronic Banking) is also known as Internet Banking or Online Banking.

E-Banking means that any user with a personal computer and a browser can get connected to his bank's website to perform any of the virtual banking functions. All the services that the bank has permitted on the Internet are displayed in the menu.

E-Shopping

E-Shopping (Electronic Shopping) or online shopping is the process of buying goods and services from merchants who sell on the Internet. Books, clothing, household appliances, toys, hardware, software and health insurance are just some of the hundreds of products, consumers can buy from an online store. Some E-shopping sites are Naaptol, Flipkart, Yebbi, Homeshop 18, etc.

E-Reservation

E-Reservation (Electronic Reservation) means making a reservation for a service via Internet. You need not personally go to an office or a counter to book/reserve railways and airways tickets, hotel rooms, tourist packages, etc.

Social Networking

It is the use of Internet based social media programs to make connections with friends, family, classmates, customers, clients, etc. It can be for social purposes, business purposes or both.

Social networking has grown to become one of the largest and most influential component of the web. The most popular social networking sites are Facebook, MySpace, Orkut, etc.

Common Social Networking Sites

LinkedIn

LinkedIn is an American site which provides business and employment oriented services. It was founded by Reid Hoffman in 2002.

LinkedIn is a platform that allows business people and professionals all over the world, regardless of their industry, to connect with other professionals.

It's great for meeting customers, getting in touch with vendors, recruiting new employees and keeping up with the latest updates in business or industry news.

Facebook

Facebook is an American social networking site which was founded in 2004 by Mark Zuckerberg. It helps the users to connect with their family, friends and one they know or want to know.

Facebook allows you to upload photos and maintain photo albums that can be shared with your friends.

It supports interactive online chat and the ability to comment on your friends's profile pages to keep in touch.

Twitter

It is an American company which provides social networking services. Besides this, Twitter also provides online news.

Twitter was founded in 2006 by Jack Dorsey, Noah Glass, Biz Stone and Evan Williams. It enables the user to send and read short 280 characters messages called tweets.

Registered users can read and post tweets while those who are not registered can only read them.

Instagram

It is a free, online photo sharing application and social network platform that was acquired by Facebook in 2012. Instagram allows users to edit and upload photos and short videos through a mobile app.

Users can add a caption to each of their posts and use hashtages and location based geotags to index these posts and make them searchable by other users within the app.

E-Commerce

E-Commerce (Electronic Commerce) includes sharing business information, maintaining business relationships and conducting business transactions by means of tele-communication networks or process of trading goods over the Internet.

Electronic Data Interchange (EDI) is the electronic transfer of a business transaction between sender or receiver.

Note *E-trading is the process of trading goods and items over the Internet.*

M-Commerce

M-Commerce (Mobile Commerce) provides the application for buying and selling goods or services through wireless Internet enabled handheld devices.

It involves new technologies, services and business models.

Note *Mobile commerce was launched in 1997 by Kevin Duffey.*

Tit-Bits

- **Cluster** is a group of servers that share work and may be able to back each other up if one server fails.
- With the **Webmail Interface**, E-mails are accessible from anywhere in the world.
- **Rich Text Formatting** helps the sender (of E-mail) format the contents of his/her E-mail message by applying font, size, bold, italic, etc.

Video-Conferencing Apps

1. Zoom

It is a proprietary software developed by Zoom Video Communications, in September, 2012. It is compatible with Windows, MacOs, iOS, Android, Chrome OS and Linux.

This platform is free for video-conferences of upto 100 participants at once, with a 40 minutes time limit. For longer or larger conferences with more features, paid subscriptions are available, costing $15-20 per month.

The highest plan supports upto 1000 concurrent participants for meetings lasting upto 30 hours.

Zoom security features include password-protected meetings, user authentication, waiting rooms, locked meetings, etc.

2. Google Meet

It is a video communciation service developed by Google, in 2017. It can run seamlessly on Android, iOS and Web platforms.

It can have upto 100 free participants for a time limit of 60 minutes. It can have 16 people on screen at a particular time. It can cost between $6 and $12 per month for paid version.

3. Microsoft Teams

It is a proprietary business communication platform developed by Microsoft, in 2017. It can schedule unlimited number of meetings and for a limited time i.e., upto 24 hours. It is compatible with Windows, MaC, iOS and Android.

Microsoft Teams requires a monthly subscription payment per user.

4. Skype

It is a proprietary tele-communications application developed by Skype Technologies (Microsoft), in August 2003. This app is compatible with Windows, Mac OS, Linux, Android, iOS, etc.

Skype can support upto 50 participants on a single video-conference, which is free. If you want to invite more than 50 people on skype for meetings, then you need to buy a paid subscription. The maximum number of participants that can be a part of the meeting is 250.

QUESTION BANK

1. The vast network of computers that connects millions of people all over the world is called
(1) LAN (2) Web
(3) Hypertext (4) Internet

2. The Internet is a system of
(1) software bundles
(2) web page
(3) website
(4) interconnected networks

3. The Internet is
(1) a large network of networks
(2) an internal communication system for a business
(3) a communication system for the Indian government
(4) All of the above

4. The Internet allows to
(1) send electronic mail
(2) view Web pages
(3) connect to servers all around the world
(4) All of the above

5. Which of the following is an example of connectivity?
(1) Internet (2) Floppy disk
(3) Power cord (4) Data

6. Internet was developed in the
(1) 1950s (2) 1960s
(3) 1970s (4) 1980s

7. Which of the following is not a type of broadband Internet connection?
(1) Cable (2) DSL (3) Dial-up (4) BPL

8. What does the acronym ISP stand for? **[IBPS Clerk 2014]**
(1) Internal Service Provider
(2) International Service Provider
(3) Internet Service Provider
(4) Internet Service Providing
(5) Internet Service Provision

9. Your business has contracted with another company to have them host and run an application for your company over the Internet. The company providing this service to your business is called an
(1) Internet Service Provider
(2) Internet Access Provider
(3) Application Service Provider
(4) Application Access Provider

10. DSL is an example of which connection?
(1) Network (2) Wireless
(3) Slow (4) Broadband

11. .... networks can be used for public internet access at hotspot such as restaurants, coffee shops, etc.
(1) Wi-Fi (2) WiMAX
(3) DSL (4) BPL

12. The standard protocol of the Internet is
(1) TCP/IP (2) Java
(3) HTML (4) Flash

13. In computing, IP address means
(1) International Pin
(2) Internet Protocol
(3) Invalid Pin
(4) Insert Pin

14. Each IP packet must contain **[IBPS Clerk 2011]**
(1) only source address
(2) only destination address
(3) source and destination addresses
(4) source or destination address
(5) None of the above

15. An IP address is .... bit number. **[SSC CGL 2017]**
(1) 8 bit (2) 16 bit (3) 32 bit (4) 64 bit

16. FTP can transfer files between any computers that have an Internet connection. Here, FTP stands for
(1) File Transfer Protocol
(2) Fast Text Processing
(3) File Transmission Program
(4) Fast Transmission Processor

17. Which of the following is the communication protocol that sets the standard used by every computer that accesses Web-based information?
(1) XML (2) DML (3) HTTP (4) HTML

18. What is the full form of HTTP? **[IBPS Clerk 2014]**
(1) HyperText Transfer Protocol
(2) HyperText Transition Protocol
(3) HyperText Transfer Program
(4) HyperText Transition Program
(5) HyperText Trivial Protocol

19. Documents converted to .... can be published on the Web. **[IBPS PO 2015]**
(1) a doc file
(2) http
(3) other than those given as options
(4) machine language
(5) HTML

20. HTML is used for designing Web pages. Here, HTML stands for **[UPSSSC Junior Engineer 2015]**

Or

The web uses the .... to request and serve web pages and programs. **[SSC CGL 2017]**
(1) High Transfer Machine Language
(2) High Transmission Markup Language
(3) HyperText Markup Language
(4) Hyper Transfer Markup Language

21. In HTML, tags consist of keywords enclosed within **[SSC CHSL 2013]**
(1) flower brackets (2) angular brackets <>
(3) parentheses () (4) square brackets [ ]

22. Telnet is a **[SSC CHSL 2012]**
(1) search engine (2) browser
(3) protocol (4) gateway

23. The .... service allows a group of Internet users to exchange their views on some common topic.
(1) nicnet (2) milnet
(3) telnet (4) usenet

24. Which protocol provides E-mail facility among different hosts? **[RBI Grade B 2014]**
(1) SMTP (2) FTP
(3) TELNET (4) SNMP
(5) None of these

25. What is the full form of VoIP? **[Clerk Mains 2017]**
(1) Voice of Internet Power
(2) Voice over Internet Protocol
(3) Voice on Internet Protocol
(4) Very optimised Internet Protocol

26. Which of the following protocols is used to receive Email? **[UPSSSC 2019]**
(a) SMTP (b) HTTP
(c) FTP (d) POP3

27. The Internet service that provides a multimedia interface to available resources is called
(1) FTP (2) world wide web
(3) telnet (4) gopher

28. The .... uses an addressing scheme known as URL indicate the location of files on the web. **[SSC CGL 2017]**
(1) java script (2) World Wide Web
(3) SQL (4) String

29. The WWW is made up of the set of interconnected .... that are linked together over the Internet.
(1) electronic documents
(2) Web pages
(3) files
(4) All of the above

30. What is a Website? **[RBI Grade B 2014]**
(1) A place from where we can get information in documents and files
(2) A site that is owned by any particular company
(3) A location on the world wide web
(4) A place from where we can access Internet
(5) None of the above

31. A Website address is a unique name that identifies a specific .... on the Web.
(1) Web browser (2) Website
(3) PDA (4) link

32. A (n) .... appearing on a Web page opens another document when clicked. **[SBI PO 2013]**
(1) anchor (2) URL
(3) hyperlink (4) reference
(5) heading

33. A reference to data that reader can directly follow by selecting or hovering is
(1) hypertext (2) hyperlink
(3) hyper media (4) hyper markup

34. A Website is a collection of **[IBPS Clerk 2012]**
(1) graphics (2) programs
(3) algorithms (4) web pages
(5) charts

35. .... is a collection of Web pages and .... is the very first page that we seen on opening of Website.
(1) Home page, Web page
(2) Website, Home page
(3) Web page, Home page
(4) Web page, Website
(5) None of the above

36. A browser is a **[RBI Grade B 2013]**
(1) tool for creating a database
(2) software program to view Web pages on the Internet
(3) printing device
(4) software program to delete a folder
(5) None of the above

37. Conference (Netscape), Netmeeting (Internet Explorer) enables (choose the option that best describes) **[RBI Grade B 2012]**
(1) sharing voice on the net
(2) live textual conferencing
(3) live audio conferencing
(4) live real time conferencing
(5) None of the above

38. To view information on the Web, you must have a **[RBI Grade B 2012]**
(1) cable modem
(2) web browser
(3) domain name server
(4) hypertext viewer
(5) None of these

39. Which key on a windows keyboard sets to full screen mode in most browsers? **[RRB NTPC 2016]**
A. F1 B. F10 C. F11 D. F12
(1) D (2) B
(3) A (4) C

40. In a web browser, which of the following is used to save frequently visited websites? **[RRB NTPC 2016]**
A. History B. Task Manager
C. Favourites D. Save as
(1) A (2) B (3) C (4) D

41. The .... which contains billions of documents called Web pages, is one of the more popular services on the Internet. **[SBI Clerk 2014]**
(1) Web server (2) Telnet
(3) Web (4) Collection
(5) None of these

42. What is URL? **[IBPS PO 2012]**
(1) A computer software program
(2) A type of programming object
(3) The address of a document or 'page' on the world wide web
(4) An acronym for unlimited resource for learning
(5) A piece of hardware

43. Which of the following is used by the browser to connect to the location of the Internet resources? **[IBPS Clerk 2011]**
(1) Linkers (2) Protocol
(3) Cable (4) URL
(5) None of these

44. An absolute .... contains the complete address of a file on the internet. **[SSC CGL 2017, UPPS Computer Assistant 2019]**
(1) JavaScript (2) URL
(3) SQL (4) String

45. Which of the following must be contained in a URL? **[IBPS PO 2012]**
(1) A protocol identifier
(2) The letters, WWW
(3) The unique registered domain name
(4) WWW and the unique registered domain name
(5) A protocol identifier, WWW and the unique registered domain name

46. URL identifies the location of a specific Web page on the Internet. Here URL stands for
(1) Uniform Read Locator
(2) Uniform Resource Locator
(3) Unicode Research Location
(4) United Research Locator
(5) None of the above

47. Which among the following terms means/refers to web address of a page?
(1) SMTP (2) IP (3) HTTP (4) URL
(5) MAC

48. The last three letters of the domain name describes the type of **[SSC FCI 2012]**
(1) organisation (domain name)
(2) connectivity
(3) server
(4) protocol

49. An educational institution would generally have the following in its domain name. **[IBPS Clerk 2011]**
(1) .org (2) .edu (3) .inst (4) .com
(5) .sch

50. Which of the following domains is used by profit business? **[SBI Clerk 2012]**
(1) .com (2) .edu (3) .mil (4) .net
(5) .org

51. Specialised programs that assist users in locating information on the Web are called **[RBI Grade B 2012]**
(1) information engines (2) locator engines
(3) Web browsers (4) resource locators
(5) search engines

52. Which among the following is a search engine?
(1) Internet Explorer (2) Flash
(3) Google (4) Firefox

53. A .... is the term used when a search engine returns a Web page that matches the search criteria. **[IBPS PO 2011]**
(1) blog (2) hit (3) link (4) view
(5) success

54. Project Loan is a search engine project by ...... for providing internet access to rural and remote areas using high altitude helium filled balloons. **[RRB NTPC 2016]**
A. Google B. Microsoft
C. Apple D. Yahoo
(1) D (2) C (3) B (4) A

55. Which of the following is always a part of E-mail address?
(1) Period (.) (2) At rate (@)
(3) Space () (4) Underscore (_)
(5) Angular Bracket (<)

56. Which one of the following is not an e-mail service provider?
(1) Hotmail (2) Gmail
(3) Bing (4) Yahoo mail
(5) Outlook

57. Junk e-mail is also called **[RBI Grade B 2012]**
(1) crap (2) spoof (3) sniffer script
(4) spool (5) spam

58. Which of the following is a valid e-mail address?
(1) name. Website@info@ed
(2) name. Website@info.in
(3) name. @Website.info.com
(3) Website. name@website.com
(5) Website@info.com

59. What is included in an E-mail address?
(1) Domain name followed by user's name
(2) User's name followed by domain name
(3) User's name followed by postal address
(4) User's name followed by street address
(5) None of the above

60. Which of the following elements are used in an e-mail to express emotions or feelings clearly?
(1) Acronyms (2) Abbreviations
(3) Rich text (4) Emoticons or smileys

61. If you receive an E-mail from someone you don't know, what should you do?
(1) Forward it to the police immediately
(2) Delete it without opening it
(3) Open it and respond to them saying you don't know them
(4) Reply and ask them for their personal information

62. Which of the following is not a term pertaining to E-mail? **[IBPS Clerk 2015]**
(1) PowerPoint (2) Inbox
(3) Sender (4) Receiver
(5) None of these

63. Storage area for E-mail messages is called
(1) folder (2) file
(3) mail box (4) directory

64. An E-mail address typically consists of a User ID followed by the.........sign and the domain name that manages the user's electronic post office box.
(1) # (2) @
(3) & (4) $

65. Video-conferencing is used for
(1) talking to each other
(2) communicating purpose
(3) live conversation
(4) All of the above

66. Who is the founder of 'facebook' which is currently the No. 1 social networking Website in India? **[SSC CGL 2013]**
(1) Orkut Buycukkokten
(2) Mark Zuckerberg
(3) Bill Gates
(4) Martin Cooper

67. The process of trading goods over the Internet is known as **[IBPS Clerk 2012]**
(1) E-selling n buying (2) E-trading
(3) E-finance (4) E-salesmanship
(5) E-commerce

68. A cookie **[IBPS Clerk 2012]**
(1) stores information about the user's web activity
(2) stores software developed by the user
(3) stores the password of the user
(4) stores the commands used by the user
(5) None of the above

69. Which of the following is most commonly used to identify return visitors to a website?
(1) Logged-in visitors
(2) Digital certificates
(3) Electronic time stamping
(4) Cookies

70. Which of the following terms is associated with Internet E-mail? **[SBI Clerk 2014]**
(1) Plotter (2) Slide Presentation
(3) Bookmark (4) Pie Chart
(5) Microsoft Excel

71. A stored link to a Web page, in order to have a quick and easy access to is later, is called **[RBI Grade B 2014]**
(1) WP-Link (2) Bookmark
(3) Field (4) Length
(5) None of these

72. A host on the Internet finds another host by its **[RBI Grade B 2014]**
(1) postal address (2) electronic address
(3) IP address (4) name
(5) None of these

ANSWERS

1. *(4)*	2. *(4)*	3. *(4)*	4. *(4)*	5. *(1)*	6. *(1)*	7. *(3)*	8. *(3)*	9. *(1)*	10. *(4)*
11. *(1)*	12. *(1)*	13. *(2)*	14. *(3)*	15. *(3)*	16. *(1)*	17. *(3)*	18. *(1)*	19. *(5)*	20. *(3)*
21. *(2)*	22. *(3)*	23. *(4)*	24. *(1)*	25. *(2)*	26. *(4)*	27. *(2)*	28. *(2)*	29. *(2)*	30. *(3)*
31. *(2)*	32. *(3)*	33. *(2)*	34. *(4)*	35. *(2)*	36. *(2)*	37. *(4)*	38. *(2)*	39. *(4)*	40. *(3)*
41. *(1)*	42. *(3)*	43. *(4)*	44. *(2)*	45. *(5)*	46. *(2)*	47. *(4)*	48. *(1)*	49. *(2)*	50. *(1)*
51. *(5)*	52. *(3)*	53. *(2)*	54. *(4)*	55. *(2)*	56. *(3)*	57. *(5)*	58. *(3)*	59. *(2)*	60. *(4)*
61. *(2)*	62. *(1)*	63. *(3)*	64. *(2)*	65. *(4)*	66. *(2)*	67. *(2)*	68. *(1)*	69. *(4)*	70. *(3)*
71. *(2)*	72. *(3)*								

CHAPTER

14

COMPUTER SECURITY

Computer security is also known as **cyber security** or **IT security**. It is a branch of information technology known as **information security**, which is intended to protect computers.

Sources of Cyber Attack

The most potent and vulnerable threat to computer users is virus attacks. A computer virus is a small software program that spreads from one computer to another and that interferes with computer operation.

The sources of cyber attack can be as follows

1. **Downloadable Programs** Downloadable files are one of the best possible sources of virus. Any type of executable file like games, screen saver are one of the major sources.
   If you want to download programs from the Internet, then it is necessary to scan every program before downloading them.
2. **Cracked Software** These softwares are another source of virus attacks. Such cracked forms of illegal files contain virus and bugs that are difficult to detect as well as to remove. Hence, it is always a preferable option to download software from the appropriate source.
3. **E-mail Attachments** These attachments are the most common source of viruses. You must handle E-mail attachments with extreme care, especially if the E-mail comes from an unknown sender.
4. **Booting from Unknown CD** When the computer system is not working, it is a good practice to remove the CD. If you do not remove the CD, it may start to boot automatically from the disk which enhances the possibility of virus attacks.

Methods to Provide Protection

There are four primary methods to provide protection

1. **System Access Control** It ensures that unauthorised users do not get into the system by encouraging authorised users to be security conscious.
2. **Data Access Control** It monitors who can access the data, and for what purpose. The system determines access rules based on the security levels of the people, the files and the other objects in your system.

3. **System and Security Administration** It performs offline procedures that make or break secure system.
4. **System Design** It takes advantage of basic hardware and software security characteristics.

Components of Computer Security

Computer security is associated with many core areas.

Basic components of computer security system are as follows

1. **Confidentiality** It ensures that data is not accessed by any unauthorised person.
2. **Integrity** It ensures that information is not altered by any unauthorised person in such a way that it is not detectable by authorised users.
3. **Authentication** Verification of a login name and password is known as authentication. It ensures that users are the persons they claim to be.
4. **Access Control** It ensures that users access only those resources that they are allowed to access.
5. **Non-Repudiation** It ensures that originators of messages cannot deny that they are not sender of the message.
6. **Availability** It ensures that systems work promptly and service is not denied to authorised users.
7. **Privacy** It ensures that individual has the right to use the information and allows another to use that information.
8. **Stenography** It is an art of hiding the existence of a message. It aids confidentiality and integrity of the data.
9. **Cryptography** It is the science of writing information in a 'hidden' or 'secret' form and in an ancient art. It protects the data during transmission and also the data stored on the disk.

Some terms commonly used in cryptography are as follows

(i) **Plain text** is the original message that is an input.

(ii) **Cipher** is a bit-by-bit or character-by-character transformation without regard to the meaning of the message.

(iii) **Cipher text** is the coded message or the encrypted data.

(iv) **Encryption** is the process of converting plain text to cipher text, using an encryption algorithm. The scrambling of code is known as encryption.

(v) **Decryption** is the reverse of encryption, i.e. converting cipher text to plain text.

Malware

Malware stands for Malicious Software. It is a broad term that refers to a variety of malicious programs that are used to damage computer system, gather sensitive information or gain access to private computer systems.

It includes computer viruses, worms, trojan horses, rootkits, spyware, adware, etc.

Some of them are described below

VIRUS

VIRUS stands for Vital Information Resources Under Siege. Computer viruses or perverse softwares are small programs that can negatively affect the computer. It obtains control of a PC and directs it to perform unusual and often destructive actions.

Viruses are copied itself and attached itself to other programs which further spread the infection. The virus can affect or attack any part of the computer software such as the boot block, operating system, system areas, files and application programs.

Note • *The first computer virus, creeper was a self-replicating program written in 1971 by Bob Thomas at VBN Technologies.*

• *The first boot sector PC virus named Brain, which was identified in the year 1986.*

Effects of VIRUS

There are many different effects that viruses can have on your computer, depending on the types of virus. *Some viruses can*

(i) monitor what you are doing.
(ii) slow down your computer's performance.
(iii) destroy all data on your local disk.
(iv) affect on computer networks.
(v) increase or decrease memory size.
(vi) display different types of error messages.
(vii) decrease partition size.
(viii) alter PC settings.
(ix) display arrays of annoying advertising.
(x) extend boot times.
(xi) create more than one partition.

Worm

A computer worm is a standalone malware computer program that replicates itself in order to spread to other computers. Often, it uses a computer network to spread itself, relying on security failures on the target computer to access it. Worms are hard to detect because they are invisible files.

For example, Bagle, I love you, Morris, Nimda, etc.

Note *Payload is a code designed in the form of a worm and for the purpose of expanding on a larger scale than the worm.*

Trojan

A Trojan, or Trojan Horse, is a non-self-replicating type of malware which appears to perform a desirable function but instead facilitates unauthorised access to the user's computer system.

Trojans do not attempt to inject themselves into other files like a computer virus. Trojan horses may steal information, or harm their host computer systems.

Trojans may use drive by downloads or install *via* online games or Internet driven applications in order to reach target computers. Unlike viruses, Trojan Horses do not replicate themselves.

For example, Beast, Sub7.Zeus, ZeroAccess Rootkit, etc.

Spyware

It is a program which is installed on a computer system to spy on the system owner's activity and collects all the information which is misused afterwards. It tracks the user's behaviour and reports back to a central source.

These are used for either legal or illegal purpose. Spyware can transmit personal information to another person's computer over the Internet.

For example, CoolWeb Search, FinFisher, Zango, Zlob Trojan, Keyloggers, etc.

Symptoms of Malware Attack

There is a list of symptoms of malware attack which indicates that your system is infected with a computer malware.

Some primary symptoms of malware attack are as follows

(i) Odd messages are displaying on the screen.
(ii) Some files are missing.
(iii) System runs slower.
(iv) PC crashes and restarts again and again.
(v) Drives are not accessible.
(vi) Anti-virus software will not run or installed.
(vii) Unexpected sound or music plays.
(viii) The mouse pointer changes its graphic.
(ix) System receives strange E-mails containing odd attachments or viruses.
(x) PC starts performing functions like opening or closing window, running programs on its own.

Some Other Threats to Computer Security

There are some other threats to computer security, which are described below

1. **Spoofing** It is the technique to access the unauthorised data without concerning to the authorised user. It accesses the resources over the network. It is also known as **Masquerade**.

   IP spoofing is a process or technique to enter in another computer by accessing its IP address.
2. **Salami Technique** It diverts small amounts of money from a large number of accounts maintained by the system.

3. **Hacking** It is the act of intruding into someone else's computer or network. Hacking may result in a Denial of Service (DoS) attack.

   It prevents authorised users from accessing the resources of the computer. A hacker is someone, who does hacking process.

4. **Cracking** It is the act of breaking into computers. It is a popular, growing subject on Internet.

   Cracking tools are widely distributed on the Internet. They include password crackers, trojans, viruses, war-dialers, etc.

Note *Cyber cracker is a person called who uses a computer to cause harm to people or destroy critical systems.*

5. **Phishing** It is characterised by attempting to fraudulently acquire sensitive information such as passwords, credit cards details, etc., by masquerading as a trustworthy person.
6. **Spam** It is the abuse of messaging systems to send unsolicited bulk messages in the form of E-mails. It is a subset of electronic spam involving nearly identical messages sent to numerous recipients by E-mails.
7. **Adware** It is any software package which automatically renders advertisements in order to generate revenue for its author. The term is sometimes used to refer the software that displays unwanted advertisements.
8. **Rootkit** It is a type of malware that is designed to gain administrative level control over a computer system without being detected.

Solutions to Computer Security Threats

Some safeguards (or solutions) to protect a computer system from accidental access are described below

Anti-virus Software

It is an application software that is designed to prevent, search for, detect and remove viruses and other malicious softwares like worms, trojans, adware and more.

It consists of computer programs that attempt to identify threats and eliminate computer viruses and other malware.

Some popular anti-viruses are

(i) Avast (ii) Avg
(iii) K7 (iv) Kaspersky
(v) Trend Micro (vi) Quick Heal
(vii) Symantec (viii) Norton
(ix) McAfee

Digital Certificate

It is the attachment to an electronic message used for security purposes. The common use of a digital certificate is to verify that a user sending a message is who he or she claims to be, and to provide the receiver with the means to encode a reply.

Digital Signature

It is an electronic form of a signature that can be used to authenticate the identity of the sender of a message or the signer of a document, and also ensure that the original content of the message or document that has been sent is unchanged.

Firewall

It can either be software based or hardware based and is used to help in keeping a network secure. Its primary objective is to control the incoming and outgoing network traffic by analysing the data packets and determining whether it should be allowed through or not, based on a pre-determined rule set.

A network's firewall builds a bridge between an internal network that is assumed to be secure and trusted, and another network, usually an external (inter) network, such as the Internet, that is not assumed to be secure and trusted. A firewall also includes or works with a proxy server that makes network requests on behalf of work station users.

Password

It is a secret word or a string of characters used for user authentication to prove identity or approval to gain access to a resource.

A password is typically somewhere between 4 to 16 characters, depending on how the computer system is setup. When a password is entered, the computer system is careful not to display the characters on the display screen, in case others might see it.

There are two common modes of password as follows

(i) **Weak Password** Easily remember just like names, birth dates, phone number, etc.

(ii) **Strong Password** Difficult to break and a combination of alphabets and symbols.

File Access Permission

Most current file systems have methods of assigning permissions or access rights to specific user and group of users. These systems control the ability of the users to view or make changes to the contents of the file system.

File access permission refers to privileges that allow a user to read, write or execute a file.

There are three specific file access permissions as follows

(i) Read permission (ii) Write permission

(iii) Execute permission

Terms Related to Security

1. **Eavesdropping** The unauthorised real time interception of a private communication such as a phone call, instant message is known as eavesdropping.
2. **Masquerading** The attacker impersonates an authorised user and thereby gain certain unauthorised privilege.
3. **Patches** It is a piece of software designed to fix problems with a computer program or its supporting data.

   This includes fixing security vulnerabilities and other bugs and improving the usability and performance.

Note *Vendor created program modifications are called patches.*

4. **Logic Bomb** It is a piece of code intentionally inserted into a computer's memory that will set off a malicious function when specified conditions are met. They are also called **slag code** and does not replicate itself.
5. **Application Gateway** This applies security mechanisms to specific applications such as File Transfer Protocol (FTP) and Telnet services.
6. **Proxy Server** It can act as a firewall by responding to input packets in the manner of an application while blocking other packets.

   It hides the true network addresses and used to intercept all messages entering and leaving the network.

Tit-Bits

- The legal right to use software based on specific restrictions is granted *via* **Software License**.
- **Software Piracy** means copying of data or computer software without the owner's permission.

QUESTION BANK

1. .... is a branch of information technology known as information security.
(1) Computer security (2) Cyber security
(3) IT security (4) All of these

2. It takes advantages of basic hardware and software security characteristics.
(1) System design
(2) Data access control
(3) System access control
(4) None of the above

3. Verification of a login name and password is known as **[IBPS Clerk 2014]**
(1) configuration (2) accessibility
(3) authentication (4) logging in
(5) Other than those given as options

4. If you are allowing a person on the network based on the credentials to maintain the security of your network, then this act refers to the process of **[IBPS PO 2016]**
(1) authentication (2) automation
(3) firewall (4) encryption
(5) None of these

5. The scrambling of code is known as
(1) encryption (2) firewalling
(3) scrambling (4) deception

6. The main reason to encrypt a file is to
(1) reduce its size
(2) secure it for transmission
(3) prepare it for backup
(4) include it in the start-up sequence

7. Cracked softwares are another source of
(1) e-mail attack (2) virus attack
(3) trojan horse (4) All of these

8. A malware is a
(1) program (2) hardware
(3) person (4) None of these

9. Softwares such as viruses, worms and trojan horses that have a malicious content, is known as **[IBPS Clerk 2014]**
(1) malicious software (malware)
(2) adware (3) scareware
(4) spyware (5) firewall

10. Viruses, trojan horses and worms are **[IBPS Clerk 2012]**
(1) able to harm computer system
(2) unable to detect if present on computer
(3) user-friendly applications
(4) harmless applications resident on computer
(5) None of the above

11. It is a self-replicating program that infects computer and spreads by inserting copies of itself into other executable code or documents.
(1) Keylogger (2) Worm
(3) Virus (4) Cracker

12. A computer virus is
(1) deliberately created
(2) created accidently
(3) produced as a result of some program error
(4) All of the above

13. ...... are often delivered to a PC through a mail attachment and are often designed to do harm. **[IBPS PO 2015]**
(1) Portals
(2) Spam
(3) Viruses
(4) Other than those given as options
(5) E-mail messages

14. Which of the following refers to dangerous programs that can be 'caught' of opening E-mail attachments and downloading software from the Internet? **[SBI PO 2014]**
(1) Utility (2) Virus (3) Honey Pot
(4) Spam (5) App

15. A program designed to destroy data on your computer which can travel to 'infect' other computers is called a **[RBI Grade B 2012]]**
(1) disease (2) torpedo
(3) hurricane (4) virus
(5) infector

16. If your computer rebooting itself, then it is likely that **[SBI Clerk 2012]**
(1) it has a virus
(2) it does not have enough memory
(3) there is no printer
(4) there has been a power surge
(5) it needs a CD-ROM

17. Computer virus is **[IBPS Clerk 2011]**
(1) a hardware (2) a windows tool
(3) a computer program (4) a system software
(5) None of the above

18. Which among the following is related to the internet and mail?
(1) Boot-Up
(2) Magnetic Tapes
(3) Applications Software
(4) Virus

19. The first PC virus was developed in
(1) 1980 (2) 1984 (3) 1986 (4) 1988

20. Which was the first PC boot sector virus?
(1) Creeper (2) Payload
(3) Bomb (4) Brain

21. The first computer virus is
(1) Creeper (2) PARAM
(3) The Famous (4) HARLIE

22. The .... of a threat measures its potential impact on a system. **[IBPS Clerk 2011]**
(1) vulnerabilities (2) counter measures
(3) degree of harm (4) susceptibility
(5) None of these

23. Which of the following is the type of software that has self-replicating software that causes damage to files and system?
(1) Viruses (2) Trojan horses
(3) Bots (4) Worms

24. Like a virus, it is also a self-replicating program. The difference between a virus and it is that it does not create copies of itself on one system it propagates through computer networks.
(1) Keylogger (2) Worm
(3) Cracker (4) None of these

25. A worm
(1) can automatically move in network
(2) can only be transferred with human intervention
(3) worms are harmless
(4) None of the above

26. Worm is a program that infects computer and spreads by inserting copies of itself into other executable code or documents.
(1) Self- attach (2) Self-replicating
(3) Non-self-replicating (4) Hacking

27. A computer virus normally attaches itself to another computer program known as a **[IBPS PO 2015]**
(1) host program (2) target program
(3) backdoor program (4) bluetooth
(5) trojan horse

28. These are program designed as to seem to being or be doing one thing, but actually being or doing another.
(1) Trojan horses (2) Keyloggers
(3) Worms (4) Crackers

29. Viruses that fool a user into downloading and/or executing them by pretending to be useful applications are also sometimes called
(1) trojan horses (2) keyloggers
(3) worms (4) crackers

30. A .... is a small program embedded inside of a GIF image.
(1) web bug (2) cookie
(3) spyware application (4) spam

31. Hackers often gain entry to a network be pretending to be at a legitimate computer.
(1) Spoofing (2) Forging
(3) IP spoofing (4) All of these

32. Attempt to gain unauthorised access to a user's system or information by pretending to be the user. **[IBPS RRB PO 2018]**
(1) Spoofing (2) Hacker
(3) Cracker (4) Phishing
(5) None of these

33. Which of the following enables to determine how often a user visited a website? **[IBPS Clerk 2014]**
(1) Hacker (2) Spammer
(3) Phish (4) Identify theft
(5) Cookie

34. A person who uses his or her expertise to gain access to other people computers to get information illegally or do damage is a **[Allahabad Bank PO 2011]**
Or
A person who uses his expertise for software. **[IBPS RRB PO 2018]**
(1) Spammer (2) Hacker
(3) Instant messenger (4) All of these
(5) None of these

35. Hackers
(1) have the same motive
(2) is another name of users
(3) many legally break into computer as long as they do not do any damage
(4) break into other people's computer

36. What is a person called who uses a computer to cause harm to people or destroy critical systems? **[IBPS Clerk 2014]**
(1) Cyber Terrorist
(2) Black-Hat-Hacker
(3) Cyber Cracker
(4) Hacktivist
(5) Other than those given as options

37. .... are attempts by individuals to obtain confidential information from you by falsifying their identity. **[IBPS Clerk 2013]**
(1) Phishing trips (2) Computer viruses
(3) Spyware scams (4) Viruses
(5) Phishing scams

38. Which of the following is a criminal activity attempting to acquire sensitive information such as passwords, credit cards, debits by masquerading as a trustworthy person or business in an electronic communication? **[IBPS Clerk 2010]**
(1) Spoofing (2) Phishing
(3) Stalking (4) Hacking
(5) None of these

39. All of the following are examples of real-security and privacy risks except **[IBPS Clerk 2014]**
(1) hackers (2) spam
(3) viruses (4) identify theft
(5) None of these

40. Junk E-mail is also called **[Union Bank of India 2011]**
(1) spam (2) spoof
(3) sniffer script (4) spool
(5) None of these

41. .... is a type of electronic spam where unsolicited messages are sent by e-mail.
(1) Trash mail (2) Cram mail
(3) Draft mail (4) Spam mail

42. Adware is something
(1) which is added to your computers
(2) by adding this performance of your computer increases
(3) software that gets different advertisement
(4) None of the above

43. It is a toolkit for hiding the fact that a computer's security has been compromised, is a general description of a set of programs which work to subvert control of an operating system from its legitimate (in accordance with established rules) operators.
(1) Rootkit (2) Keylogger
(3) Worm (4) Cracker

44. An anti-virus is a(n)
(1) program code
(2) computer
(3) company name
(4) application software

45. Anti-virus software is an example of
(1) business software
(2) an operating system
(3) a security
(4) an office suite

46. A digital signature is a/an **[SBI Clerk 2011]**
(1) scanned signature
(2) signature in binary form
(3) encrypting information
(4) handwritten signature
(5) None of the above

47. To protect yourself from computer hacker intrusions, you should install a **[RBI Grade B 2012]**
(1) firewall (2) mailer
(3) macro (4) script
(5) None of these

48. Which one of the following is a key function of firewall? **[SBI PO 2010]**
(1) Monitoring (2) Deleting
(3) Copying (4) Moving
(5) None of these

49. Mechanism to protect network from outside attack is
(1) firewall (2) anti-virus
(3) digital signature (4) formatting

50. A firewall operated by **[SBI Clerk 2010]**
(1) the pre-purchase phase
(2) isolating intranet from extranet
(3) screening packets to/from the network and provide controllable filtering of network traffic
(4) All of the above
(5) None of the above

51. Coded entries which are used to gain access to a computer system are called
(1) Entry codes
(2) Passwords
(3) Security commands
(4) Codewords

52. Password enables users to
(1) get into the system quickly
(2) make efficient use of time
(3) retain confidentiality of files
(4) simplify file structure

53. Which of the following is the combination of numbers, alphabets along with username used to get access to user account?
(1) Password (2) Username
(3) Titlename (4) Host-Id

54. .... refers to privileges that allow a user to read, write or execute a file.
(1) Authentication
(2) File access permission
(3) Password
(4) Firewall

55. The unauthorised real-time interception of a private communication such as a phone call, instant message is known as
(1) replay
(2) eavesdropping
(3) patches
(4) payloads

56. Vendor created program modifications are called **[Allahabad Bank PO 2011]**
(1) patches (2) anti-viruses
(3) hales (4) fixes
(5) overlaps

57. Which of the following is a computer's memory, but unlike a virus, it does not replicate itself ? **[SBI PO 2011]**
(1) Trojan Horse (2) Logic Bomb
(3) Cracker (4) Firewall
(5) None of these

58. They are also called slag code and does not replicate itself.
(1) Time (2) Anti-virus
(3) Logic bomb (4) All of these

59. It hides the true network addresses and used to intercept all messages entering and leaving the network.
(1) Logic bomb (2) Firewall
(3) Patches (4) Proxy server

60. The legal right to use software based on specific restrictions is granted *via* a **[RBI Grade B 2012]**
(1) software privacy policy
(2) software license
(3) software password manager
(4) software log
(5) None of the above

61. .... refers to the unauthorised copying and distribution of software. **[IBPS Clerk 2014]**

Or

Illegal copying and distribution of software is **[IBPS RRB PO 2018]**
(1) hacking (2) software piracy
(3) software literacy (4) cracking
(5) copyright

ANSWERS

1. *(4)*	2. *(1)*	3. *(3)*	4. *(1)*	5. *(1)*	6. *(2)*	7. *(2)*	8. *(1)*	9. *(1)*	10. *(1)*
11. *(3)*	12. *(1)*	13. *(3)*	14. *(2)*	15. *(4)*	16. *(1)*	17. *(3)*	18. *(4)*	19. *(3)*	20. *(4)*
21. *(1)*	22. *(3)*	23. *(4)*	24. *(2)*	25. *(1)*	26. *(2)*	27. *(5)*	28. *(1)*	29. *(1)*	30. *(3)*
31. *(3)*	32. *(1)*	33. *(1)*	34. *(2)*	35. *(4)*	36. *(3)*	37. *(1)*	38. *(2)*	39. *(2)*	40. *(1)*
41. *(4)*	42. *(3)*	43. *(1)*	44. *(4)*	45. *(3)*	46. *(3)*	47. *(1)*	48. *(1)*	49. *(1)*	50. *(3)*
51. *(2)*	52. *(3)*	53. *(1)*	54. *(2)*	55. *(2)*	56. *(1)*	57. *(2)*	58. *(3)*	59. *(4)*	60. *(2)*
61. *(2)*									

CHAPTER

15

OVERVIEW OF FUTURE TECHNOLOGY

'Future Technology' is a term generally used to describe a new technology, but it may also refer to the continuing development of an existing technology. It can have slightly different meaning when used in different areas, such as media, business, science or education.

This term commonly refers to technologies that are currently developing or that are expected to be available within the next 4 to 5 years. It is usually reserved for technologies that are creating, or expected to create, significant social or economic effects.

Introduction to Internet of Things (IoT)

IoT is a network in which all physical objects are connected to the Internet through network devices and exchange data. IoT allows objects to be controlled remotely across existing network infrastructure.

The goal of IoT is to extend to Internet connectivity from standard devices like computer, mobile, tablet to relatively dumb devices like a toaster.

Components of IoT

1. **Sensors** Sensors or devices are key components that help you to collect real time data from the surrounding environment.

   All this data may have various levels of complexities. It could be a simple temperature monitoring sensor or it may be in the form of the video feed.

2. **Connectivity** All the collected data is sent to a cloud infrastructure. The sensors should be connected to the cloud using various media of communication. These communication media include Mobile or Satellite networks, Bluetooth, Wi-Fi, WAN, etc.

3. **Data Processing** Once the data is collected and it gets to the cloud, the software performs processing on the gathered data.

   This process can be just checking the temperature, reading on devices like AC or heaters. However, it can sometimes also be very complex like identifying objects using computer vision on video.

4. **User Interface** The information made available to the end user in some ways, that can achieve by triggering alarms on their phones or notifying through text or E-mails. Also, a user sometimes might also have an interface through which he/she can actively check in on their IoT system.

Advantages of IoT

1. **Technical Optimisation** IoT technology helps a lot in improving technologies and making them better.
2. **Reduce Waste** IoT offers real time information leading to effective decision-making and management of resources.
3. **Improved Customer Engagement** IoT allows you to improve customer experience by detecting problems and improving the process.
4. **Improved Data Collection** Traditional data collection has its limitations and it's designed for passive use. With the help of IoT, limitation of data collection has reduced.

Disadvantages of IoT

1. **Security** As the IoT systems are inter-connected and communicate over networks, the system offer little control despite any security measures. It can reduce the various kinds of network attacks.
2. **Privacy** Even without the active participation of user, IoT system provides substantial personal data in maximum detail.
3. **Complexity** The designing, developing, maintaining and enabling the large technology to IoT system is quite complicated.

Big Data Analytics

It is the process of collecting, organising and analysing large sets of data to discover patterns and other useful information. Big data analytics can help organisations to better understand the information contained within the data and well also help to identify the data that is most important to the business and future business decisions.

Characteristics of Big Data Analytics

1. **Variety** Variety of big data analytics refers to structured, unstructured and semi-structured data, i.e. gathered from multiple sources. While in the past, data could only be collected from spreadsheets and databases, today data comes in an array of forms such as E-mails, PDFs, Photos, etc.
2. **Velocity** It essentially refers to the speed at which data is being created in real time.

   In a broader prospect, it comprises the rate of change and linking of incoming data sets at varying speeds.
3. **Volume** Big data indicates huge volumes of data that is being generated on a daily basis from various sources like social media platforms, business processes, machines, networks, etc.

Applications of Big Data Analytics

1. **Government** When government agencies are harnessing and applying analytics to their big data, they have improvised a lot in terms of managing utilities, running agencies, dealing with traffic congestion or preventing the crimes.
2. **Heathcare** Big data analytics had already started to create a huge difference in the healthcare sector. With the help of predictive analytics, medical professionals can now able to provide personalised healthcare services to individual patient.
3. **Banking** The banking sector relies on big data for fraud detection. Bit data tools can efficiently detect fraudulent acts in real time such as misuse of credit/debit cards, etc.
4. **Manufacturing** Using big data analytics, manufacturing industry can improve product quality and output by minimising waste.

Virtual Reality

It is a computer interface which tries to mimic real world beyond the flat monitor to give an immersive 3D visual experiences.

It is an artificial environment that is created with software and presented to the user in such a way that the user suspends belief and accepts it as a real environment.

On a computer, virtual reality is primarily experienced through two of the five senses, i.e. sight and sound.

Virtual Reality (VR) technology is applied to advance fields of machine, engineering, education, design, training and entertainment.

Applications of Virtual Reality

1. **In Gaming** Virtual technology's devices are used for virtual gaming experiences. Along with this, devices such as Wi-Fi Remote, Playstation Move/Eye, Kinect are based on virtual reality which track and send input of the players to the game.
2. **In Healthcare** Healthcare is one of the applications where virtual reality could have the most significant impact. Healthcare professional can now use virtual models to prepare them for working on a real body.
3. **In Education** Virtual reality has been adopted in education too. It improves teaching and learning process. With virtual reality, a large group of students can interact with one another within a three dimensional environment.
4. **In Entertainment** Virtual reality is being used in the entertainment industry to boost experiences with 3D films and increase emotional connection with them and/or the characters.
5. **In Business** Virtual reality has also been adopted in business. It is now being used for virtual tours of a business environment, training of new employees and this also gives new employees a 360° view of every product.

Artificial Intelligence (AI)

AI is an area of computer science that emphasises the creation of intelligent machines that work and react like humans.

The term may also be applied to any machine that exhibits traits associated with a human mind such as learning and problem-solving.

Knowledge engineering is a core part of AI research. Machines can often act and react like humans only if they have abundant information relating to the world. Artificial intelligence must have access to objects, categories, properties and relations between all of them to implement knowledge engineering.

Types of Artificial Intelligence

1. **Weak AI** It embodies a system designed to carry out one particular job. Weak AI systems include video games such as the chess and personal assistants such as Amazon's Alexa.
2. **Strong AI** These are the systems that carry on the tasks considered to be human like. These tend to be more complex and complicated systems. These kinds of systems can be found in applications like self-driving cars or in hospital operating rooms.

Applications of Artificial Intelligence

1. **In Business** Robotic process automation is being applied to highly repetitive tasks normally performed by humans.
2. **In Gaming** Over the past few years, AI has become an integral part of the gaming industry. Infact, one of the biggest accomplishments of AI is in the gaming industry.
3. **In Healthcare** Companies are applying machine learning to make better and faster diagnoses than humans. One of the best known technologies is IBM's Watson. It understands natural language and can respond to questions asked from it.

4. **In Banking** A lot of banks have already adopted AI based systems to provide customer support, detect anomalies and credit card frauds. AI solutions can be used to enhance security across a number of business sectors, including retail and finance.
5. **In Autonomous Vehicles** Just like humans, self-driving cars need to have sensors to understand the world around them and a brain to collect, processes and choose specific actions based on information gathered.

Blockchain Technology

The blockchain is an encrypted, distributed database that records data. It is a digital ledger of any transactions, contracts that need to be independently recorded.

In financial sector, with blockchain technology the participants can interact directly and can make transactions across the internet without the interference of a third party.

With all the fraud resistant features, the blockchain technology holds the potential to revolutionise various business sectors and make processes smarter, secure, transparent and more efficient compared to the traditional business processes.

Advantages of Blockchain Technology

1. It allows smart devices to speak to each other better and faster.
2. It allows the removal of intermediaries that are involved in record keeping and transfer of assets.
3. It provides durability, reliability and longevity with decentralised network.
4. The data that is entered in blockchain based systems is immutable which prevents against fraud through manipulating transactions and the history of data.
5. It brings everyone to the highest degree of accountability.

Challenges of Blockchain Technology

1. To verify all the transactions, huge power, i.e. electricity is required.
2. Blocks in a chain must be verified by the distributed network and it can take time. So, transaction speed can be an issue.

3D Printing / Additive Manufacturing

3D printing is a manufacturing process where a 3D printer creates three dimensional objects by depositing materials layer by layer in accordance to the object's 3D digital model.

It uses data Computer Aided Design (CAD) software or 3D object scanners to direct hardware to deposit material, layer upon layer, in precise geometric shapes. As its name implies, additive manufacturing adds material to create an object.

How does 3D Printing Work?

Here are the steps taken in creating a 3D object

1. Produce a 3D model using CAD or equivalent 3D design software.
2. Convert the drawing to the STL (Standard Tessellation Language) file format, which is a format developed for 3D printers.
3. Transfer the STL file to the computer that controls the 3D printer. From there, you can specify the size and orientation for printing.
4. It prepare for a new print job based on the requirement of the 3D printer. This may include refilling whichever additive you are using to make your object.
5. Begin the building process. Since, each layer is usually about 0-1 mm thick, this can be take anywhere from hours to days to complete depending on the object's size.
6. Remove the object from the printer and avoid any contact with toxins or hot surfaces.

7. Performs any post processing needed, which may involve brushing off residue or washing the object.
8. Use your new printed object.

Examples of 3D Printing

- Architectural scale model and maquettes.
- Eyewear.
- Dental Products.
- Design (lamps, furniture, etc).
- Reconstructing bones and body parts in forensic pathology.
- Reconstructing heavily damaged evidence. retrieved from a crime scene.

Robotics Process Automation (RPA)

RPA is the use of specialised computer programs, known as software robots, to automate and standardise repeatable business processes.

Robotic process automation does not involve any form of physical robots. Software robots mimic human activities by interacting with applications in the same way that a person does. Robot process automation enables business professionals to easily configure software robots to automate repetitive, routine work between multiple systems, filling in automation gaps to improve business processes.

Applications of RPA

1. **Customer Service** RPA can help companies offer better customer service by automating contact center tasks, including verifying E-signatures, uploading scanned documents and verifying information for automatic approvals or rejections.
2. **Healthcare** Medical organisation can use RPA for handling patient records, claims, customer support, account management, billing, reporting and analytics.
3. **Supply Chain Management** RPA can be used for procurement, automating order processing and payments, monitoring inventory levels and tracking shipments.
4. **Financial Services** Companies in the financial services industry can use RPA for foreign exchange payments, automating account opening and closing, managing audit requests and processing insurance claims.
5. **Accounting** Organisations can use RPA for general accounting, operational accounting, transactional reporting and budgeting.

Fifth Generation (5G)

5G standard is for broadband cellular networks, which cellular phone companies began deploying worldwide in 2019. It is designed to improve network connections by addressing the legacy issues of speed, latency and utility, which the earlier generations and the current generation of mobile networks could not address.

5G is promised to deliver data speed at a rate 100 times faster than 4G networks.

Globally, 5G network deployment is rapidly moving from trials to early commercialisation. In India, network operators like Airtel, Vodafone, Idea, Reliance, Jio, etc., have already partnered with vendors like Ericsson, Huawai and Samsung for planned trials sometime by the end of year 2020, before the service's forecast commercial rollout in 2020.

Advantages of 5G

1. **Greater Speed in Transmission** Speed in transmissions can approach 15 or 20 Gbps. By being able to enjoy a higher speed, we can access files, programs and remote applications in direct without waiting.
2. **Lower Latency** Latency is the time that elapses since we give an order on our device until the action occurs. In 5G, the latency will be ten times less than in 4G, being able to perform remote actions in real time.
3. **Greater Number of Connected Devices** With 5G, the number of devices that can be connected to the network increases greatly, it will go to millionaire scale per square kilometer.

All connected devices will have access to instant connections to the internet, which in real time will exchange information with each other.

4. **New Technology Options** As speed of network has improved, more and more tasks are being transitioned to the world of smart devices from the world of computers. With the rising network speeds, this could open new doors for smart devices that may not have been available.

Disadvantages of 5G

1. **Obstruction can Impact Connetivity** The range of 5G connectivity is not great as the frequency waves are only able to travel a short distance. Added to this setback is the fact that 5G frequency is interrupted by physical obstructions such as trees, towers, walls and buildings. The obtrusions will either block, disrupt or absorb the high frequency signals. To counter this setback, the telecom industry is extending cell towers to increase the broadcast distance.
2. **Limitation of Rural Access** While 5G might bring about real connectivity for the predominantly urban areas, those living in the rural area, they will not necessarily benefit from the connection.
3. **Battery Drain on Devices** When it comes to cellular devices connected to 5G, it seems the batteries are not able to operate for a significant period of time. The battery technology needs to advance to allow for this enhanced connectivity, where a single charge will power a cellphone for a full day.

   Alongside depleted batteries, users are reporting that cellphones are getting increasing hot when operating on 5G.

QUESTION BANK

1. Which of the following is a term generally used to describe a new technology, but it may also refer to the continuing development of an existing technology?
(1) Future technology
(2) Future skills
(3) IoT
(4) Future processing

2. Future technology is usually reserved for .... that are creating, or expected to create, significant social or economic effects.
(1) processing (2) skills
(3) things (4) technologies

3. Which of the following objects to be controlled remotely across existing network infrastructure?
(1) Future skills (2) IoT
(3) Cloud computing (4) Saas

4. ...... are key components that help you to collect live data from the surrounding environment.
(1) Sensors (2) Connectivities
(3) User interfaces (4) None of these

5. IoT system provides substantial personal data in ...... detail.
(1) minimum (2) maximum
(3) medium (4) All of these

6. Big data analytics is used in
(1) government (2) healthcare
(3) banking (4) All of these

7. Which of the following is the process of collecting, organising and analysing large sets of data to discover patterns and other useful information?
(1) Future skills (2) IoT
(3) Big data analytics (4) User interface

8. ...... of big data analytics refers to structured, unstructured and semi-structured data that is gathered from multiple sources.
(1) Feature (2) Analysis
(3) Privacy (4) Variety

9. Virtual reality is primarily experienced through ...... of the five senses.
(1) Two (2) Three
(3) Four (4) One

10. Which technology devices is used for virtual gaming experiences?
(1) Future skills (2) Virtual
(3) Big data analytics (4) Blockchain

11. Virtual reality technology is applied to advance fields of
(1) medicine (2) engineering
(3) education (4) All of these

12. ...... is an area of computer science that emphasises the creation of intelligent machines that work and react like humans.
(1) Artificial intelligence
(2) Introduction to things
(3) Future skills
(4) Robotics

13. Which type of artificial intelligence embodies a system designed to carry out one particular job?
(1) Weak AI (2) Strong AI
(3) Both (1) and (2) (4) None of these

14. AI is important because it can help to solve immensely difficult issues in
(1) entertainment (2) education
(3) health (4) All of these

15. Which of the following is an encrypted and distributed database that records data?
(1) Automation
(2) Blockchain
(3) Artificial intelligence
(4) Future skills

16. Blockchain mechanism brings everyone to the highest degree of ....
(1) Accountability (2) Availability
(3) Performance (4) Analytics

17. Additive manufacturing uses ...... software.
(1) System (2) Application
(3) Utility (4) CAD

18. Example(s) of 3D printing is/are
(1) Eyewear
(2) Dental products
(3) Architectural Scale Model
(4) All of the above

19. RPA is the use of specialised computer programs known as ......
(1) future skills
(2) user interface
(3) software robot
(4) artificial intelligence

20. What is/are the business benefit(s) of RPA?
(1) Increased accuracy
(2) No interruption of work
(3) Low technical barriers
(4) All of the above

21. ......can help companies offer better customer service by automating contact center tasks.
(1) RPA (2) Interface
(3) Additive (4) Blockchain

ANSWERS

1. *(1)*	2. *(4)*	3. *(2)*	4. *(1)*	5. *(2)*	6. *(4)*	7. *(3)*	8. *(4)*	9. *(1)*	10. *(2)*
11. *(4)*	12. *(1)*	13. *(1)*	14. *(4)*	15. *(2)*	16. *(1)*	17. *(4)*	18. *(4)*	19. *(3)*	20. *(4)*
21. *(1)*									

CHAPTER

16

MISCELLANEOUS

IT Gadgets

A gadget is a device that has a specific function, in addition usually has small dimensions.

Some IT gadgets are as follows

1. Smartphone

Smartphone is a cell phone that allows you to do more than make phone calls and send text messages. Smartphones use browsers and other softwares like a computer system. There is a touch screen in smartphone to interact with user means use to enter data or information.

In turn, a smartphone also offers capabilities such as support for biometrics, video chatting, digital assistants and much more.

Smartphones are run with the help of mobile operating systems such as Android, Symbian, iOS, BlackBerry and Windows mobile.

2. Smart Band

Smart bands are called smart bracelets or connected bracelets. In most cases, they have a simple form and their main function is to track and analyse your movements during the day.

Most smart bands have a pedometer and sometimes also an optical heart rate sensor and various other sensors.

3. Bluetooth Speaker

Bluetooth speakers are a type of wireless speakers that are aimed at improving convenience and comfort of listening to music.

These speakers work with the wireless technology. They use short wavelength UHF radiowaves in the ISM band from 2.4 to 2.485 GHz and builds Personal Area Network (PAN).

4. Smart Watch

Smart watch is a wearable computing device that closely resembles a wrist watch. Many smart watches are connected to a smart phone that notifies the user of incoming calls, e-mail messages and notifications from applications.

Some smart watches are able to make calls. Smart watches can be smart bands with pedometers and heart rate monitors to help users track their health.

5. Google Glass

It is a wearable computing device which comes with a head mounted display, in the form of eye glasses. The google glasses function as a hands free smart phone, letting users access the mobile internet browser, camera, maps, calendar and other apps by voice commands.

6. Drone Camera

It is the device that captured of still images and video by a remotely-operated or autonomous Unmanned Aerial Vehicle (UAV), also known as Unmanned Aircraft System (UAS) or more commonly as a drone.

7. Spy Pen

Spy pen is an ordinary pen with a hidden digital camera concealed inside, allowing the user to take video, images often with the pen placed in a shirt pocket or held in a hand. This type of device is usually used for protection, safety and even investigation.

Mobile Applications

Mobile applications (also known as mobile apps) are software programs developed for mobile devices such as smartphones and tablets.

Most Widely used Mobile Apps in India

1. BHIM (Bharat Interface for Money) App

This app is used to make simple, easy and quick payment transactions using UPI (Unified Payment Interface). BHIM app was launched by PM Narendra Modi on 30th December, 2016.

It has been named after the architect of the India's Constitution Dr. B R Ambedkar, the BHIM app is an aggregator of UPI services across various banks.

The aim to launch the BHIM app is to make cashless payments.

Key features of BHIM app

- Money can be transfered using mobile number or account number.
- It helps to receive and transfer money directly into bank accounts.
- Its two factor authentication ensures your transactions are safe and secure.
- It provides transaction history.

2. IRCTC Connect App

IRCTC (Indian Railway Catering and Tourism Corporation) has released its official Android App called IRCTC Connect on 9th October, 2014.

Key features of IRCTC Connect app

- User can check the schedule of trains.
- User can check the availability of the seat in any train.
- It can keep the passengers up-to-date for their train journey.

3. MyGov App

It was launched on 26th July, 2014. Google became the first multinational firm to collaborate with MyGov.

Key features of MyGov app

- MyGov provides you a readymade interface to connect with the government on regular basis.
- It also gives you the opportunity to connect and engage with government representatives through live chats.

4. DigiLocker App

It is a digital locker to store all official documents that linked to both Aadhaar Card and cellphone numbers.

It was launched by Prime Minister on 1st July, 2015. Initially, it had 100 MB space and was later increased to 1 GB.

Key features of DigiLocker app

- It provides an online account with 1GB storage space to Aadhaar holders.
- These documents can be shared by residents with governments or other registered organisations.

5. GARV (Grameen Vidyutikaran) App

GARV app is used to monitor the progress of the rural electrification scheme and provide real-time updates.

This app was launched in October, 2015. GARV app is an important part of the Digital India Initiative of the Government and will contribute in further development of the villages.

Key features of GARV app

- Using this app, user can know that which village will be electrified next.
- You can also check the progress status of any village.

6. mPassport Seva App

It is a easy to use app that provides all the functions as available over the Passport Seva Portal such as New User Registration, existing user login, etc.

This app was launched on the occasion of Sixth Passport Seva Divas on 26th June, 2018.

Key features of mPassport Seva app

- Users are able to search for a Passport Seva Kendra or District passport cell.
- mPassport Seva app lets you check both passport application status and RTI status.

7. Voter Helpline App

This app provides the convenience to all the people for finding their names in the electoral roll, submitting online forms, checking status of the application, filling complaints and receiving the reply.

Voter helpline app was launched in February, 2019. The main objective of this app is to motivate and educate voters.

Key features of Voter Helpline app

- It provides a single point of service and information delivery to voters across the country.
- Voter can register to vote for new voter registration.

8. Google Maps

It is a web based service that provides detailed information about geographical regions and sites around the world. It offers satellite imagery, aerial photography, street maps, 360° interactive panoramic views of streets, etc.

Key features of Google Maps app

- Provides route planner, allowing users to find available directions through driving, or walking.
- Began offering traffic data as a coloured overlay on top of roads.

Digital Financial Tools

A new era of financial system in India was started. In this era, efforts were made up to improve methodology and responsibilities of financial system.

Financial tools are terms used to describe organisations that deal with the management of money.

Some terms that used in digital financial tools are

UPI (Unified Payment Interface)

UPI is a digital mode that helps you transfer funds from one bank to another without using any account number, bank name, account type and IFSC code. It facilitates users to access multiple bank accounts with a single mobile application.

UPI has been launched by the National Payments Corporation of India, also known as NPCI. In conjunction with the Reserve Bank of India and Indian Banks' Association, NPCI has framed this network.

It is similar in mechanisms like the RuPay system through which debit and credit cards function.

Note *There are 4 or 6 digits required to set UPI pin.*

e-Wallet

e-Wallet (Mobile Wallet) is a type of prepaid account in which a user can store his/her money for any future online transaction. An e-Wallet is protected with a password.

With the help of an e-Wallet, one can make payments for groceries, online purchases and flight tickets among others. An e-Wallet needs to be linked with the individual's bank account to make payments. The main objective of e-Wallet is to make paperless money transaction easier.

Types of e-Wallet

There are various types of e-Wallet as follows

Paytm

Paytm is India's largest mobile commerce platform launched in 2010 by Vijay Shekhar Sharma. Paytm Wallet, because of its amazing marketing and operation strategies, has been able to capture maximum market share of this industry.

The wallet can be used to sent money directly to bank accounts as well. Paytm is the first company in India to receive a license from the Reserve Bank of India (RBI) to start a payment bank.

Freecharge

This service was launched in September, 2015 and has ever since introduced many attractive features. This will enable all customers to send and receive funds through the UPI system.

Freecharge UPI will allow users to initiate fund transfers instantly on a 24/7 basis on all 365 days in a year, including bank holidays.

Mobikwik

It is a digital wallet that can be used for a number of online payments including transferring money, accepting payments, mobile recharge, payment of utility bills, such as electricity, DTH, online shopping, etc.

Mobikwik has received an approval from the Reserve Bank of India (RBI) and has tied up with a number of retails and online merchants in the country.

Oxigen

It is a digital wallet service through which users can avail all the services offered by Oxigen. It is an application based service that can be used on all types of smartphone such as Android, Windows and IOs.

Oxigen wallet is a semi-closed wallet as per RBI guidelines. You can transfer funds from your wallet to your bank account.

Airtel Money

Airtel Money is the Mobile Wallet from the successful and popular telecom company Airtel.

It allows you to use your smartphone as an electronic wallet to make and receive payments. Originally launched in 2012, this app offers customers with an efficient alternative to cash transactions.

Citrus Wallet

It is an app that lets you send money to and receive from anyone who has a phone number or E-mail. It lets your transfer money to friends, colleagues and family members within seconds.

You can pay canteen, movie, travel and party bills with ease. You can even see all your past transactions and keep a track of your spending patterns.

SBI Buddy

SBI had launched the Mobile Wallet Buddy in August 2015, in 13 different languages in collaboration with Master Card.

It is a digital platform by which customers can simply send or ask money from any of their contacts even if they do not have an SBI account.

PayZapp

PayZapp offered by HDFC bank is an ideal mobile payment wallet.

With PayZapp, you can shop on your mobile at partner apps, bus and movie tickets, groceries, book flight tickets and hotels, pay bills and recharge your mobile.

With the HDFC PayZapp e-Wallet app, customers do not need to depend on card based transactions and can enjoy secure and convenient payments.

PhonePe

PhonePe wallet has launched by Sameer Nigam and Rahul Chari.

It provides an online payment system based an Unified Payments Interface (UPI), which is a new process in electronic funds transfer launched by National Payments Corporation of India (NPCI).

Using PhonePe, users can send and receive money, recharge mobile, data cards, buy gold and shop online and offline.

QUESTION BANK

1. ...... is a device that has a specific function, in addition usually has small dimensions.
(1) Software (2) Gadget
(3) Keyboard (4) Scanner

2. Which of the following is an IT gadget?
(1) Keyboard (2) Wrist watch
(3) Smart watch (4) Joystick

3. Smart band is also known as
(1) Smart bracelet
(2) Connected bracelet
(3) Both (1) and (2)
(4) Smart watch

4. Which of the following is a wearable computing device which comes with a head mounted display in the form of eyeglasses?
(1) Google glass (2) Drone camera
(3) Spy pen (4) Smart goggle

5. This IT gadget is used for protection, safety and even investigation.
(1) Drone camera (2) Smart watch
(3) Bluetooth speaker (4) Spy pen

6. Smart watches can be smart bands with
(1) pedometers (2) heart rate monitors
(3) Both (1) and (2) (4) None of these

7. Smart phone also offers capability(ies) such as
(1) support for biometrics
(2) video chatting
(3) digital assistants
(4) All of the above

8. Bluetooth speakers work with the
(1) Wireless technology
(2) Wired technology
(3) Both (1) and (2)
(4) None of the above

9. BHIM app is used to make simple, easy and quick payment transactions using
(1) Password (2) UPI
(3) Phone number (4) Aadhar number

10. App launched by IRCTC was known as
(1) IRCTC Connect (2) IRCTC App
(3) IRCTC Launcher (4) IRCTC Booking

11. Paytm is India's largest mobile payment and commerce platform founded by
(1) Aditya Sharma (2) Vijay Shekhar Sharma
(3) Sidhartha Sharma (4) Shekhar Verma

12. This mobile app reduces the use of physical documents and fake documents. What is this?
(1) GARV app (2) DigiLocker app
(3) MyGov app (4) OnlineRTI app

13. UPI has been launched by
(1) RBI (2) IFSC
(3) USSD (4) NPCI

14. Which of the following is a system that facilitates users to access multiple bank accounts with a single mobile application?
(1) UPI (2) AEPS
(3) USSD (4) OTP

15. How many digits are there to set UPI Pin?
(1) 3 (2) 7 (3) 5 (4) 6

16. e-Wallet is also known as .... protected with a password.
(1) Pocket wallet (2) Mobile wallet
(3) Prepaid wallet (4) None of the above

17. Which of the following facilities is available under e-Wallet?
(1) Cash back (2) Rewards
(3) Both (1) and (2) (4) None of the above

18. Which e-Wallet is the first company in India to receive a license from RBI to start a payment bank?
(1) Freecharge (2) Mobikwik
(3) Airtel Money (4) Paytm

19. Which bank offered the e-Wallet app PayZapp?
(1) ICICI (2) HDFC
(3) SBI (4) PNB

20. .... provides an online payment system based on Unified Payment Interface (UPI).
(1) PayZapp (2) PhonePe
(3) SBI Buddy (4) Citrus

21. Who has launched the Paytm e-Wallet?
(1) Vijay Shekhar Sharma
(2) Sameer Saxena
(3) Sameer Nigam
(4) Rahul Chari

22. PhonePe wallet has been launched by
(1) Sameer Nigam (2) Rahul Chari
(3) Both (1) and (2) (4) None of these

23. Oxigen wallet is a ...... wallet as per RBI guidelines.
(1) Open (2) Closed
(3) Semi-closed (4) Semi-open

24. SBI Buddy has launched the Mobile Wallet Buddy in ......
(1) 10 languages (2) 13 languages
(3) 17 languages (4) 22 languages

ANSWERS

1. *(2)*	2. *(3)*	3. *(3)*	4. *(1)*	5. *(4)*	6. *(3)*	7. *(4)*	8. *(1)*	9. *(2)*	10. *(1)*
11. *(2)*	12. *(2)*	13. *(4)*	14. *(1)*	15. *(4)*	16. *(2)*	17. *(3)*	18. *(4)*	19. *(2)*	20. *(2)*
21. *(1)*	22. *(3)*	23. *(4)*	24. *(2)*						

PRACTICE SET 1

1. Which of the following is an example of non-volatile memory?
   (1) ROM (2) RAM (3) LSI (4) VLSI
2. Which of the following is a unit of measurement used in computer system?
   (1) Byte (2) Megabyte
   (3) Gigabyte (4) All of these
3. Which command is used to copy files?
   (1) Copy (2) Disk copy
   (3) Type (4) All of these
4. Which of the following is/are fundamental component(s) of IoT?
   (1) Sensors (2) Connectivity
   (3) Data processing (4) All of these
5. Which is not an advantage of using computerised spreadsheets?
   (1) Flexibility moving entries
   (2) Speed of calculation
   (3) Ability to generate tables
   (4) Cost of initial setup
6. To select several cells or ranges that are not touching each other, what would you do while selecting?
   (1) Hold down the Ctrl key
   (2) Hold down the Shift key
   (3) Hold down the Alt key
   (4) Hold down Ctrl + Shift key
7. Which of the following are selected in PowerPoint to play a PowerPoint slide show for previewing?
   (1) View, Slide Sorter (2) View, Slide
   (3) View, Slide Show (4) View, Outline
8. Which of the following are used in MS-PowerPoint, in order to see all the slides on one screen?
   (1) View, Slide Sorter
   (2) View, Slide
   (3) View, Master
   (4) View, Slide Show
9. Which of the following is not a property of fibre optic cabling?
   (1) Transmits at faster speed than copper cabling
   (2) Easier to capture a signal from than copper cabling
   (3) Very resistant to interference
   (4) Carries signals as light waves
10. What does fibre use to transmit data?
    (1) Vibrations (2) Sound
    (3) Electrical current (4) Light
11. To cut the selected text, these keys should be pressed.
    (1) Ctrl + C (2) Ctrl + D
    (3) Ctrl + V (4) Ctrl + X
12. It is the abuse of messaging systems to send unsolicited bulk messages in the form of e-mails.
    (1) Spam (2) Adware
    (3) Hacking (4) Cracking
13. .... is a software that is designed to prevent, detect and remove viruses.
    (1) Firewall (2) Digital certificate
    (3) Anti-virus software (4) Password
14. The secondary storage devices can only store data, but they cannot perform
    (1) arithmetic operations
    (2) fetch operations
    (3) logic operations
    (4) All of the above
15. Which of the following is/are the type(s) of QR Code?
    (1) Static QR Code (2) Dynamic QR Code
    (3) Both (1) and (2) (4) None of these
16. In computer science, by information we mean
    (1) any output coming out from computer
    (2) processed data put in an intelligent form
    (3) a report printed by the computer
    (4) plural of data

17. DEL command is used to
(1) delete files
(2) delete directory
(3) delete labels
(4) delete contents of file

18. C++ language was developed by
(1) Dennis Ritchie
(2) Charles Babbage
(3) Niklaus Wirth
(4) Bjarne Stroustroup

19. The bar which shows your current status in the document is called
(1) status (2) standard
(3) format (4) title

20. You can delete one character to the left of cursor using ...... key.
(1) backspace (2) delete
(3) edit (4) format

21. You can use .... alignment to centralise your text.
(1) right (2) centre
(3) left (4) All of these

22. In MS-Word, Spell Check is under which menu?
(1) Edit (2) Review
(3) Tool (4) Format

23. Grammatical errors are shown in which colour?
(1) Red (2) Green
(3) Blue (4) Black

24. This part of operating system manages the essential peripherals, such as the keyboard, screen, disk drives and parallel and serial ports.
(1) Basic input/output system
(2) Secondary input/output system
(3) Peripheral input/output system
(4) Marginal input/output system

25. The following are all computing devices, except
(1) notebook computers
(2) cellular telephones
(3) digital scanners
(4) personal digital assistants

26. It performs basic tasks such as controlling input and output devides, processing of instructions, controlling and allocating memory, managing files.
(1) The platform
(2) Application software
(3) Operating system
(4) The motherboard

27. Servers are computers that provide resources to other computers connected to a
(1) mainframe (2) network
(3) supercomputer (4) client

28. A Database Management System (DBMS) is a
(1) hardware system used to create, maintain and provide controlled access to a database
(2) hardware system used to create, maintain and provide uncontrolled access to a database
(3) software system used to create, maintain and provide uncontrolled access to a database
(4) software system used to create, maintain and provide controlled access to a database

29. When data changes in multiple lists and all lists are not updated, this causes
(1) data redundancy
(2) information overload
(3) duplicate data
(4) data inconsistency

30. Words that a programming language has set aside for its own use.
(1) Control words (2) Reserved words
(3) Control structures (4) Reserved keys

31. A .... is a software program used to view web pages.
(1) Site (2) Host (3) Link (4) Browser

32. Mobile Wallet Buddy app had launched by
(1) SBI (2) HDFC
(3) RBI (4) NPCI

33. Which term identifies a specific computer on the Web and the main page of the entire site?
(1) URL (2) Website Address
(3) Hyperlink (4) Domain Name

34. Which one of the following is a valid binary number?
(1) 120 (2) 459 (3) 10101 (4) 10108

35. Process to verify the username and password is known as
(1) logic (2) checkin
(3) authentication (4) authorisation

36. The unit of speed used for super computer is
(1) KB (2) FLOPS (3) GB (4) EB

37. HTTP stands for
(1) HyperText Transfer Protocol
(2) HighText Transfer Protocol
(3) HyperTechnical Transfer Protocol
(4) HyperText Test Protocol

38. 23 will be written in binary as
(1) 10111 (2) 11111
(3) 10011 (4) 11011

39. Which one of the following is a good password?
(1) My date of birth (2) My school name
(3) My name (4) Timepass_09

40. It is also known as temporary memory.
(1) ROM (2) RAM
(3) DVD (4) CD

41. Which of the following is a correct syntax of URL?
(1) udinra.com (2) .udinra.com
(3) udinra.html.com (4) @udinra.

42. Which of the following is the communication protocol that sets the standard used by every computer that accesses Web based information?
(1) XML (2) DML
(3) HTTP (4) HTML

43. Which software will you use to write a business letter?
(1) MS-Word (2) MS-Excel
(3) MS-PowerPoint (4) MS-Access

44. An operating system is said to be multitasking if
(1) more than one programs can run simultaneously
(2) more than one users can work simultaneously
(3) Either (1) or (2)
(4) None of the above

45. What is E-commerce?
(1) Buying and selling takes place over Internet
(2) Buying and selling takes place over phone call
(3) Buying and selling takes place over both Internet and phone call
(4) Buying and selling takes place over either Internet or phone call

46. The default extensions of Microsoft Word 2007 and Microsoft Excel 2007 files are
(1) .doc,.xsl (2) .doc,.xml
(3) .docx,.xlsx (4) .docx,.xml

47. 30,000 bytes is nearly equal to
(1) 30 KB (2) 3MB
(3) 3GB (4) 3TB

48. EDI stands for
(1) Electronic Data Internet
(2) Electronic Data Interchange
(3) Electric Device Internet
(4) Electric Data Interchange

49. Which command is used to permanently delete files or folders?
(1) Shift + Delete (2) Ctrl + Delete
(3) Alt + Delete (4) Delete

50. While working with MS-DOS, which command transfers a specific file from one disk to another?
(1) Copy (2) Diskcopy
(3) Time (4) Rename

ANSWERS

1. *(1)*	2. *(4)*	3. *(1)*	4. *(4)*	5. *(4)*	6. *(1)*	7. *(3)*	8. *(1)*	9. *(2)*	10. *(4)*
11. *(4)*	12. *(1)*	13. *(3)*	14. *(4)*	15. *(3)*	16. *(2)*	17. *(1)*	18. *(4)*	19. *(1)*	20. *(1)*
21. *(2)*	22. *(2)*	23. *(2)*	24. *(1)*	25. *(2)*	26. *(3)*	27. *(2)*	28. *(4)*	29. *(4)*	30. *(2)*
31. *(4)*	32. *(1)*	33. *(1)*	34. *(3)*	35. *(3)*	36. *(2)*	37. *(1)*	38. *(1)*	39. *(4)*	40. *(2)*
41. *(1)*	42. *(3)*	43. *(1)*	44. *(1)*	45. *(1)*	46. *(3)*	47. *(1)*	48. *(2)*	49. *(1)*	50. *(1)*

PRACTICE SET 2

1. First Supercomputer developed in India was
(1) PARAM (2) Aryabhatta
(3) Buddha (4) CRAY-1

2. Which of the following is an example of computer software?
(1) Impact printer (2) Console
(3) Device driver (4) OCR

3. Programmers use a variety of .... to communicate instructions to the computer.
(1) programming languages
(2) system languages
(3) high level languages
(4) low level languages

4. Which of the following displays the contents of the active cell?
(1) Active cell (2) Formula bar
(3) Menu bar (4) Name box

5. A software used to convert source program instructions to object instructions is known as
(1) compiler (2) assembler
(3) interpreter (4) language processor

6. In computers, IC chip is used which is made of
(1) chromium (2) iron oxide
(3) silica (4) silicon

7. PhonePe Wallet launched by
(1) Sameer Nigam (2) Airtel
(3) HDFC (4) None of these

8. Which of the following is a part of central processing unit?
(1) Printer (2) Keyboard
(3) Mouse (4) ALU

9. Which of the following statements is wrong?
(1) Windows XP is an operating system
(2) Linux is owned and sold by Microsoft
(3) Photoshop is a graphical design tool by Adobe
(4) Linux is a free and open source software

10. Pointing device includes the following except
(1) maouse (2) light pen
(3) trackball (4) keyboard

11. The term 'operating system' means
(1) a set of programs which controls computer working
(2) the way a user operates the computer system
(3) conversion of high level language to machine language
(4) the way computer operator works

12. The physical arrangement of elements on a page is referred to as the document's
(1) feature (2) format
(3) pagination (4) grid

13. Most Websites have a main page, the......which acts as a doorway to the rest of the Website pages.
(1) search engine (2) home page
(3) browser (4) URL

14. Input, output and processing devices grouped together represent a(n)
(1) mobile device
(2) information processing cycle
(3) circuit board
(4) computer system

15. Which type of computer could be found in a digital watch?
(1) Mainframe computer
(2) Supercomputer
(3) Embedded computer
(4) Notebook computer

16. Which of the following is not true about computer files?
(1) They are collection of data saved to a storage medium
(2) Every file has a file name
(3) A file extension is established by the user to indicate the file's contents
(4) Files usually contain data

17. All of the following are examples of real security and privacy risks except
(1) hackers (2) spam
(3) viruses (4) identity theft

18. What type of technology allows you to use your finger, eye or voice print to secure your information resources?
(1) Haptics (2) Caves
(3) Biometrics (4) RFID

19. Main memory is
(1) Random Access Memory
(2) Random Only Memory
(3) Serial Access Memory
(4) Storage Memory

20. The smallest and fastest computer, imitating brain working is
(1) Supercomputer
(2) Quantum computer
(3) Param-1000
(4) IBM chips

21. A Compact Disc (CD) is which type of data storage?
(1) Magnetic (2) Optical
(3) Electrical (4) Electro-mechanical

22. Which of the following is not a language for computer programming?
(1) Windows (2) Pascal
(3) Basic (4) Cobol

23. First computer mouse was built by
(1) Douglas Engelbart
(2) William English
(3) Oaniel Coogher
(4) Robert Zawacki

24. Java Language was developed by
(1) Ada Byron (2) Bill Gates
(3) Blaise Pascal (4) James Gosling

25. Which of the following is not one of the four major data processing functions of a computer?
(1) Gathering data
(2) Processing data into information
(3) Analysing the data or information
(4) Storing the data or information

26. When you connect to this service your computer is communicating with a server at your Internet Service Provider (ISP). What does this refer?
(1) Modem (2) Internet
(3) Intranet (4) Server

27. A collection of related files is called a
(1) character (2) field
(3) database (4) record

28. Hard disk drives and CD drives are examples of
(1) backup (2) storing
(3) storage (4) All of these

29. You would use ...... software to create spreadsheets, type documents and edit photos.
(1) application (2) utility
(3) system (4) operating

30. Which of the following is a computer that support hundreds or thousands of users simultaneously?
(1) Super (2) Macro
(3) Mini (4) Mainframe

31. Which device is a microprocessor-based computing device?
(1) Personal computing
(2) Mainframe
(3) Workstation
(4) Server

32. An E-mail account includes a storage area, often called a/an
(1) attachment (2) hyperlink
(3) mailbox (4) IP address

33. Data becomes......when it is presented in a format that people can understand and use it.
(1) processed (2) graphs
(3) information (4) presentation

34. A set of computer programs that helps a computer monitor itself and function more efficiently is a/an
(1) windows
(2) system software
(3) DBMS
(4) application software

35. A ...... converts all the statements in a program in a single batch and the resulting collection of instructions is placed in a new file.
(1) converter (2) compiler
(3) interpreter (4) instruction

36. The advantages(s) of IoT is/are
(1) Technical optimisation
(2) Improved data collection
(3) Reduce waste
(4) All of the above

37. Which one of the following is not a broadband communication medium?
(1) Microwave (2) Fibre optic cable
(3) Twisted pair (4) Co-axial cable

38. Which of the following performs modulation and de-modulation?
(1) Co-axial cable (2) Satellite
(3) Modem (4) Optical fibre

39. The earliest calculating device is
(1) Abacus (2) Difference Engine
(3) Clock (4) Pascaline

40. The function of Esc key is
(1) to end the action
(2) to go to last action
(3) to repeat the last action
(4) to begin the action

41. This device is usually used for protection, safety and even investigation.
(1) Drone camera (2) Spy pen
(3) Tablet (4) All of these

42. The memory sizes in mainframe computers and advanced technology micro computers are expressed as
(1) bytes (2) kilobytes
(3) bits (4) megabytes

43. Computer virus is a
(1) hardware
(2) windows tool
(3) a computer program
(4) a system software

44. Each model of a computer has a unique
(1) assembly language
(2) machine language
(3) high level language
(4) All of the above

45. A website is a collection of
(1) graphics (2) programs
(3) algorithms (4) web pages

46. To move the cursor to the end of the document, press
(1) Ctrl + Esc
(2) Ctrl + End
(3) Ctrl + B
(4) Ctrl + C

47. The shortcut method to print documents is
(1) Ctrl + A (2) Ctrl + B
(3) Ctrl + P (4) Ctrl + C

48. Viruses, Trojan horses and worms are
(1) able to harm computer system
(2) unable to detect if affected on computer
(3) user-friendly applications
(4) harmless applications resident on computer

49. Which of the following is used to browse Internet?
(1) Skype (2) Facebook
(3) Google (4) Firefox

50. Internet banking is done over
(1) Internet (2) mobile
(3) laptop (4) computer

ANSWERS

1. *(1)*	2. *(3)*	3. *(1)*	4. *(2)*	5. *(4)*	6. *(4)*	7. *(1)*	8. *(4)*	9. *(2)*	10. *(4)*
11. *(1)*	12. *(2)*	13. *(2)*	14. *(4)*	15. *(3)*	16. *(3)*	17. *(2)*	18. *(3)*	19. *(1)*	20. *(2)*
21. *(2)*	22. *(1)*	23. *(1)*	24. *(4)*	25. *(3)*	26. *(2)*	27. *(4)*	28. *(4)*	29. *(1)*	30. *(4)*
31. *(1)*	32. *(3)*	33. *(3)*	34. *(2)*	35. *(2)*	36. *(4)*	37. *(1)*	38. *(3)*	39. *(1)*	40. *(1)*
41. *(2)*	42. *(4)*	43. *(3)*	44. *(2)*	45. *(4)*	46. *(2)*	47. *(3)*	48. *(1)*	49. *(4)*	50. *(1)*

PRACTICE SET 3

1. What are the contents that are lost on turning OFF the computer?
(1) Storage (2) Input
(3) Output (4) Memory

2. Assembly language is a
(1) machine language
(2) high level programming language
(3) low level programming language
(4) language for assembling computers

3. The binary system is a number system to the base
(1) 2 (2) 4
(3) 8 (4) 10

4. Which of the following is not an example of hardware?
(1) Scanner (2) Printer
(3) Monitor (4) Interpreter

5. What happens when we try to delete the files on the floppy?
(1) The files get moved to the recycle bin
(2) Files on a floppy cannot be deleted
(3) The files get deleted and can be restored again from Recycle Bin
(4) The files get deleted and cannot be restored again

6. Paytm wallet was launched by
(1) Sameer Nigam
(2) Rahul Chari
(3) Vijay Shekhar Sharma
(4) Vijay Bhatkar

7. Computer system is comprised of
(1) hardware, programs, information, people and network
(2) hardware, software, procedures, networks and people
(3) hardware, programs, information, people and procedures
(4) hardware, programs, processors, procedures, networks and people

8. Press .... to move the insertion point to the address box or to highlight the URL in the address.
(1) Alt + D (2) Alt + A
(3) Shift + Tab (4) Tab + Ctrl

9. In analog computer,
(1) input is first converted to digital form
(2) input is never converted to digital form
(3) output is displayed in digital form
(4) All of the above

10. VGA stands for
(1) Video Graphics Array
(2) Visual Graphics Adapter
(3) Virtual Graphics Access
(4) Volatile Graphics Adapter

11. Which of the following memory chips is faster?
(1) There is no certainty
(2) DRAM
(3) SRAM
(4) DRAM is faster for larger chips

12. An improvement on the ENIAC was made possible with the help of the mathematician
(1) John Von Neumann (2) Albert Federer
(3) Lord Smith (4) Tim Shown

13. A person who used his or her expertise to gain access to other people's computers to get information illegally or to do damage is a
(1) spammer (2) hacker
(3) instant messenger (4) programmer

14. Which of the following is an example of storage devices?
(1) Magnetic disks (2) Tapes
(3) DVDs (4) All of these

15. The basic computer processing cycle consists of
(1) input, processing and output
(2) systems and application
(3) data, information and applications
(4) hardware, software and storage

16. Video processor consists of ...... and ......, which store and process images.
(1) CPU and VGA (2) CPU and memory
(3) VGA and memory (4) VGI and DVI

17. .... are specially designed computers that perform complex calculations extremely rapidly.
(1) Servers (2) Supercomputers
(3) Laptops (4) Mainframes

18. Which of the following domains is used by profit business?
(1) .com (2) .edu (3) .mil (4) .net

19. To reload a Web page, press the ...... button.
(1) redo (2) reload
(3) restore (4) refresh

20. Where are you likely to find an embedded operating system?
(1) On a desktop operating system
(2) On a networked PC
(3) On a network server
(4) On a PDA

21. A popular way to learn about computers without ever, going to a classroom is called
(1) I-learning (2) isolated learning
(3) E-learning (4) E-commerce

22. It ensures that data is not accessed by any unauthorised person.
(1) Integrity (2) Authentication
(3) Confidentiality (4) Access control

23. In 5G, speed of transmission can approx
(1) 5 or 7 Gbps (2) 7 or 10 Gbps
(3) 10 or 15 Gbps (4) 15 or 20 Gbps

24. Mobile commerce is best described as
(1) the use of kiosks in marketing
(2) transporting products
(3) buying and selling goods/services through wireless handheld devices
(4) using notebook PC's in marketing

25. A(n) .... is composed of several computers connected together to share resources and data.
(1) Internet (2) network
(3) backbone (4) hyperlink

26. Which of the following is a storage device that uses rigid, permanently installed magnetic disks to store data/information?
(1) Floppy disk (2) Hard disk
(3) Permanent disk (4) Optical disc

27. Which of the following contains chips connected to the system board and is also a holding area for data instructions and information?
(1) Program (2) Mouse
(3) Internet (4) Memory

28. The smallest unit of information about a record in a database is called a
(1) cell (2) field
(3) record (4) query

29. A(n) .... is a special visual and audio effect applied in PowerPoint to text or content.
(1) animation (2) flash
(3) wipe (4) dissolve

30. Which of the following is a programming language for creating special programs like Applets?
(1) Java (2) Cable
(3) Domain name (4) Net

31. The piece of hardware that converts your computer's digital signal to an analog signal that can travel over telephone lines is called a
(1) red wire (2) blue cord
(3) tower (4) modem

32. Personal computers can be connected together to form a
(1) server (2) supercomputer
(3) network (4) enterprise

33. You can keep your personal files/folders in
(1) My folder (2) My doucments
(3) My files (4) My text

34. Which of the following is a graphic package?
(1) CorelDraw (2) MS-Word
(3) MS-Excel (4) All of these

35. Default paper size of Word documents is
(1) letter (2) A4
(3) A3 (4) Both (1) and (3)

36. Which PowerPoint view displays each slide of the presentation as a thumbnail and is useful for rearranging slides?
(1) Slide Sorter (2) Slide Show
(3) Slide Master (4) Notes Page

37. Example of impact printer is
(1) jet printer
(2) thermal printer
(3) laser printer
(4) daisy wheel printer

38. Notification area is found on which side of the desktop?
(1) Left (2) Right
(3) Centre (4) Both (1) and (2)

39. Which shortcut key is used to search for a file or a folder?
(1) F1 (2) F2
(3) F3 (4) F5

40. Which of the following is not a layer of OSI model?
(1) Host to network (2) Application
(3) Network (4) Transport

41. Who invented Linux?
(1) J Presper Eckert and John W Mauchly
(2) Dennis M Ritchie
(3) Seymour Papert
(4) Linus Torvalds

42. Which command is used to search all the text files in any drive?
(1) File1.txt (2) *.txt
(3) _*.txt (4) File2.txt

43. Motherboard is also known as
(1) electronic board
(2) Printed Circuit Board (PCB)
(3) combined device board
(4) Both (1) and (3)

44. The collection of links throughout the Internet creates an interconnected/network called
(1) WWW (2) Web
(3) World Wide Web (4) All of these

45. Every computer has a(n) .... many ....
(1) operating system, client system
(2) operating system, instruction sets
(3) application programs, operating system
(4) operating system, application programs

46. .... are basically questions based on the data available in a database.
(1) Forms (2) Queries
(3) Tables (4) Reports

47. Which number system is used by computer to store data and perfom calculations?
(1) binary (2) octal
(3) decimal (4) hexadecimal

48. Cache is a
(1) permanent memory
(2) temporary memory
(3) storage device
(4) Both (2) and (3)

49. Zoom app is compatible with
(1) Windows (2) MacOS
(3) iOS (4) All of these

50. What is 'Quick Heal'?
(1) Antivirus (2) Vaccine
(3) Program (4) Software

ANSWERS

1. (4)	2. (3)	3. (1)	4. (4)	5. (4)	6. (3)	7. (3)	8. (1)	9. (2)	10. (1)
11. (3)	12. (1)	13. (2)	14. (4)	15. (1)	16. (2)	17. (2)	18. (1)	19. (4)	20. (4)
21. (3)	22. (2)	23. (4)	24. (3)	25. (2)	26. (2)	27. (4)	28. (2)	29. (1)	30. (1)
31. (4)	32. (3)	33. (2)	34. (1)	35. (2)	36. (1)	37. (4)	38. (2)	39. (3)	40. (1)
41. (4)	42. (2)	43. (2)	44. (4)	45. (4)	46. (2)	47. (1)	48. (2)	49. (4)	50. (1)

PRACTICE SET 4

1. Devices that enter information and let you communicate with the computer are called
(1) software (2) output devices
(3) hardware (4) input devices

2. Which among the following was the first graphical Web browser?
(1) Mosaic (2) WAIS
(3) CERN (4) Gopher

3. The free available known repair of software bug on Internet is called
(1) version (2) add on
(3) tutorial (4) patch

4. The first computer virus is
(1) Creeper (2) PARAM
(3) The Famous (4) HARLIE

5. What is the function of the central processing unit of a computer?
(1) Creates invoices
(2) Performs calculations and processing
(3) Deletes data
(4) Corrupts the data

6. The feature that keeps track of the right margin is
(1) find and replace (2) wordwrap
(3) right justified (4) left justified

7. When a real-time telephone call between people is made over the Internet using computers, it is called
(1) a chat session
(2) an e-mail
(3) an instant message
(4) internet telephony

8. An electronic device, operating under the control of information, that can accept data, process the data, produce output and store the results for future use, is called
(1) input (2) computer
(3) software (4) hardware

9. In ER diagram, relationship type is represented by
(1) ellipse (2) dashed ellipse
(3) rectangle (4) diamond

10. Which of the following will be used if a sender of E-mail wants to bold, italic, etc., the text message?
(1) Rich signature (2) Rich text
(3) Rich format (4) Both (2) and (3)

11. It is a set of one or more attributes that can uniquely identify tuples within the relation.
(1) Primary key (2) Candidate key
(3) Foreign key (4) Alternate key

12. All of the logic and mathematical calculations done by the computer happen in/on the
(1) system board
(2) central control unit
(3) motherboard
(4) central processing unit

13. The operating system called UNIX is typically used for
(1) desktop computers (2) laptop computers
(3) supercomputers (4) web servers

14. The ...... file format is a method of encoding pictures on a computer.
(1) HTML (2) JPEG
(3) FTP (4) URL

15. Which of the following is a program that uses a variety of different approaches to identify and eliminate spam?
(1) Directory search
(2) Anti-spam program
(3) Web server
(4) Web storefront creation package

16. To access properties of an object, the mouse technique to use is
(1) dragging (2) dropping
(3) right-clicking (4) shift-clicking

17. Computers use the ...... number system to store data and perform calculations.
(1) binary (2) octal
(3) decimal (4) hexa-decimal

18. ...... are attempts by individuals to obtain confidential information from you by falsifying their identity.
(1) Phishing trips (2) Computer viruses
(3) Spyware scams (4) Viruses

19. Why is it unethical to share copyrighted files with your friends?
(1) It is not unethical, because it is legal
(2) It is unethical because the files are being given for free
(3) Sharing copyrighted files without permission breaks copyright laws
(4) It is not unethical because the files are being given for free

20. Google Meet can have upto 100 free participants for a time limit of
(1) 20 minutes (2) 30 minutes
(3) 40 minutes (4) 60 minutes

21. The processor is a ...... chip plugged onto the motherboard in a computer system.
(1) LSI (2) VLSI
(3) ULSI (4) XLSI

22. To change selected text to all capital letters, click the Change Case button, then click
(1) Sentence Case
(2) Lower case
(3) Upper case
(4) Capitalise each word

23. An online discussion group that allows direct 'live' communication is known as
(1) web crawler
(2) chat group
(3) regional service provider
(4) hyperlink

24. The cost of a given amount of computing power has......dramatically with the progress of computer technology.
(1) stayed the same
(2) changed proportionally with the economy
(3) increased
(4) decreased

25. Another name for a pre-programmed formula in Excel is
(1) range (2) graph (3) function (4) cell

26. If your computer keeps re-booting itself, then it is likely that
(1) it has a virus
(2) it does not have enough memory
(3) there is no printer
(4) there has been a power surge

27. A program for viewing web pages is called
(1) word processor (2) spreadsheet
(3) protocol (4) a browser

28. The term used to describe the instructions that tell the computer what to do is ....
(1) hardware (2) software
(3) storage (4) input/output

29. Codes consisting of lines of varying widths or lengths that are computer-readable are known as
(1) an ASCII code (2) a magnetic tape
(3) an OCR scanner (4) a bar code

30. What type of keys are 'Ctrl' and 'Shift'?
(1) Adjustment (2) Function
(3) Modifier (4) Alpha-numeric

31. In Word, you can change page margins by
(1) dragging the scroll box on the scroll bars
(2) deleting the margin boundaries on the ruler
(3) dragging the margin boundaries on the ruler
(4) clicking the right mouse button on the ruler

32. Assembly instructions are in the form of
(1) binary digits (2) mnemonics
(3) general english (4) All of these

33. The speed of clock frequency or microprocessor is measured in
(1) hertz (2) baud rate
(3) cps (4) bits

34. UPI (Unified Payment Interface) has been launched by
(1) RBI (2) HDFC
(3) NPCI (4) SBI

35. What type of device is a $3\frac{1}{2}$ inch floppy drive?
(1) Input (2) Output
(3) Software (4) Storage

36. What utility do you use to transfer files and exchange messages?
(1) Web browsers (2) WWW
(3) E-mail (4) Hypertext

37. Which unit controls the movement of signals between CPU and I/O?
(1) ALU (2) Control unit
(3) Memory unit (4) Secondary storage

38. What are different views to display a table in MS-Access?
(1) Pivot table (2) Design view
(3) Datasheet view (4) All of these

39. The three main parts of the processor are
(1) ALU, Control Unit and Registers
(2) ALU, Control Unit and RAM
(3) Cache, Control Unit and Registers
(4) Control Unit, Registers and RAM

40. Portable computer, also known as laptop computer, weighing between 4 and 10 pounds is called
(1) PDA
(2) Supercomputer
(3) Mainframe computer
(4) Notebook computer

41. All the characters, that a device can use are called its
(1) skill set
(2) character alphabet
(3) characters codes
(4) character set

42. .... is a technique that is used to send more than one call over a single line.
(1) Digital transmission
(2) Infrared transmission
(3) Digitising
(4) Multi-plexing

43. Supercomputers
(1) are smaller in size than mainframe computers
(2) are common in majority of households
(3) contain thousands of microprocessors
(4) are rarely used by researchers due to their lack of computing capacity

44. Which of the following is the second largest measurement of RAM?
(1) Terabyte (2) Megabyte
(3) Byte (4) Gigabyte

45. The systems BIOS and ROM chips are called
(1) software (2) firmware
(3) hardware (4) bootware

46. Today, the common form of RAM is built with
(1) transistors
(2) vacuum tubes
(3) semi-conductors ICs
(4) super conductors ICs

47. A modern electronic computer is a machine that is meant for
(1) doing quick mathematical calculations
(2) input, storage, manipulation and outputting of data
(3) electronic data processing
(4) performing repetitive tasks accurately

48. Speakers and headphones are .... devices.
(1) Input (2) Input/Output
(3) Software (4) Output

49. Which type of memory holds the program to start up the computer?
(1) ROM (2) RAM
(3) Cache (4) Static

50. The PC (Personal Computer) and the Apple Macintosh are examples of two different
(1) platforms (2) applications
(3) programs (4) storage devices

ANSWERS

1. *(4)*	2. *(1)*	3. *(4)*	4. *(1)*	5. *(2)*	6. *(3)*	7. *(4)*	8. *(2)*	9. *(4)*	10. *(4)*
11. *(1)*	12. *(4)*	13. *(4)*	14. *(2)*	15. *(2)*	16. *(3)*	17. *(1)*	18. *(1)*	19. *(3)*	20. *(4)*
21. *(2)*	22. *(3)*	23. *(2)*	24. *(4)*	25. *(3)*	26. *(1)*	27. *(4)*	28. *(2)*	29. *(4)*	30. *(3)*
31. *(3)*	32. *(2)*	33. *(1)*	34. *(3)*	35. *(4)*	36. *(3)*	37. *(2)*	38. *(4)*	39. *(1)*	40. *(4)*
41. *(4)*	42. *(4)*	43. *(3)*	44. *(4)*	45. *(2)*	46. *(3)*	47. *(2)*	48. *(2)*	49. *(1)*	50. *(1)*

PRACTICE SET 5

1. What is Telnet?
   (1) Network or telephone
   (2) Television network
   (3) Remote login
   (4) All of the above

2. In Word, when you indent a paragraph, you
   (1) push the text in with respect to the margin
   (2) change the margins on the page
   (3) move the text up by one line
   (4) move the text down by one line

3. How do you measure character size?
   (1) Text (2) Data
   (3) Font (4) File

4. A key that will erase information from the computer's memory and characters on the screen is
   (1) edit key (2) delete key
   (3) backspace key (4) shift key

5. Logic chip is also known as
   (1) Program
   (2) Memory
   (3) Microprocessor
   (4) ROM

6. A removable magnetic disk that holds information is
   (1) floppy disk (2) hard drive
   (3) monitor (4) portable

7. Which keys enable the input of number quickly?
   (1) Ctrl, Shift and Alt
   (2) Function keys
   (3) The numeric keypad
   (4) Arrow keys

8. To exit the program without leaving the application, what is to be done?
   (1) File (2) Edit
   (3) Copy (4) Close

9. .... provides process and memory management services that allow two or more tasks, jobs or programs to run simultaneously.
   (1) Multi-tasking (2) Multi-threading
   (3) Multi-processing (4) Multi-computing

10. Which ports connect special types of music instruments to sound cards?
    (1) BUS (2) CPU
    (3) USB (4) MIDI

11. To insert a copy of the clipboard contents, whatever was last cutted or copied at the insertion point, what is to be done?
    (1) Paste (2) Stick in
    (3) Fit in (4) Push in

12. The contents of .... are lost when the computer turns OFF.
    (1) storage (2) input
    (3) output (4) memory

13. Tangible, physical computer equipment that can be seen and touched, is called
    (1) hardware (2) software
    (3) storage (4) input/output

14. The.........enables you to simultaneously keep multiple Web pages open in one browser window.
    (1) tab box (2) pop-up helper
    (3) tab row (4) address bar

15. The main memory of a computer can also be called
    (1) primary storage
    (2) internal memory
    (3) primary memory
    (4) All of the above

16. Junk e-mail is also called
    (1) spam (2) spoof
    (3) sniffer script (4) spool

17. Internet requires
(1) an international agreement to connect computers
(2) a local area network
(3) a commonly agreed set of rules to communicate between computers
(4) a world wide web

18. When speaking of computer input and output, input refers to
(1) any data processing that occurs from new data input into the computer
(2) data or information that has been entered into the computer
(3) the transmission of data that has been input into the computer
(4) Both (2) and (3)

19. What resides on the motherboard and connects the CPU to other components on the motherboard?
(1) Input unit (2) System bus
(3) ALU (4) Primary memory

20. PayZapp offered by .... is an ideal mobile payment wallet.
(1) HDFC Bank (2) SBI Bank
(3) ICICI Bank (4) PNB Bank

21. In an ER diagram, attributes are represented by
(1) rectangle (2) square
(3) ellipse (4) triangle

22. The .... performs simple mathematics for the CPU.
(1) ALU (2) DIMM (3) Bus (4) Register

23. Connection or link to other documents or Web pages that contain related information is called
(1) dial-up (2) electronic commerce
(3) hyperlink (4) E-cash

24. A DVD is an example of a/an
(1) hard disk
(2) optical disc
(3) output device
(4) solid-state storage device

25. Use this when you want to make all letters capital without having to use the Shift key for each character. What does this refer here?
(1) Shifter (2) Upper case
(3) Caps lock key (4) Icon

26. A device that reads the information contained on a disk and transfers it to the computer's memory. What is it?
(1) Monitor (2) Screen
(3) Keyboard (4) Disk drive

27. Which of the following is not the major function of a computer?
(1) Processing data into information
(2) Storing data or information
(3) Accepting data
(4) Analysing data or information

28. The main job of a CPU is to
(1) carry out program instructions
(2) store data/information for future use
(3) process data and information
(4) Both (1) and (3)

29. Which of the following is an example of optical disc?
(1) Digital versatile discs
(2) Magnetic disks
(3) Memory disks
(4) Data bus disks

30. The .... folder retains copies of message that you have started but are not yet ready to send.
(1) inbox (2) outbox
(3) drafts (4) sent items

31. ...... moves the cursor one space to the right or puts spaces in between words.
(1) Control key (2) Space bar
(3) Printer (4) Mouse

32. In Excel, which one is a pre-recorded formula that provides a shortcut for complex calculations?
(1) Value (2) Data Series
(3) Function (4) Field

33. Which of the following computer's memories is characterised by low cost per bit stored?
(1) Primary (2) Secondary
(3) Magnetic tape (4) All of these

34. To change written work already done, what is to be used?
(1) File (2) Edit
(3) Cut (4) Close

35. ...... is the process of dividing the disk into tracks and sectors.
(1) Tracking (2) Formatting
(3) Crashing (4) Allotting

36. All of the following terms are related to spreadsheet software except
(1) worksheet (2) cell
(3) formula (4) virus detection

37. The term used for set of instructions which allow computer to perform more than one task, is
(1) hardware (2) software
(3) humanware (4) firmware

38. Which is a shortcut method to insert a new worksheet in MS-Excel?
(1) Ctrl+W (2) Ctrl+N
(3) Ctrl+IW (4) Shift+F11

39. How many bits are there in ASCII codes?
(1) 8 (2) 10 (3) 12 (4) 16

40. The basic unit of a worksheet into which you enter data in Excel is called a
(1) tab (2) cell
(3) box (4) range

41. You can use ...... to copy selected text and ...... to paste it in a document.
(1) Ctrl+C, Ctrl+V (2) Ctrl+C, Ctrl+P
(3) Ctrl+S, Ctrl+S (4) Shift+C, Alt+P

42. Computer software can be defined as
(1) the computer and its associated equipment
(2) the instructions that tell the computer what to do
(3) computer components that act to accomplish a goal
(4) an interface between the computer and the network

43. Which of the following is not a function category in Excel?
(1) Logical (2) Data series
(3) Financial (4) Text

44. A search engine is a program to search
(1) for information
(2) Web pages
(3) Web pages for specified index terms
(4) Web pages for information using specified search terms

45. A ...... is a set of rules.
(1) resource locator (2) domain
(3) hypertext (4) protocol

46. Data or information used to run the computer is called
(1) software (2) hardware
(3) peripheral (4) CPU

47. The device which helps you to communicate with computer is called
(1) input device (2) output device
(3) software device (4) Both (1) and (2)

48. In order to avoid memorising E-mail address you should use
(1) browser
(2) search engine
(3) list of birth date
(4) address book

49. Computers gather data, which means they allow users to ...... data.
(1) present (2) store
(3) output (4) input

50. To be able to boot, the computer must have a/an
(1) compiler (2) loader
(3) operating system (4) assembler

ANSWERS

1. *(3)*	2. *(2)*	3. *(3)*	4. *(2)*	5. *(3)*	6. *(1)*	7. *(3)*	8. *(4)*	9. *(1)*	10. *(4)*
11. *(1)*	12. *(4)*	13. *(1)*	14. *(3)*	15. *(4)*	16. *(1)*	17. *(3)*	18. *(4)*	19. *(2)*	20. *(1)*
21. *(3)*	22. *(1)*	23. *(3)*	24. *(2)*	25. *(3)*	26. *(4)*	27. *(4)*	28. *(4)*	29. *(1)*	30. *(3)*
31. *(2)*	32. *(3)*	33. *(2)*	34. *(2)*	35. *(2)*	36. *(4)*	37. *(2)*	38. *(4)*	39. *(1)*	40. *(2)*
41. *(1)*	42. *(2)*	43. *(2)*	44. *(4)*	45. *(4)*	46. *(1)*	47. *(4)*	48. *(4)*	49. *(4)*	50. *(3)*

ABBREVIATION

A

ADC Analog to Digital Convertor
ARP Address Resolution Protocol
AH Active Hub
AI Artificial Intelligence
ALGOL Algorithmic Language
ALU Arithmetic Logic Unit
APCI Application layer Protocol Control Information
API Application Program Interface
ARPANET Advanced Research Projects Agency Network
ASCII American Standard Code for Information Interchange
ATM Automated Teller Machine
ADF Automatic Document Feeder

B

BINAC Binary Automatic Computer
Bcc Blind Carbon Copy
BMP Bitmap
BASIC Beginner's All purpose Symbolic Instruction Code
BCD Binary Coded Decimal
BCR Bar Code Reader
BD Blu-ray Disc
Bin Binary
BIOS Basic Input/Output System
B2B Business-to-Business
Bit Binary Digit
BLOG Web Log
BPI Bytes/Bits Per Inch
BPL Broadband over Power Line
BPS Bits Per Second
BHIM Bharat Interface for Money

C

Cc Carbon Copy
CMOS Complementary Metal Oxide Semi-conductor
CAD Computer Aided Design
COBOL Common Business Oriented Language
CD Compact Disc
C-DAC Centre for Development of Advanced Computing
CPU Central Processing Unit
CRT Cathod Ray Tube
CSS Cascading Style Sheet
CU Control Unit
CTCP Client-To-Client Protocol
CD-R Compact Disc Recordable
CD-ROM Compact Disc Read Only Memory
CD-RW Compact Disc ReWritable
CD-R/W Compact Disc-Read/Write
CG Computer Graphics
CGI Common Gateway Interface
CLI Command Line Interface
CLR Common Language Runtime
CDMA Code Division Multiple Access

D

DAC Digital to Analog Convertor
DB Database
DBA Database Administrator
DBMS Database Management System
DCL Data Control Language
DFS Distributed File System
DFD Data Flow Diagram
DHTML Dynamic HyperText Markup Language
DMA Direct Memory Access
DNS Domain Name System
DPI Dots Per Inch

DRAM	Dynamic Random Access Memory
DSL	Digital Subscriber Line
DTP	Desktop Publishing
DVD	Digital Video Disc/Digital Versatile Disc
DVD-R	Digital Video Disc-Recordable
DVD-ROM	DVD-Read Only Memory
DVD-RW	DVD-Rewritable
DVR	Digital Video Recorder
DOS	Disk Operating System

E

EBCDIC	Extended Binary Coded Decimal Interchange Code
E-Commerce	Electronic Commerce
EDP	Electronic Data Processing
EDSAC	Electronic Delay Storage Automatic Calculator
EEPROM	Electrically Erasable Programmable Read Only Memory
E-Mail	Electronic Mail
ENIAC	Electronic Numerical Integrator And Computer
EOF	End Of File
EPROM	Erasable Programmable Read Only Memory
EXE	Executable
EDI	Electronic Data Interchange

F

FAT	File Allocation Table
FAX	Facsimile
FDC	Floppy Disk Controller
FDD	Floppy Disk Drive
FIFO	First In First Out
FORTRAN	Formula Translation
FPU	Floating Point Unit
FTP	File Transfer Protocol
FXP	File Exchange Protocol
FLOPS	Floating Point Operations Per Second

G

Gb	Gigabit
GB	Gigabyte
GIF	Graphics Interchange Format
GIGO	Garbage In Garbage Out
GPU	Graphics Processing Unit
GSM	Global System for Mobile communication
GUI	Graphical User Interface

H

HLL	High Level Language
HPFS	High Performance File System
HDD	Hard Disk Drive
HSM	Hierarchical Storage Management
HTML	HyperText Markup Language
HTTP	HyperText Transfer Protocol

I

IM	Instant Message
IMAP	Internet Message Access Protocol
iOS	iPhone Operating System
IP	Internet Protocol
ISDN	Integrated Services Digital Network
ISOC	Internet Society
ISP	Internet Service Provider
ISR	Interrupt Service Routine
IT	Information Technology
IMEI	International Mobile Equipment Identity
IoT	Internet of Things

J

JPEG	Joint Photographic Experts Group
JRE	Java Runtime Environment
JS	Java Script

K

Kb	Kilobit
KB	Kilobyte
KHz	Kilohertz
Kbps	Kilobit Per Second

L

LAN	Local Area Network
LCD	Liquid Crystal Display
LDU	Liquid Display Unit
LED	Light Emitting Diode
LPI	Lines Per Inch
LISP	List Processing

M

MAN	Metropolitan Area Network
Mb	Megabit
MB	Megabyte
MBR	Master Boot Record
MAC	Media Access Control
MPEG	Moving Picture Experts Group
MMS	Multimedia Messaging Service
MIME	Multipurpose Internet Mail Extensions
MSN	Microsoft Network
MDI	Multiple Document Interface
MICR	Magnetic Ink Character Recognition
MIPS	Million Instructions Per Second
MIDI	Musical Instrument Digital Interface

N

NFS	Network File System
NIC	Network Interface Card
NOS	Network Operating System

O

OCR	Optical Character Recognition
OMR	Optical Mark Reader
OOP	Object Oriented Programming
OS	Operating System
OSS	Open Source Software
OLE	Object Linking and Embedding
OTP	One Time Password

P

P2P	Peer-to-Peer
PAN	Personal Area Network
PAP	Password Authentication Protocol
PC	Personal Computer
PD	Pen Drive
PCL	Printed Command Language
PDF	Portable Document Format
PDL	Program Design Language
PIO	Programmed Input/Output
PLA	Programmable Logic Array
PnP	Plug and Play
POS	Point Of Sales
PPM	Pages Per Minute
PPP	Point-to-Point Protocol
PPTP	Point-to-Point Tunneling Protocol
PROM	Programmable Read Only Memory
PSTN	Public Switched Telephone Network
PSU	Power Supply Unit
POST	Power On Self Test

Q

QoS	Quality of Service
QBE	Query By Example
QR	Quick Response

R

RPA	Robotics Process Automation
RAID	Redundant Array of Independent Disks
RAM	Random Access Memory
RDBMS	Relational Database Management System
RIP	Routing Information Protocol
ROM	Read Only Memory
RPG	Report Program Generator
RTOS	Real Time Operating System
RTF	Rich Text Format

S

SaaS	Software as a Service
SAN	Storage Area Network
SCSI	Small Computer System Interface
SDL	Simple DirectMedia Layer
SMTP	Simple Mail Transfer Protocol
SNOBOL	String Oriented and Symbolic Language
SP	Service Pack
SQL	Structured Query Language
SRAM	Static Random Access Memory
SNMP	Simple Network Management Protocol
SIM	Subscriber Identification Module

T

TCP	Transmission Control Protocol
TDMA	Time Division Multiple Access
TTA	True Tap Audio
TTF	True Type Font
TTS	Text-To-Speech
TTY	Tele Type
TFT	Thin-Film Transistor
TB	Terabytes

U

UI User Interface
UPS Uninterruptible Power Supply
URI Uniform Resource Identifier
URL Uniform Resource Locator
URN Uniform Resource Name
USB Universal Serial Bus
ULSI Ultra Large Scale Integration
UNIVAC Universal Automatic Computer
UAS Unmanned Aircraft System

V

VB Visual Basic
VDD Virtual Device Driver
VGA Video Graphics Array
VLAN Virtual Local Area Network
VM Virtual Memory
VMS Video Memory System
VPN Virtual Private Network
VT Video Terminal
VR Virtual Reality
VSNL Videsh Sanchar Nigam Limited
VDU Visual Display Unit
VoIP Voice over Internet Protocol
VLSI Very Large Scale Integration
VRAM Video Random Access Memory

W

WAN Wide Area Network
WAP Wireless Application Protocol
Wi-Fi Wireless Fidelity
WiMAX Worldwide Interoperability for Microwave Access
WINS Windows Internet Naming Service
WLAN Wireless Local Area Network
WMA Wireless Media Audio
WMV Wireless Media Video
WPA Wi-Fi Protected Access
WWAN Wireless Wide Area Network
WWW World Wide Web
WLL Wireless Local Loop
WORM Write Once Read Many

X

XHTML eXtensible HyperText Markup Language
XML eXtensible Markup Language
XNS Xerox Network Services
XUL XML User interface Language

Y

YB Yottabyte

Z

ZIFS Zero Insertion Force Socket
ZIP Zone Information Protocol
ZISC Zone Instruction Set Computer
ZMA Zone Multicast Address
ZNA Zone Network Administration
ZB Zettabyte

GLOSSARY

Access Time The time interval between the instance at which data is called from a storage device and the instance when delivery begins.

Accumulator A local storage area called a register, in which the result of an arithmetic and the logic operations is formed.

Active Cell It refers to the currently selected cell in a spreadsheet. It can be identified by a bold outline that surrounds the cells.

Active Window It is the currently focused window in the current window manager.

Algorithm In computing, an algorithm is a procedure for accomplishing some tasks which given an initial state, will terminate in a defined end-state.

Alphanumeric A character set that contains letters, digits and other special characters such as @, $, +, *, %, etc.

Analog Computer A computer that operates on data which is in the form of continuous variable physical quantities.

Animation It is the process of making the illusion of motion and change by means of the rapid display of a sequence of static image that minimally differ from each other.

Antivirus It consists of computer programs that attempt to identify threat and eliminate computer viruses and other malicious software (malware).

Application Software It is a sub-class of computer software that employs the capabilities of a computer directly to a task that the user wishes to perform.

Archive It provides backup storage.

Arithmetic Logic Unit (ALU) It is a part of the execution unit, a core component of all CPUs. ALUs are capable of calculating the results of a wide variety of basic arithmetical and logical computations.

Artificial Intelligence (AI) Fifth generation computing devices, based on artificial intelligence, are still in development, though there are some applications, such as voice recognition, that are being used today.

ASCII (American Standard Code for Information Interchange) It is a character set and a character encoding based on the Roman alphabet as used in Modern English and other Western European languages.

Assembler A program that translates mnemonic statement into executable instructions.

Attribute The characteristics of an entity are called its attributes.

Authentication Any process by which a system verifies the identity of the user who wants to access it.

Auxiliary Memory It is also known as secondary memory that is not directly addressable by the CPU.

Backspace Key This key is used to delete the text. Backspace will delete the text to the left of the cursor.

Backup A copy of a file or other item of data made in case the original is lost and damaged.

Bandwidth The maximum amount of data that can travel in a communication path in a given time, measured in bits per second (bps).

Bar Code It is a machine-readable representation of information in a visual format on a surface.

Big Data Analytics It is the process of collecting, organising and analysing large sets of data to discover patterns and other useful information.

Blockchain It is an encrypted distributed database that records data.

Binary Coded Decimal (BCD) A coding system in which a 4 digit binary number represents each decimal digit from 0 to 9.

Bit It is the most basic information unit used in computing and information theory.

Blog It is a discussion or informational site published on the world wide web.

Bomb A type of virus designed to activate at a specific date and time on your computer.

Bluetooth It permits a wireless exchange of information between computers, cell phones and other electronic devices.

Booting It is a boot strapping process which starts the operating system when a computer is switched ON.

Browser A special software that enables users to read/view Web pages and jump from one Web page to another.

Buffering The process of storing data in a memory device, allowing the devices to change the data rates, perform error checking and error re-transmission.

Bug It is an error, flaw, failure, or fault in a computer program or system that produces an incorrect or unexpected result.

Bus A circuit that provides a communication path between two or more devices of a digital computer system.

Byte It is commonly used as a unit of storage measurement in computers, regardless of the type of data being stored.

Cell A box in a spreadsheet, in which you can enter a single piece of data.

Central Processing Unit (CPU) It performs the actual processing of data. The CPU is generally called by its generic name 'Processor'. It is also known as the brain of computer.

Channel A communication channel can be a physical link, such as a cable that connects two stations in a network or it can consist of some electromagnetic transmission.

Chatting Typing text into a message box on a screen to engage in dialog with one or more people via the Internet or other network.

Chip A tiny wafer of silicon containing miniature electric circuits that can store millions of bits of information.

Client-Server It is a network architecture which separates the client from the server. Each instance of the client software can send requests to a server or application server.

Command It is a directive to a computer program acting as an interpreter of some kind, in order to perform a specific task.

Compile It is the process of converting high level language to machine language.

Compiler It is a computer program that translates a series of instructions from high level language to machine language.

Cookie A packet of information that travels between a browser and the web server.

Communication Protocol It is a system of rules that allow two or more entities of a communication system to transmit information.

Computer Network It is a system for communication among two or more computers.

Computer Graphics These are visual presentations on a computer screen. Examples are photographs, drawings, line arts, graphs or other images.

Control Panel It is the part of Windows menu, accessible from the Start menu, which allows users to view and manipulate basic system settings and controls.

Computer Worm It is a self-replicating computer program, similar to a computer virus.

Control Unit It is the part of a CPU that directs its operation. The output of this unit control the activity of the rest of the device.

Crawler It is an Internet bot that systematically browse the world wide web, typically for the purpose of Web indexing. It is also called a Web spider.

Cryptography The conversion of data into a secret code for transmission over a public network.

Cut To remove an object from a document.

Data It is a collection of facts and figures which are not in directly usable form.

Database It is a collection of logically related information in an organised way so that it can be easily accessed, managed and updated.

Data Entry Direct input of data in the appropriate data fields of a database known as data entry.

Database Management System (DBMS) It is a collection of various programs. It provides a systematic way to create, retrieve, update and manage data.

Data Processing Converting data into information, is called data processing.

Data Redundancy It is a condition created within a database or data storage technology in which the same piece of data is held in two separate places.

Debugging A methodical process of finding and reducing the number of bugs, or defects are known as debugging.

Degree The number of fields associated with the database table or relation.

Desktop Publishing (DTP) It combines a personal computer, page layout software and a printer to create publications on small economic scale.

Display Unit A device with a screen that displays characters or graphics representing data in a computer memory.

Device Driver It is a computer program that enables another program, typically, an operating system to interact with a hardware device.

Dial-up Line A line through which communication established.

Digital Computer A computer that operates with numbers expressed directly as digits.

Direct Access It is the capability of the computer equipment to obtain data from a storage device.

Directory In computing, a directory is an entity in a file system which contains a group of files and other directories.

Domain Name A unique name that identifies a particular Website and represents the name of the server where the Web pages reside.

Dots Per Inch (DPI) It is defined as the measure of the resolution of a printer, scanner or monitor. It refers to the number of dots in one inch line.

Download It refers to the act of transmitting data from a remote computer on the Internet or other network to one's own computer.

Drag and Drop In computer graphical user interface, drag and drop is the action of clicking on a virtual object and dragging it to a different location or onto another virtual object.

DVD It is an optical disc storage media format that can be used for data storage including movies with high quality video and sound.

Dynamic RAM (DRAM) It is a type of random access memory which stores each bit of data in a separate capacitor.

EBCDIC (Extended Binary Coded Decimal Interchange Code) It is an 8-bit character encoding used on IBM mainframe operating systems, like Z/OS, S/390, AS/400 and i5/OS.

E-Commerce (Electronic Commerce) It is a type of industry where buying and selling of products or services is conducted over electronic systems such as the Intranet and other computer network.

Editing The process of changing information by inserting, deleting, replacing, rearranging and reformation.

Electronic Data Processing (EDP) A data processing through equipment that is predominantly electronic such as digital computer.

Electronic Mail (E-Mail) It is a method of composing, sending, storing and receiving messages over electronic communication systems.

Encryption In cryptography, encryption is the process of encoding messages (or information) in such a way that hackers cannot read it, but the authorised users can access it.

End User Any individual who uses the information generated by a computer based system.

Entity It is something that has certain attributes or properties which may be assigned values.

Error Message It is information displayed when an unexpected condition occurs usually on a computer or other device.

Excel It allows users to create spreadsheets much like paper ledgers that can perform automatic calculations.

Exe (.exe) It is a common filename extension denoting an executable file (a program) in the DOS, MS-Windows.

Execution Time The total time required to execute a program on a particular system.

Expansion Slot It is a socket on the motherboard that is used to insert an expansion card which provides additional features to a computer.

Extranet A technology that permits the users of one organisation's Intranet to enter portions of another organisation's Intranet in order to conduct business transactions or collaborate on joint projects.

Fax It stands for 'Facsimile'. It is used to transmit a copy of a document electronically.

Field The attributes of an entity are written as fields in the table representation.

File A collection of information stored electronically and treated as a unit by a computer. Every file must have its own distinctive name.

File Allocation Table (FAT) It is the name of a computer file system architecture. The FAT file system is a legacy file system which is simple and robust.

File Manager It is an operating system utility that provides a user interface to work with file systems.

Firewall A security system usually consisting of hardware and software that prevents unauthorised persons from accessing certain parts of a program database or network.

Flowcharts These are the means of visually representing the flow of data through an information processing system, the operations performed within the system and the sequence in which they are performed.

Foreign Key A field in a database table, which links it to another related table.

Format To set margins, tabs, font or line spacing in layout of a document.

FORTRAN It stands for Formula Translation. The language was designed at IBM for scientific computing.

Freeware A form of software distribution where the author retains copyright of the software but makes the program available to others at no cost.

File Transfer Protocol (FTP) This protocol is used to transfer files from one place to another on Internet.

Function Key A special key on a computer keyboard or a terminal devices keyboard that is used to perform specific functions. Many keyboards have function keys labelled from F1 to F12.

Gadget It is a device that has a specific function in addition usually has small dimensions.

Garbage In Garbage Out (GIGO) It pertains to the fact that most computer errors are not machine errors, they are data errors caused by incorrect input data.

Gateway A device that is used to join together two networks having different base protocols.

Gigabyte (GB) It is a unit of information or computer storage equal to approximately one billion bytes.

Gigahertz (GHz) A measurement unit used to identify the speed of the central processing unit. One gigahertz is equal to 1 billion cycles per second.

Graphics Interchange Format (GIF) A simple file format for pictures and photographs, that are compressed so they can be sent quickly.

Graphic Tablet It is an input device which is used to create images, etc.

Graphical User Interface (GUI) It is a method of interacting with a computer through a metaphor of direct manipulating of graphical images and widgets in addition to text.

Hacker A computer criminal who penetrates and tempers with computer programs or systems.

Hang To crash in such a way that the computer does not respond to input from the keyboard or mouse.

Hard Copy It is a printed copy of information from a computer.

Hard Disk It is a non-volatile data storage device that stores data on a magnetic surface layered onto disk platters.

Hardware The mechanical, magnetic, electronic and electrical components that comprises a computer system such as CPU, monitor, keyboard, mouse, etc.

High-Level Programming Language It is a programming language that is more user-friendly, to some extent platform-independent and abstract from low-level computer processor operations such as memory accesses.

Home Page A starting point or a doorway to the Website. It refers to the Web page that identifies a Website and contains the hyperlink to other Web pages in the Website.

Host Computer A computer that provides information or a service to other computers on the Internet. Every host computer has its own unique host name.

Hub A network device that connects multiple computers on a LAN, so that they can communicate with one another.

Hybrid Computer These computers are made by taking the best features of the analog computer and digital computer.

Hyperlink An image or portion of text on a Web page that is linked to another Web page.

HyperText Markup Language (HTML) It is mainly used for designing Websites.

HyperText Transfer Protocol (HTTP) It is an important protocol used on the world wide web for moving hypertext files across the Internet.

Icon A symbol (such as picture or a folder) that represents a certain function on your computer. When the user clicks on the icon, the appropriate function is executed.

Information It is the summarisation of data according to a certain pre-defined purpose.

Input In order to give instructions to a computer, the information has to be supplied to it.

Instant Messaging (IM) A chat program that lets people communicate over the Internet in real time.

Instruction A command or order given to a computer to perform a task.

Interface A device or program that helps a user to communicate with a computer.

Interpreter A program that converts and executes the source code into machine code line by line.

Internet A vast computer network linking smaller computer networks worldwide.

Internet of Things (IoT) It is a network in which all physical objects are connected to the Internet through network devices and exchange data.

Internet Surfing To search something on Internet is called Internet surfing.

Internet Service Provider (ISP) It is a business organisation that offers users to access the Internet and related services.

Integrated Circuits Multiple electronic components combined on a silicon chip.

Java A programming language, used to create mobile applications, softwares, etc.

Javascript It is an object oriented programming language used to create interactive effects in a Web browser.

JPEG (Joint Photographic Experts Group) It is a commonly used method of lossy compression for digital photography.

Joystick It is a computer peripheral or general control device consisting of a handheld stick that pivots about one end and transmits its angle in two or three dimensions to a computer.

Kernel It is the fundamental part of a program, such as an operating system, that resides in memory at all times.

Keyboard This is the standard input device attached to all computers. The layout of keyboard is just like the traditional typewriter of the type QWERTY.

Key Stroke It is the process of pressing button in keyboard.

Kilobyte (KB) It is a unit of information or computer storage equal to 1024 bytes.

LAN (Local Area Network) In LAN, the connected computers are geographically close together. They are either in the same building or within a smaller area.

Laptop It is a small, lightweight and portable battery-powered computer that can fit onto your lap. They each have a thin, flat and liquid crystal display screen.

Light Pen A light sensitive style for forming graphics by touching coordinates on a display screen, thereby seeming to draw directly on the screen.

Link A communication path between two nodes or channels.

LINUX It is an open source operating system, meaning that the source code of the operating system is freely available to the public.

List Processing (LISP) A high level programming language suitable for handling logical operations and non-numeric applications.

Log In It is the process by which an individual gains access to a computer system by identifying and authenticating themselves.

Log Off It is a process of withdrawal from function after performing program.

Low Level Language It is a assembly language which is used in computer. It was mostly used in first generation computers.

Machine Language The language of computer also called binary language. Instructions in this language are written as a sequence of 0's and 1's.

Main Memory A volatile and speedy memory. It is divided into two parts RAM and ROM.

Malware It is a software that disrupts normal computers functions or sends a user's personal data without the user authorisation.

Mass Storage It is referred to storage where large volume of backup/data is stored.

Megabyte (MB) 1 Megabyte is equal to 1048576 bytes, usually rounded off to one million bytes. It is also called a 'meg'.

Memory Temporary storage for information, including applications and documents.

Menu Bar The horizontal strip across the top of an application's window. Each word on the strip has a context sensitive drop-down menu containing features and actions that are available for the application in use.

Merge Combining two or more files into a single file.

Microcomputer A microprocessor-based computer, consisting of CPU, internal semi-conductor memory, input and output sections and a system bus, all on one, or several monolithic IC chips inserted into one or several PC boards.

Microprocessor A complete Central Processing Unit (CPU) contained on a single silicon chip.

MIDI (Music Instrument Digital Interface) It allows a computer to store and replay a musical instrument's output.

Minicomputer Considered to be more capable than a microcomputer but less powerful than a mainframe.

Mnemonic A symbolic label or code remainder that assists the user in remembering a specific operation or command in assembly language.

Modem (Modulator/Demodulator) It refers to specific equipment that provides a means of communication between two computer systems over conventional telephone lines.

Monitor The visual readout device of a computer system. A monitor can be in several forms; a Cathode Ray Tube (CRT), a Liquid Crystal Display (LCD), or a flat-panel, full-color display.

Multitasking It can work with several programs or interrelated tasks simultaneously that share memories, codes, buffers and files.

Multithreading It is a facility available in an operating system that allows multiple functions from the same application packages.

Multimedia Software programs that combine text and graphics with sound, video and animation. A multimedia PC contains the hardware to support these capabilities.

Network It is an inter-connection of two or more than two computers.

Network Interface Card (NIC) This is a part of the computer that allows it to talk to other computers via a network protocol like TCP/IP.

Nibble A sequence of four adjacent bits, or a half-byte. A hexa-decimal or BCD coded digit can be represented by a nibble.

Node The end point of a network branch or the junction of two or more branches.

Non-Volatile Memory A memory where stored data remain undisturbed by the removal of electrical power.

Notebook A portable computer, that can fit into a briefcase. It is used as personal computer. It is also called laptop.

Object Something that contains both the data and the application that operate on that data.

Offline It refers to the state in which a computer is temporarily or permanently unable to communicate with another computer.

Online It refers to the state of being connected to the networked computer system or the Internet.

Operating System A set of instructions that tells a computer how to operate when it is turned ON. It sets up a filing system to store files and tells the computer how to display information on a video display.

Output Data that come out of a computer device.

Patch A small program that improves an existing piece of software or corrects an error in it.

Personal Computer (PC) A single-user computer containing a Central Processing Unit (CPU) and one or more memory circuits.

Piracy The illegal copying of software or other creative works.

Pixels An acronym derived from picture element. The smallest element (a dot) on a display screen.

Plug-In This is a program that your browser uses to manipulate a downloaded file.

Portrait A term that designates the position of conventional printing across the width of a page.

Post Office Protocol (POP) A protocol that specifies how a personal computer can connect to a mail server on the Internet and download E-mail.

Primary Key It is a key that uniquely identifies each tuple or row in a table.

Process A collection of code, data and other system resources including atleast one thread of execution that performs a data processing task.

Program A set of instructions to perform a specific task.

Programming Language A vocabulary and set of grammatical rules for instructing a computer to perform specific tasks.

Printer A mechanical device for printing a computer's output on paper.

Protocol A set of rules that defines exactly how information is to be exchanged between two systems over Internet.

Pseudocode It is a short hand way of describing a computer program.

Query A request for information from a database.

Random Access Memory (RAM) A volatile, semi-conductor storage structure that accesses temporary data with a random or direct accessing method. Data in this memory can be read by the CPU directly.

Read Only Memory (ROM) A semi-conductor memory whose data cannot be erased, or overwritten; it can only be accessed (read) for use by the CPU.

Record A collection of all the information pertaining to a particular entity instance.

Register A temporary storage unit for quick, direct accessibility of a small amount of data for processing.

Remote Server A network computer that allows a user on the network from a distant location to access information.

Robotics Process Automation (RPA) It is the use of specialised computer programs, known as software robots, to automate and standardise repeatable business processes.

Router A network device that enables the network to re-route messages it receives that are intended for other networks. The network with the router receives the message and sends it on its way exactly as received.

Routing The process of choosing the best path throughout the LAN.

Scanner An electronic device that uses light-sensing equipment to scan paper images such as text, photos, illustrations and translate the images into signals that the computer can then store, modify, or distribute.

Search Engine Software that makes it possible to look for and retrieve information on the Internet, particularly the Web. Some popular search engines are AltaVista, Google, HotBot, Yahoo!, Web Crawler and Lycos.

Sector A section of a recording track on a magnetic disk.

Sequential Access It is a class of data storage device that reads stored data in a sequence.

Server A computer that shares its resources and information with other computers on a network.

Shareware A software that is not free but is available for a free trial period.

Simplex Transmission of data in one direction only.

Software The set of computer programs, procedures and associated documentation related to the effective operation.

Source Code (Source Program) A set of computer instructions in hard-copy or stored form.

Spam Irrelevant or unsolicited messages sent over Internet, typically to large number of users, for the purpose of advertising, phishing, spreading malwares, etc.

Spreadsheet Software that allows one to calculate numbers in a format that is similar to pages in a conventional ledger.

Static RAM It is a type of RAM, that contains its contents only whenever current supply is ON.

Sub-Program A particular part of a program that complete the special work.

Supercomputer The largest mainframe computer featuring exceptionally high speed operation while manipulating huge amount of information.

TCP/IP (Transmission Control Protocol/Internet Protocol) This is a large grouping of programs and standards that govern how information moves around the Internet.

Terabyte (TB) It is about a trillion bytes. Actually, it's 2^{40} or 10095111627776 bytes.

Terminal This is what you look at when you are on the Internet. It's your computer screen.

Time Sharing It refers to the allocation of computer resources in a time dependent fashion to run several programs simultaneously.

Topology The structure of the network including physical connection such as wiring schemes and logical interactions between network devices.

Trackball Input device that controls the position of the cursor on the screen.

Uniform Resource Locator (URL) The specific Internet address for a resource such as an individual or an organisation.

Unix This is an operating system developed by AT & T. It is a big push that it allows one server to serve many different end users at one time.

Upgrade The process of improve hardware and software functionality.

Upload The process of transferring information from a computer to a Website (or other remote location on a network).

UPS (Universal Power Supply or Uninterruptible Power Supply) An electrical power supply that includes a battery to provide enough power to a computer during an outage to back-up data and properly shut down.

User A person who uses or operates something.

User-Friendly A software program that has been designed to easily direct the user through the operation or application of a program.

Validation The process of making sure that the forms and documents from a particular transaction are correct.

Video Tele-conferencing A remote 'face-to-face chat,' when two or more people using a webcam and an Internet telephone connection chat online. The webcam enables both live voice and video.

Virus A piece of computer code designed as a prank or malicious act to spread from one computer to another by attaching itself to other programs.

Virtual Reality (VR) It is the use of computer technology to create a simulated environment.

Volatile Memory A memory whose contents are irretrievably lost when power is removed. If data in RAM must be saved after power shutdown, back-up in non-volatile memory (magnetic disk, tape, or CD-R) is essential.

Website A collection of web pages or hyperlinked webpages which onwned by an individual, company or an organisation.

Window A portion of a computer display used in a graphical interface that enables users to select commands by pointing to illustrations or symbols with a mouse.

Wide Area Network (WAN) It is a tele-communication network or computer network that extends over a large geographical distance.

Word Processor A computer system or program for setting, editing, revising, correcting, storing and printing text.

World Wide Web ('WWW' or 'Web') A network of servers on the Internet that uses hypertext-linked databases and files. It was developed in 1989 by Tim Berners-Lee, a British computer scientist and is now the primary platform of the Internet.

Workgroup Persons sharing files and data between themselves.

Workstation The work area and/or equipment used for computer operations, including Computer-Aided Design (CAD). The equipment generally consists of a monitor, keyboard, printer and/or plotter and other output devices.

X-Y Plotter A computer-driven printing mechanism that draws coordinate points in graph form.

ZOOM The enlarging or reducing an image displayed on a computer process of proportionately monitor.

ZIP (Zone Information Protocol) This is an application that allows for the compression of application files.

Printed in the USA
CPSIA information can be obtained
at www.ICGtesting.com
LVHW060359310723
753624LV00010B/154